Karen!

All my best of
good channel
fortune!

Ken Hobeck
7/31/98

# Managing Channels of Distribution

# Managing Channels of Distribution

## The Marketing Executive's Complete Guide

## Kenneth Rolnicki

AMACOM
American Management Association

New York • Atlanta • Boston • Chicago • Kansas City • San Francisco • Washington, D.C.
Brussels • Mexico City • Tokyo • Toronto

This publication is designed to provide accurate and authoritative
information in regard to the subject matter covered. It is sold with the
understanding that the publisher is not engaged in rendering legal,
accounting, or other professional service. If legal advice or other expert
assistance is required, the services of a competent professional person
should be sought.

Library of Congress Cataloging-in-Publication Data

Rolnicki, Kenneth.
    Managing channels of distribution; the marketing executive's
complete guide / Kenneth Rolnicki.
       p.   cm.
    Includes index.
    ISBN 0-8144-0335-2
    1. Marketing channels—Management.   I. Title.
HF5415.129.R65   1997
658.8'4—dc21                                        97-31322
                                                    CIP

Printing number

10  9  8  7  6  5  4  3  2

*To*
**Marilyn,** *my wife,*
*and*
**Melissa** *and* **Heather,**
*our two daughters,*
*whose support, admiration,*
*and, above all, love encouraged me to*
*successfully persevere through the arduous*
*yet rewarding publishing process*

# Contents

# List of Exhibits

# Preface

The world of marketing channels is a dynamic, ever-evolving place that offers some of the most exciting challenges known to business professionals. Whenever a new opportunity to make money appears, a new channel is often created. In some fast-changing markets like cellular phones or computers, business possibilities emerge so rapidly that a channel's overall architecture can be completely transformed in as little as a year.

This profusion of alternatives is tempestuous and sometimes frustrating for channel managers, who must decide which channels are correct for their company, product, and marketplaces; whether their company can afford to use the new channels; and whether working through multiple channels will create new profits or could lead to product overdistribution and distributor conflict.

I've been facing questions like these for more than thirty years now. Sometimes my answers have been right; sometimes I've been off the mark. Fortunately, I've succeeded many more times than I've been mistaken. And along the way, I've carefully noted the reasons *why* various channels succeeded or failed. The pages that follow distill my channelmaster experience into principles and recommendations that will definitely help increase your channel success rate. The material will also help reduce your frustration level and boost your excitement about being involved in this dynamic business field.

You will also note that at the end of each chapter (for your professional sporting appetite) is a mini-case pertinent to the subject matter covered in that section.

Throughout this book, I stress the importance of creating and nurturing strong channel relationships. Treat your partners with respect and concern, make decisions fairly and equitably, and communicate honestly, and you will build relationships of great closeness—closeness that will see you through good times and bad. A bonding relationship will also help you achieve your Number 1 goal as a channelmaster: securing the greatest possible share of your distributors' resource commitment. Without a credible relationship, a lasting commitment is not possible.

Quite frankly, few distributors are so dependent on a manufacturer that they cannot exist without that manufacturer's sales revenue and profit contribution. The same holds true for most manufacturers. Neither party wants to operate in such concentrated levels of channel dependence. That is why earning and maintaining as much business trust as possible is critical to an efficient and reliable channel system.

*Value* is just as important as trust, as my colleague Phil Kotler, Distinguished Professor of Marketing at Northwestern University's J. L. Kellogg Graduate School of Management, points out:

> *Marketing is not the art of finding clever ways to dispose of what you make. Marketing is the art of creating genuine customer value. It is the art of helping your customers become better off.*

In channels of distribution, as in all of marketing, Phil Kotler's marketing wisdom rings true. Create genuine value for your distributors and your end users, and your channel of distribution will positively react to your efforts. Make creating genuine customer value your business as a channelmaster, and you will gain the highest possible level of trust and confidence from your distributors, as well as the greatest personal and business success.

# Acknowledgments

I have benefited greatly from the experience and contributions of several individuals who and organizations that shared their insights and perspectives with me. Without question, their valuable input has substantially enhanced this book. I shall forever be indebted to them. My thanks to:

❐ Acquisitions Editors Mary Glenn and Ellen Kadin, Development Editor Jacqueline Flynn, and Copy Editor Jacqueline Laks-Gorman of AMACOM Books, who steadfastly guided me through the publishing process from conception through production.

❐ My Chicago-based Development Editor, Anne Basye, to whom I owe a very special debt of gratitude for her in-depth and persistent efforts to perfect this text.

❐ Mike Sivilli, Associate Editor at AMACOM, who took on the project midstream, put the finishing literary (among other) touches on the book, worked in his unique fast-paced and optimistic way, and produced the final product.

❐ Finally, a special note of appreciation to my colleagues who graciously provided me with a wealth of marketing channel information and data. At the J. L. Kellogg Graduate School of Management at Northwestern University, they include Professor Philip Kolter, Professor Louis Stern, Professor James Anderson, and Professor Anthony J. Paoni. My thanks as well to Attorney Richard O. Becker; William Brinkworth, Chairman/CEO, Global Trade Net Ltd.; William C. Fath, President, W. C. Fath Associates; and Frank Lynn, Chairman, Frank Lynn and Associates.

*Merci beaucoup!*

# Chapter 1

# Pivotal Marketing Channel Concepts

This is a book about indirect marketing channels. It is designed to help you become a "channelmaster," one who can build and manage a strong, profitable network of channels that sell products and services for you and your company.

From an operational standpoint, a *marketing channel* is the path a product or service takes as it moves from the manufacturer to its end user or consumer. The very basic channel structure shown in Exhibit 1-1 was the rule in the years following World War II. In those days, the path between manufacturer and consumer was a straight one. A manufacturer faced only one decision: whether to use a *direct* or an *indirect* channel of distribution (COD).

If the manufacturer selected a direct channel, it hired a sales force to get the product on the shelves or into the hands of consumers. In the 1950s, for example, the only way to buy an IBM typewriter was to order one from IBM salespeople who called on offices. If the manufacturer was too small to hire a proprietary sales force, it opted for an indirect channel and hired a distributor to sell to end users. In the 1950s, sales agents, not employees, invited housewives to parties to purchase Tupperware products. Tupperware sales agents and their parties were their indirect channel.

As time passed, the path between manufacturer and end user developed a thousand twists and turns. In fact, today it is less like a path and more like a wheel, with the manufacturer at the "hub" connected to the end user at the "tire" by dozens of direct and indirect channel "spokes."

Exhibit 1-2 shows how the number and complexity of indirect channels has multiplied. Today, IBM's hub-spokes-wheel sales channel includes a direct sales force that sells mainframe computers; system integrators and value-added resellers that handle its minicomputers and midrange systems; and value-added resellers, dealers, resellers, and retail-

**Exhibit 1-1.** Basic channel structure.

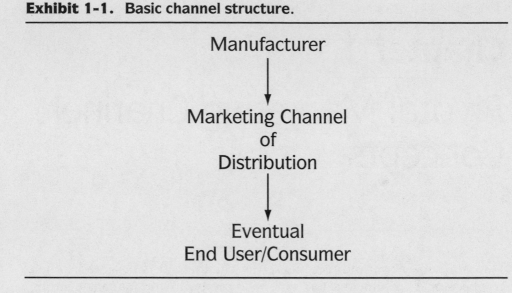

Manufacturer

Marketing Channel
of
Distribution

Eventual
End User/Consumer

ers that sell personal computers. The sheer number of choices makes creating and managing these channels challenging—even frustrating!

## Why Manufacturers Use Indirect Channels

The traditional, direct sales route offers a number of advantages to the manufacturer. For one thing, the manufacturer controls its sales force. The manufacturer's management can tell its salespersons where to sell, what to sell, how to sell, and how much to charge. Management can dictate activities that support the company image. And, of course, the sales force is completely committed to its employer. It sells the manufacturer's products and no one else's.

But a direct-employed sales force is not appropriate for every company and certainly isn't appropriate for every stage in a company's evolution. A small company may not be able to afford its own sales force. It may need to utilize an indirect channel until its sales and profit performance improve enough to afford the fixed expense of a direct sales force in the field. In addition, it would be unprofitable to have your direct salespeople spend time on smaller customers. Indirect channels of distribution can afford to engage the smaller customer by selling many other manufacturers' product lines to that same customer group. By doing so, they spread the same cost of sales over several product lines.

Generally speaking, when a specific territory produces between

**Exhibit 1-2.** A chronicle of distribution marketing showing how the number and complexity of channels has multiplied.

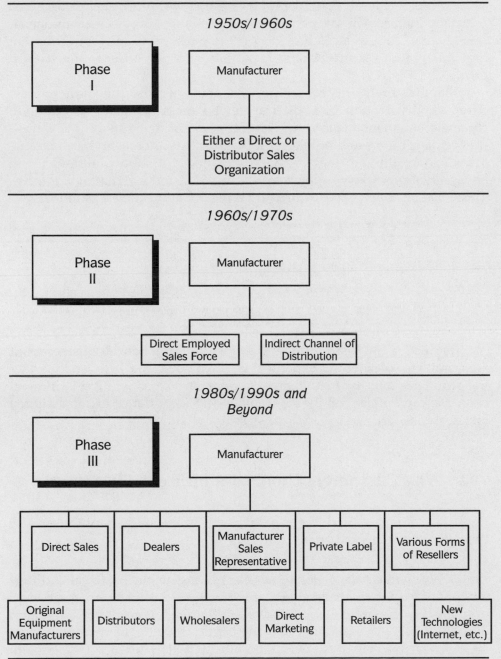

*1950s/1960s*

Phase I

Manufacturer

Either a Direct or Distributor Sales Organization

*1960s/1970s*

Phase II

Manufacturer

Direct Employed Sales Force

Indirect Channel of Distribution

*1980s/1990s and Beyond*

Phase III

Manufacturer

Direct Sales

Dealers

Manufacturer Sales Representative

Private Label

Various Forms of Resellers

Original Equipment Manufacturers

Distributors

Wholesalers

Direct Marketing

Retailers

New Technologies (Internet, etc.)

$2 million and $2.5 million in annual sales, the expense of an employed salesperson can be justified. Of course, product line profitability has to be at an acceptable level. (Each company sets its own profit standards.) As a company increases in sales revenue and profit size, so do the commensurate channel choices available. Most companies eventually conclude that they must pursue indirect channels of distribution in order to survive and grow.

Manufacturers also use indirect channels because they save money. After all, distribution is a cost transfer business. By using distribution channels, the manufacturer can transfer some of the costs of doing business to distributors and resellers. Marketing costs are most typically transferred down through the channel, as Exhibit 1-3 shows (although you always incur some marketing costs for national and international efforts). These passed-down expenditures are typically apportioned as follows:

| | |
|---|---|
| Inventory | 40% |
| Sales | 30 |
| Order Handling | 20 |
| Credit | 10 |
| | 100% |

Because many distributors are fragile, entrepreneurial businesses, it is essential to consider this expense mix when you create sales and marketing strategies and internal channel support systems. Selling via indirect channels can be justified by the number and importance of the assigned business tasks transferred to the distributor channel.

## Why Customers Buy From Indirect Channels

End users purchase products and services from indirect channels because they offer a number of benefits:

❑ *The convenience of one-stop shopping.* Imagine having to call a different manufacturer whenever you wanted to buy a saw, a hammer, or a box of nails. That's what life would be like if there were no indirect channels of distribution. A retail outlet like The Home Depot lets a consumer meet *all* of his or her hardware needs, because it sells several products from many different manufacturers. A customer can save time and money by choosing from a wide selection of products instead of items from only one manufacturer's line.

**Exhibit 1-3.** Transferring market costs down through the channel.

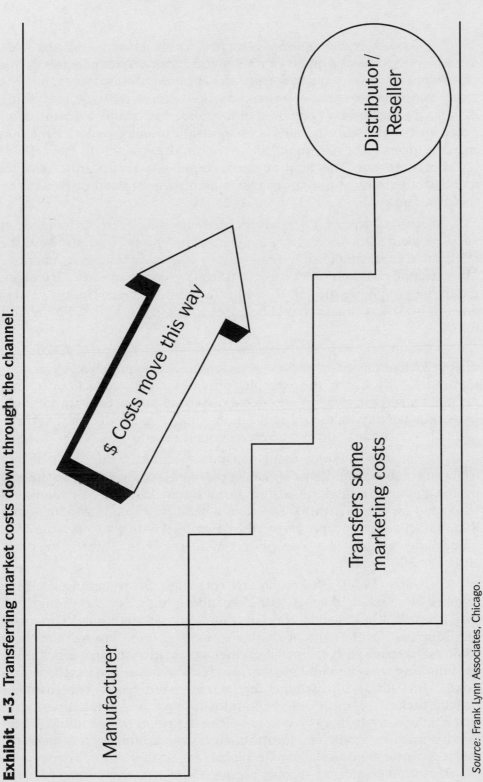

*Source:* Frank Lynn Associates, Chicago.

❏ *Customer service and technical support.* Indirect channels can provide service and technical support promptly and locally. Where required, this can be provided on a quick reaction, local market basis. For example, a small computer store can offer inexperienced computer users everything they need to use a new computer with confidence. It can set up the computer, install the software, and offer postsale training—all services that manufacturers like Compaq or IBM do not make available to the individual computer user. This kind of rapid, competent, and nearby technical and customer service assistance is often highly desired and demanded by the customer.

❏ *Logistical support.* Channels of distribution that carry inventory can supply a local market with close-by physical inventory. They also have the ability to "break bulk" down to smaller, customer-requested amounts. Thus, a small company stocking up on cleaning compounds deals with an industrial supply distributor instead of a manufacturer. The distributor buys in bulk and breaks that bulk down to the level desired by the end user.

❏ *Ease of doing business.* Consumers can rely on indirect CODs to conduct tasks that manufacturers do not, cannot, or are not interested in performing locally. Sears, for example, provides credit, collection, billing, emergency service, local product or service consultation, order processing, physical inventory, sales and application engineering, and sales and marketing to consumers—so manufacturers don't have to.

❏ *Community presence.* Many consumers faithfully support and buy from their local neighborhood resellers, dealers, and retailers because of professional association, friendship, social ties, or other deeply rooted relationship factors. Whether they live in a big city, a small town, or something in between, most people would rather deal with someone who lives around the corner than a power direct mail retailer that lives at the other end of an 800 number.

❏ *Greater channel efficiency.* Many corporations are cutting back the number of suppliers they use and demanding higher quality from those they keep. This is a channel concept commonly referred to as "Diminishing Supplies." More efficient channels of distribution are helping these companies accomplish their cost-savings goals. In response, distributors are bundling several manufacturers' products into a single purchase proposal with additional discounts for increased purchases. The customer usually makes a blanket order commitment over an extended period of time that effectively blocks any competitive distributors and, in turn, competitive manufacturers' entrance into such an account. In "channelese," this is commonly known as *bundle power.*

This kind of indirect channel creates a win-win environment for the manufacturer, distributor, and end user. The manufacturer efficiently moves its product through the channel to the end user. The distributor locks in an end user to purchasing several product lines over a specified period of time. Last, the end user reduces its procurement costs by limiting the number of suppliers with which it has to deal.

## Direct vs. Indirect Channels of Distribution

Exhibit 1-4 shows the vast array of channels that deliver products and services from manufacturer to end user or consumer, in both consumer and industrial markets. Every year, new channels are created in response to new product, market, or buying behavioral influences. These new customer-satisfying business organizations are usually entrepreneurial in nature. They arise when entrepreneurs notice a need, see an opportunity to make money, and respond by creating a new kind of channel. Many are simply an improvement on a previous channel form. But no matter how new the channel, it probably falls into one of two categories: either (1) it takes ownership of the manufacturer's product, or (2) it doesn't.

When a channel does *not* take ownership, the manufacturer retains control over how products are priced and where they are shipped. In exchange for this control, the manufacturer performs many tasks that an ownership channel would manage. For example, a manufacturer may:

- ❒ Offer return provisions.
- ❒ Maintain readily available inventory.
- ❒ Ensure rapid delivery.
- ❒ Offer credit.
- ❒ Provide for emergency service.
- ❒ Offer some degree of product customization.
- ❒ Include packaging and special handling.
- ❒ Provide technical assistance.
- ❒ Maintain market information.
- ❒ Offer storage space.
- ❒ Process orders and billing.
- ❒ Provide market sales coverage.

A manufacturer that maintains product ownership can dictate pricing and control product during all three phases of the sales process: (1) presale, (2) transaction, and (3) postsale (see Exhibit 1-5).

Exhibit 1-6 shows the specific business tasks generally performed by direct and indirect sales channels, depending on whether the channel as-

**Exhibit 1-4.** The different channels delivering products and services from manufacturer to consumers or end users.

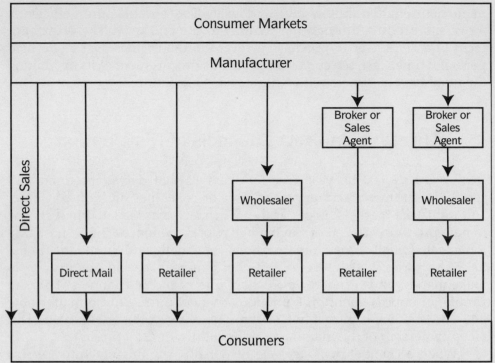

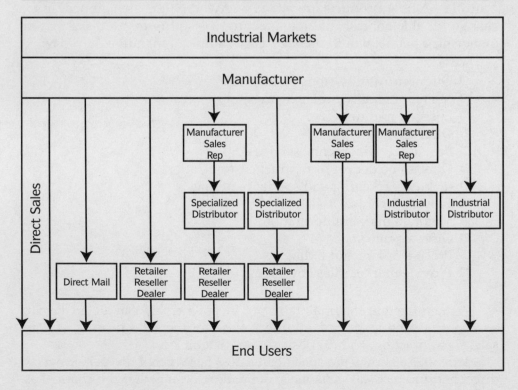

**Exhibit 1-5.** The three phases of the sales process.

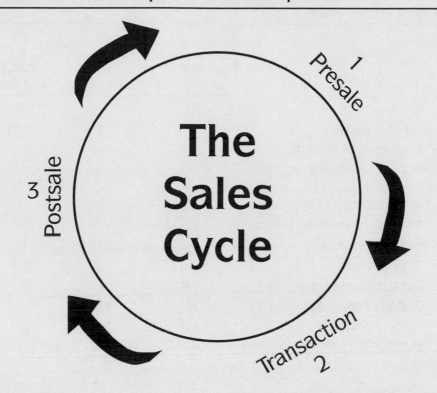

sumes ownership of the product. Obviously, a channel that handles a great number of important tasks deserves a substantial compensation package from the manufacturer.

## Channel Definitions

Before we go further, let's define the various kinds of indirect channels and their activities. A summary of these channels is shown in Exhibit 1-7.

### Indirect Channels That Take Ownership

***distributor, industrial and consumer products***   A company that purchases products from a manufacturer and resells them directly to an end user or another business in the same or related marketplace.

***distributor, high-technology products***   An organization that buys products from a manufacturer and resells them to another channel member (dealer, value-

**Exhibit 1-6.** The business functions/tasks performed by direct and indirect sales channels.

| Business Function/Task | Direct | Indirect | |
|---|---|---|---|
| | Employed Direct Sales Force | Product Ownership | Product Nonownership |
| 1.  Fixed expense | yes | no | no |
| 2.  Variable expense | no | yes | yes |
| 3.  Takes ownership of product | yes | yes | no |
| 4.  Product bears full sales cost | yes | no | no |
| 5.  Sales cost spread over several product lines | no | yes | yes |
| 6.  Receives payment for product | yes | yes | no |
| 7.  Order acceptance | yes | yes | no |
| 8.  Commissioned | yes | no | yes |
| 9.  Discount from manufacturer | no | yes | no |
| 10.  Customer invoicing/billing | yes | yes | no |
| 11.  Ships to customer | yes | yes | no |
| 12.  Inventories product | yes | yes | no |
| 13.  Determines price | yes | yes | no |
| 14.  Managerial control | yes | no | no |
| 15.  Has a sales force | yes | yes | yes |
| 16.  Control over company image | yes | no | no |
| 17.  Bureaucratic | yes | no | no |
| 18.  Entrepreneurial | no | yes | yes |
| 19.  Possible intrachannel conflict | yes | yes | yes |
| 20.  Sells only one product line | yes | no | no |

added reseller, system integrator) which, in turn, sells these same products to its customers.

*private label*   Product is adapted for the reseller. A manufacturer affixes the customer's corporate identification and otherwise cosmetically alters the product to the customer's requirements.

*stocking manufacturer sales representative*   A hybrid form of a manufacturer sales representative that carries limited physical inventory for key customers but performs only the normal sales functions for other manufacturers' product lines. This dual role can and often does cause conflict among customers as well as with noninventoried manufacturer principals that view a stocking rep as a potential competitor.

**Exhibit 1-7.** Categories of direct and indirect channels.

| Direct | Indirect | |
|---|---|---|
| *Product Ownership* | *Product Ownership* | *Product Nonownership* |
| • Direct sales force<br>• National account sales<br>• Direct mail<br>• Telemarketing<br>• Manufacturer's catalog | • Distributor<br>• Private label<br>• Stocking manufacturer sales representative<br>• Original equipment manufacturer (OEM)<br>• Catalog house<br>• Telemarketing company<br>• Wholesaler<br>• Master distributor<br>• Reseller<br>• Retailer<br>• Dealer<br>• Value-added reseller (VAR)<br>• Value-added dealer<br>• System integrator<br>• Phantom channel of distribution | • Manufacturer sales representation<br>• Broker<br>• Independent sales agent<br>• Export management company (EMC)<br>• Synthetic channel of distribution<br>• Fulfillment channel |

*original equipment manufacturer (OEM)*   A manufacturer that sells a part of its product to another producer that then includes that part or subassembly into its finished product.

*catalog house*   A company that purchases and stocks products, frequently of the same category, and offers them to the end user buying public via some printed or electronic catalog. Quill Office Supply is a good example.

*telemarketing company*   Performs the same functions as a catalog house, but sells through telecommunications.

*wholesaler*   A distributor that sells into the consumer marketplace.

*master distributor*   A distributor that sells to a lower-level counterpart. Manufacturers that establish master distributors often require increased inventory, more sophisticated marketing expertise, a national presence, and technical and strategic planning capability. For example, Procter & Gamble now sells only to those distributors that can buy P&G products in 500-case lots or more. Distributors that cannot afford to buy in these quantities must purchase from one that does.

*reseller*   An industrial or high-technology company that purchases a product or a service either direct from a manufacturer or from a distributor, depending on the sales volume levels or services required by the manufacturer. The higher the potential sales volume or the more sophisticated or technical the services needed, the more likely the reseller will purchase directly from the manufacturer. Resellers that provide fewer services and garner lower sales volume deal with distributors in the channel. Also called a *dealer.*

*retailer*   A company that performs the same functions as a reseller but operates in the consumer arena.

*dealer*   Another name for reseller.

*value-added reseller (VAR)*   Performs the same functions as a reseller with the important exception that it also bundles or adds product and service value to provide a true one-step shop or system solution to its customers. An example is the computer shop that sells, sets up, and installs a complete LAN system for small businesses.

*value-added dealer*   Similar to a value-added reseller, it usually offers less technical expertise and a smaller library of lower-end products.

*system integrator*   Similar to a value-added reseller, this kind of company offers a high degree of technical knowledge about complicated, system-oriented products. IBM system integrators sell minicomputers and midrange computers that facilitate work for a thousand people. Sound contracting system integrators can outfit a night club, civic auditorium, or church with all the microphones, mixers, and amplifiers it needs.

## Direct Channels That Take Ownership

*direct sales force*   The manufacturer's employed direct sales force that sells products to the end user.

*national account sales*   Exists where a manufacturer has a direct sales arrangement with a large national customer. While the sales contracts may be negotiated at corporate headquarters, local service or installation may also be required. For example, a company might sell power protection products to Wal-Mart and then install the product at each of its stores.

## Indirect Channels That Do Not Take Ownership

*manufacturer sales representative*   A business organization that primarily provides sales expertise and marketing efforts, such as direct mail, exhibit booth assistance, or customer open houses and seminars, thereby giving the manufacturer local market coverage that couldn't be achieved otherwise. The manufacturer retains direct responsibility for credit billing, collection, shipment, advertising, public relations, and national direct mail.

*broker*   Similar to a manufacturer sales representative, except this type of company centers its sales activity in the consumer marketplace. (E.g.: food, apparel products.)

*independent sales agent*   Same as a broker or manufacturer sales representative but primarily concentrated in the consumer marketplace. (E.g.: Insurance agents.)

*export management company (EMC)*   The international version of a manufacturer sales representative that concentrates on certain international geographic theaters, such as Latin America, Europe, or Asia.

***synthetic channel of distribution***   A channel created by farming out tasks to different companies that specialize in the performance of a particular business function. A manufacturer might contract with an order fulfillment house for order processing and shipment or use a service company to provide postsale warranty administration. All channel tasks are provided by these companies; the manufacturer provides only the product.

## The Channelmaster's Job

Being a channel marketing executive today is challenging. Channels change in the blink of an eye. Channel conflict lurks everywhere—but so does the opportunity for success.

To succeed, you need to become what I call a *channelmaster*. You need to know how to create a new channel, locate sound channel partners, and manage fruitful and positive channel relationships. It's hard work—but it's what makes channel marketing such an exciting and dynamic field.

A channelmaster is a sales and marketing manager with a legion of attributes he or she can call on when necessary.

What attributes should a channelmaster possess?

- ❐ Creative
- ❐ Organized
- ❐ A team player
- ❐ A teacher and coach
- ❐ An above-average communicator
- ❐ Ethical
- ❐ Politically astute
- ❐ Reliable and trustworthy
- ❐ A skilled mediator
- ❐ Personable and easy to relate to
- ❐ Compassionate
- ❐ Intelligent
- ❐ An expert on indirect channels
- ❐ Aggressive
- ❐ Tactical
- ❐ Strategic
- ❐ Consistent
- ❐ A channel defender
- ❐ A leader
- ❐ A general manager

The channelmaster is also a change agent, as Professor Louis Stern, J. L. Kellogg Graduate School of Management at Northwestern University, points out. Thus, he or she "must have power, credibility, political skills and, most importantly, tenacity" in order to manage the change process that is triggered whenever a company adds a new channel.

Sound like a hard role to fill? It is. In my experience, there aren't many true channelmasters. I've been in channel marketing for more than thirty years, and I didn't become a channelmaster until I'd spent five years swimming upstream. But what I've learned is in this book. Study it, and you'll be on your way to getting your channelmaster diploma.

The rest of this chapter covers the basic concepts that influence the way you design, manage, and communicate with a channel. With these concepts under your belt, you'll be prepared for the step-by-step process of channel design to come.

## The Primary Business Challenge

As channelmaster, you set up and manage a complex network of distributors and resellers that sell your product along with those of many other manufacturers. Those distributors have a number of resources they can invest in your line if they choose, depending on how important you are to them. Exhibit 1-8 shows how distributor activities vary depending on your rank. At the low end, few distributor resources are committed. But the more important you become, the more eager the distributor is to invest dollars in your inventory and sales and marketing time in your mutual success.

*Your primary job as channelmaster is to achieve a disproportionate share of your COD's resource commitment, through crafting a business relationship that benefits both parties.* Throughout this book are ways you can strengthen your relationship, make your line more important to your distributors, and increase your "share of mind" with your channel members. Pay attention, channelmaster! This is your most important task!

## Know What Your Customer Desires

Before you can set up a channel, you need to know what your end customer wants. That's why every intelligent channel strategy begins with a customer segmentation analysis. Find out *who* your end users are and how they behave. How do they use the product? What are their needs? Are they loyal users? What is their lifestyle? Pinpoint their social class, and try to understand their opinions, activities, and attitudes. What are their demographics? Dig up data on their age, gender, income, education, ethnic origin, occupation, and location. Find these facts first—and then match the channel to those needs.

**Exhibit 1-8.** **Impact of product line importance on distributor behavior.**

*Your Importance to the Distributor:*
% of Distributor Sales Represented by Your Products

| | *Low Importance:* | *Medium Importance:* | *High Importance:* | *High Strategic Importance:* |
|---|---|---|---|---|
| | 1% of sales | 5% of sales | 10% of sales | 40% of sales |
| Distributor Activities | Fill orders | Sell your product | Sell your product proactively | Your are strategically linked to the distributor's future |
| | Probably use your support minimally | Use your support if easily incorporated into its business | Use your support enthusiastically | |
| | Probably not change any aspects of its business for you | Rebel if you are hard to do business with | May modify components of its business for you | |

*Source:* Frank Lynn and Associates, Chicago.

## Find Out What Your Distributor Desires

Before you begin seeking and selecting distributors, acquaint yourself with the ingredients that distributors look to manufacturers to supply. Make sure you supply these business requirements, and you will find it easier to secure resource commitment from your channel. Here are the core competencies distributors look for:

❏ *Quality product.* No distributor wants to represent a poor quality manufacturer. If one product is below standard, customers may perceive that the distributor's entire product mix suffers from the same poor quality. That's a market image the distributor wants to avoid at all costs.

❐ *Adequate compensation.* If your company cannot or will not meet a distributor's margin demands, then the distributor will refuse to deal with you. It's just that simple!

❐ *Committed manufacturer field salespeople.* Without question, the ultimate success or failure of your channel marketing program rests with your field salespeople. They are literally the *last* lines of communication and management between the manufacturer and the distributor, and they are responsible for implementing your business policies and procedures. Your distributors want salespeople who are company representatives, channel defenders, trainers, and field sales managers, all wrapped up in one convenient package. They want to deal with salespeople who execute your company's business philosophy while working to achieve satisfaction for the distributor. They want salespeople who help them develop marketing strategies; pass along customer testimonials, sales success stories, marketing trends, and emerging market opportunities; and help them with joint sales calls, product expertise, sales contests, and motivation.

❐ *Competent internal support system.* One of the principal ingredients in a lasting relationship is the resourcefulness of your internal channel support systems, such as customer service, technical support, training, and marketing services support. For example, one of the quickest ways to turn off a distributor is to provide an inadequate level of sales and marketing support. Distributors commit their resources to manufacturers they can trust and rely on.

❐ *Reputable manufacturer image.* The adage "we're known by the company we keep" truly applies here. A manufacturer must constantly work on improving its image. Quality product, superior media communications, competent factory personnel, and respected manufacturer managerial capabilities all contribute to the image that is conveyed to the channel of distribution and, in turn, the end user.

These are the core concerns of every distributor—the components that distributors use to evaluate manufacturers. To attract and retain good distributors, take these elements into account as you create marketing plans for your channels.

## Select a Market Coverage Strategy

The channelmaster needs to decide upon the correct market coverage strategy for his or her channel. Exhibit 1-9 illustrates three basic ways to approach a market through indirect channels:

1. *Intensive:* Covering a market by authorizing several distributors to sell products in a given geographic area or market segment

**Exhibit 1-9.** Three channel market coverage strategies.

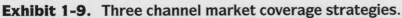

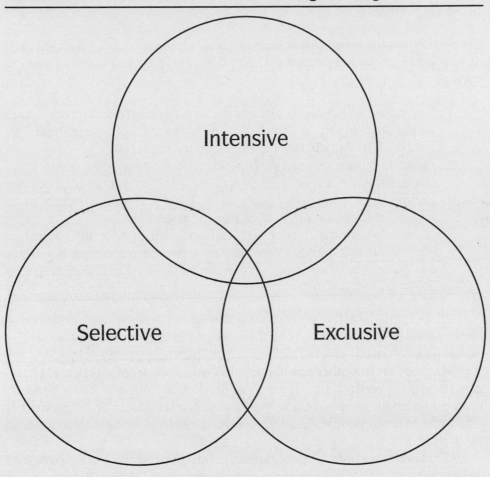

2. *Selective:* Selecting only those distributors that meet certain channel selection criteria to sell products in a given market
3. *Exclusive:* Authorizing only one distributor per geographic area or market segment to sell products

Conceivably, you *could* employ a combination of coverage strategies, such as exclusivity in one area and selectivity in another.

Selecting the best approach is not difficult because the supply of top-notch distributors may be limited in your target market. You want to work with what I call *eagle* distributors—distributors whose competence is unquestioned and whose integrity is unblemished. The availability of these distributors significantly influences your market coverage decision.

## Structure Your Sales Organization to Either General or Niche Markets

There are also three options for structuring your sales organization, each of which offers varying degrees of specialization and expertise in a vertical market:

1. *Geographic:* Where each distributor or set of distributors is assigned a specific territory in which it is authorized to sell your products. Exhibit 1-10 depicts this type of sales organization.
2. *Product:* Where selected distributors that have the required expertise are authorized to sell a specific product or group of products. Exhibit 1-11 is an illustration of this type of sales organization, which achieves a moderate degree of specialization.
3. *Market:* Where distributors are authorized to sell to specific industries or vertical markets, thus enabling the manufacturer to achieve a high degree of customer expertise. Exhibit 1-12 is an example of this type of sales organization.

As a channelmaster, you have to closely evaluate which of the three forms of sales organization is best for your company. Your decision depends on how much specialization your distributors need to develop.

Markets, on the other hand, come in two fundamental types: (1) horizontal, and (2) vertical. In a horizontal market, a company or its product is all things to all people. In a vertical market, a company or its product is all things to *some* people. Most channels are set up to deal with vertical markets.

Whether you choose a geographic, product, or market sales structure is determined by the complexity of your product and how much customer support, training, and other forms of support it requires.

If your product is simple—say, a piece of luggage—you need not create a structure that lends itself to specialization. But if you're selling something much more complex—like medical equipment or computer products—you need to pursue a specialized, strategic channel approach. You need channels that can offer expertise and experience to your end users. Your sales organization should be structured to achieve that.

Vertical market customers want specialized attention because they have particular satisfaction requirements. Consider the simple surge protector. In the horizontal market of consumer computer owners, a surge protector is sold to computer owners in order to protect data from sudden surges in home electrical supply. But in the industrial market, selling strategies vary. Selling a surge protector to a hospital is quite different from

*(text continues on page 22)*

**Exhibit 1-10.** A geographic sales organization.

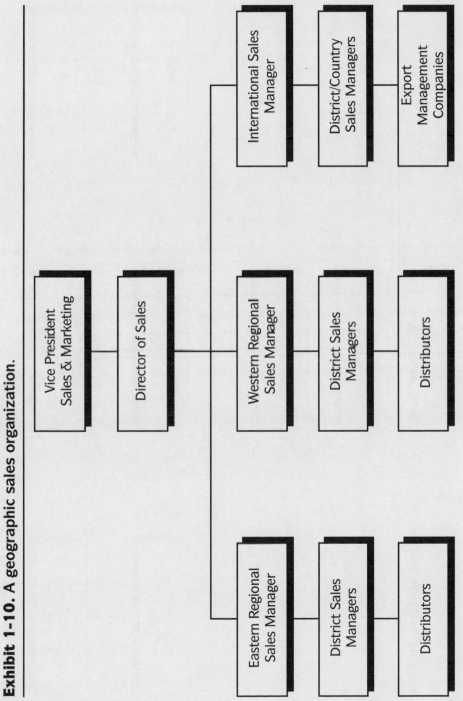

**Exhibit 1-11.** A product-specialized sales organization.

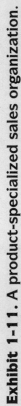

**Exhibit 1-12. A market-specialized sales organization.**

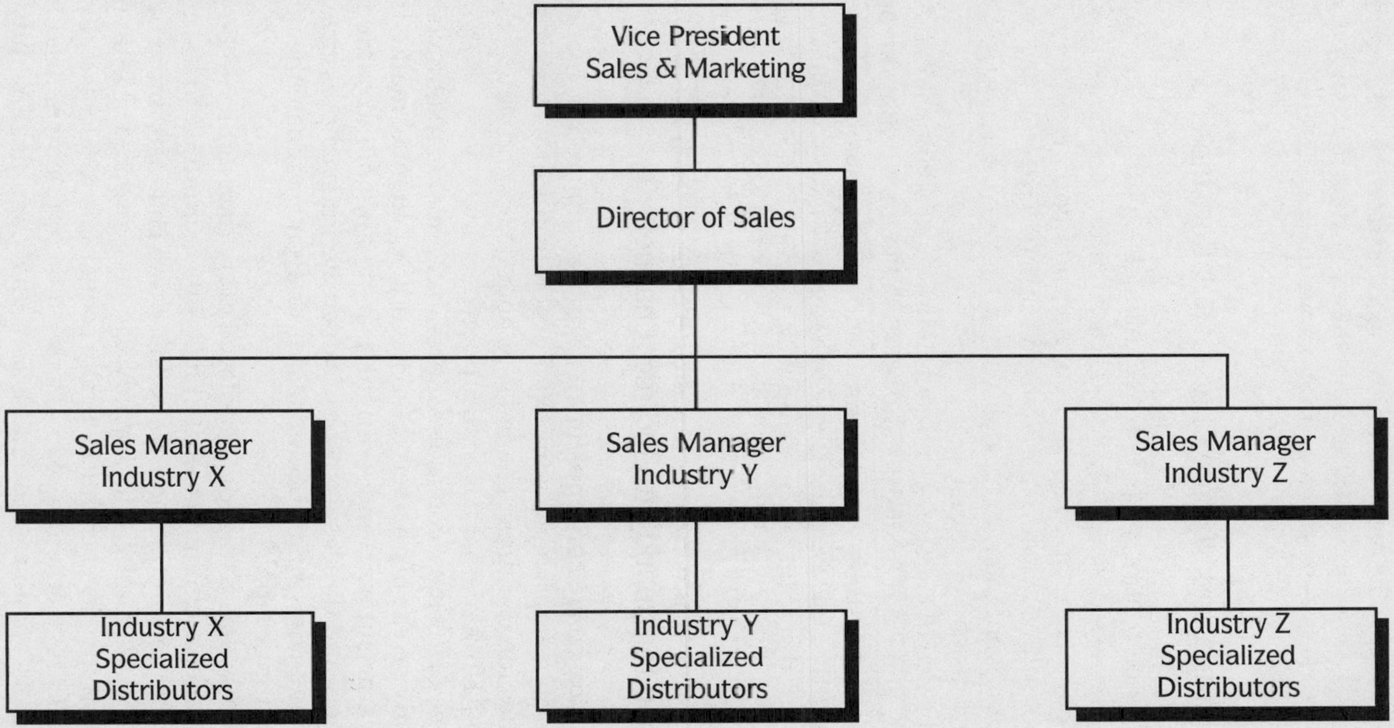

selling one to a telecommunications company. A surge protector thus takes on very different technical specifications in different industries. That's why it is necessary to have different distributors reaching each of those markets—distributors that know the needs and requirements of each market's end users.

## Understand and Nurture Channel Relationships

You do not control your indirect channels—you *manage* them. Unlike a direct-employed sales force, your distributors are not at your beck and call. They may or may not call on the leads you give them. They may or may not sell what you want them to sell. They may or may not charge the price you want them to charge. They may even decide to sell a competing product instead of yours!

The key to managing channels is building relationships. As a channel-master, you need to understand all of the factors that influence a channel relationship. Put simply, these factors are the major business issues and practices that make up the fabric of a successful alliance between manufacturer and distributor. They are the managerial glue that keeps a channel bonded together. And *you* are the one who keeps it glued for longevity!

## Make Sure Your Corporate Culture Supports the Decision to Expand Into Indirect Channels

Before you create and implement a strategic marketing channel plan, you must fully comprehend your true corporate culture. Does it support a direct sales force, indirect channels, or both direct and indirect sales organizations? How emphatic is that support?

One of the most common failures in channel marketing occurs when a company gives only lip service to its indirect channel marketing program. Lukewarm support and outright fear and ignorance among company managers and direct salespeople can create internal pressure, causing the company to downplay, deemphasize, or even terminate the newly created distributor group.

This business tragedy is replayed every day, but it can be prevented if management communicates that it is fully committed to indirect channels of distribution and demonstrates that those channels are to be folded into the corporate family. The tragedy can be prevented if everyone at every administrative level enthusiastically cooperates to successfully implement the full COD marketing plan. Cynics and complainers need to be able to voice their opinions, but enthusiasm and commitment must eventually persuade or silence them.

What kind of culture does your company support? What groundwork needs to be done before you can launch a successful indirect channel program?

## Have the Direct Sales Force and the Indirect Channel of Distribution Report to One Functional Manager

Say you command your direct salespeople to pursue and develop only businesses above a certain sales revenue benchmark—*Fortune* 1000 and midsize businesses with an annual sales potential of $200,000 or more. But what happens when a powerful distributor also decides to penetrate *Fortune* 1000 corporations? Conflict explodes between your direct sales force and the distributor, creating a most uncomfortable and adversarial environment.

One way to avoid this kind of conflict is by *designing* your channel in a way that minimizes or eliminates this kind of head-butting. A second, essential tactic is to have both direct and indirect channels of distribution report to *one* functional sales and marketing manager. Doing so discourages intrachannel conflict and can help mediate conflicts when they arise.

If each channel reports to a different manager, there will be two political camps in often heated adversarial roles. This is definitely *not* desirable. Why battle the enemy within when it's more productive to direct your managerial energies to combating direct competition in the field?

### Observe the Total Channel Equation

The best relationships occur when the channelmaster observes the Total Channel Equation.

---

**The Total Channel Equation**

Manufacturer = Channel = End User

---

Every time you make a decision, consider its impact on all three participants in the channel. Very often a channel marketing manager makes a decision without thoroughly thinking through the consequences. Suppose intense competition forces you to lower your entire pricing schedule—both suggested list prices and channel prices. Now let's say that distributor A has $100,000 of your product, purchased at the previously higher price. Because of its overpriced product, Distributor A is not a happy channel member. A better approach would be to first estimate how much physical inventory is present in the channel, and then protect the distributor's inventory commitment by announcing a price protection policy that would credit distributors for the difference between the old high price and the new lower price.

There is a very definite cause and effect relationship in the total channel equation. All three parts must be fully considered prior to taking any managerial action. All three parts must also be considered during every step of the Channel Design Sequence, the subject of Chapter 2.

## Why Channel Programs Fail

Channel consultants Frank Lynn and Associates created the following list of the top ten reasons why channel programs fail. Sounds gloomy—until you realize that each of these mistakes can be avoided with careful planning and forethought. Find out how to avoid them in the chapters listed after each reason.

1. *Ignoring end user buying patterns and needs.* A true death wish. See Chapter 5 to find out how to discover end user satisfaction requirements and buying patterns.

2. *Assuming your direct sales force will support indirect channels for the good of the company.* Get real—this "conflict eternal" will always exist. Deal with it fairly and equitably. Chapter 3 tells how to uncover internal conflict. Chapter 9 tells how to enhance the relationship between your indirect and direct channels.

3. *Expecting channels to change for you.* Distributors are most reluctant to move out of their comfort zone. Find ways to motivate them in Chapter 11.

4. *Sticking with traditional channels too long.* A frequent and fatal mistake. Chapter 9 tells when it's appropriate to leave an old channel behind.

5. *Not realizing or building your importance (or lack thereof) to the channel.* This is channel ignorance and arrogance. Find out all about it in Chapter 10 on power and conflict.

6. *Being casual about selecting and evaluating your distributors/dealers/reps.* The "warm body syndrome" spells sales failure. All of Part I helps you establish criteria and select the distributors that best meet your needs.

7. *Not understanding the economics of channel marketing.* You have to be able to afford the channel's profit requirement. Find out if you can during your preliminary research, discussed in Chapter 8.

8. *Hoping that one channel can sell to every customer and market.* The

primary reason for having multiple channels of distribution is to reach vertical markets.

9. *Avoiding channel conflict instead of accepting and managing it.* Channel conflict will not go away. Address and manage it by following the principles discussed in Chapter 10.

10. *Not developing strategic "business closeness" relationships.* Channel bonding can easily spell success or failure. Find out how to create it in Chapter 9.

---

**Ken's Words of Wisdom**

❐ If at all possible, pursue sales and marketing specialization (vertical marketing).
❐ To be a true channelmaster, one must be able to feel the business pain and pleasure of each channel member.

---

## *Case:* The Conflict Eternal: Direct vs. Indirect Channels of Distribution

Your company is in the second phase of a new product development cycle and has correctly identified a clear need for a totally new indirect channel of distribution to market a low-priced, new-to-the-world product. You have accepted a very significant promotion from direct sales account manager to national marketing manager for the future, indirect COD. Furthermore, you also envision your established, employed, direct sales force selling the same unit to its existing base of customers.

So far, everything has gone well. To establish the new channel, you have executed the eleven steps of the Channel Design Sequence (discussed in Chapter 2) by signing twenty-four regional and two national distributors to market this exciting new product line. Wisely, you approach your counterpart in charge of the direct sales force to solicit her immediate and complete support. Surprisingly, she snaps back that already your "bottom-feeding" distributors have not only taken away direct account business but have sold these same captured customers other products that are fiercely competitive to the other product lines your company sells.

The same direct sales manager goes on to loudly reprimand you for not being selective in choosing your twenty-six distributors. She sees you as the primary cause of this internal channel conflict. She flatly refuses to support your sales and marketing efforts and openly states that she and her field salespeople will do everything possible to see that your distributor sales organization has a short channel life.

What is to be done? One thing is certain: Your managerial equal has significant internal power, and that justifiably concerns you. Now what? Specifically, what actions will you take to alleviate this corporate war?

## Case interpretational points:

◻ Two basic questions must be answered: (1) Why did this happen in the first place? (2) Why wasn't every marketing manager in the company involved with not only the creation but also the execution of this indirect channel program?

◻ Attempt first to resolve this sensitive issue on the same level of management. Failing that, this matter must be brought up to your immediate superior and perhaps a managerial tribunal for resolution.

◻ Immediately open the lines of communication among all levels of management in both the direct and indirect channels. Establish meetings where open and constructive dialogue can go on.

◻ Top management commitment to the indirect channel program must be firmly communicated to all concerned parties.

◻ Institute a compensation system that pays direct salespeople for all indirect sales within their assigned territory. In return, the direct salespeople must provide an appropriate level of sales and marketing support (training, joint sales calls, technical and customer services that can be verified by their call reports and your field distributors' contacts).

◻ Above all, establish a mediating system where interchannel conflict can be quickly and fairly heard and resolved. Try forming a management council made up of both direct and indirect internal and external marketing managers.

# Part I
# Crafting Your Channel

# Chapter 2

# Channel Design Sequence

A well-crafted, well-executed channel design plan is a powerful weapon in any company's arsenal. With a plan in place, you can provide superior value and service to both types of customers you serve: distributors and end users. Without a plan, you flounder.

I define channel design as creating a totally new channel or modifying an existing channel of distribution structure. There are eleven steps involved in creating a new channel or reorganizing an existing one through the Channel Design Sequence discussed in this chapter. Proceeding in an orderly manner through these eleven steps gives you can excellent shot at success. Neglecting steps or taking shortcuts endangers your plans and places your channel in jeopardy.

## The Uses and Benefits of Effective Channel Design

The main objective of a channel design effort is to efficiently select and entice "golden eagles"—the very best candidates in your channel environment. Your ability to deal with eagles determines the ultimate success or failure of your marketing efforts. Make no mistake, channelmaster!

Investing attention in the channel design process pays off amply every time. Carefully following all eleven steps helps you:

❒ Establish selection criteria that identify the best channel candidates.
❒ Minimize conflict by weeding out potential antagonists and choosing the most cooperative and least conflictual distributors.
❒ Avoid legal entanglements by filtering out trouble-making, channel-destroying undesirables while maintaining the highest legal and ethical standards.

Go slowly. Take your time. Resist the urge to hurry. For example, if internal pressures force you to fill a geographic territory or market area with a mediocre distributor, you will be condemned to mediocre sales performance. You will also need to devote a great deal of your managerial attention to repairing a mistake that should never have been made in the first place. And what do you think your competitors will do while you are wasting your time managing this situation? They will concentrate their firepower in that territory or market to achieve a stronger position. And during this time, you will experience "sales leakage"—a loss of revenue and profits going to your field opponents.

Another consequence of rushed and therefore incomplete channel of distribution plans is a shallow and one-sided marketing program that clearly exhibits a manufacturer's lack of knowledge in the way a distributor conducts business. No wonder the distributor greets this with shrugged shoulders. The distributor justifiably feels that this is just another manufacturer that will load it with inventory and then disappear into the sunset—known in channel circles as another manufacturer with short-range, tactical thinking. How typical. . . .

When you proactively and strategically think through the Channel Design Sequence, you can construct a two-way mutually beneficial program. Your selection criteria and enticing administrative policies will be strong evidence of your full understanding of your distributor's part of the channel equation. You position yourself as a channelmaster, and you position your company's image and products as most desirable and trustworthy additions to your eagle distributor's inventory.

Investing in a comprehensive design also enables you to identify and deal with a competitive market blockade. When approaching a new market, you frequently find that your competition has blocked your entrance into the market by locking up the eagle distributors. They clearly have the "early mover" advantage. Faced with this dilemma, you have three choices:

1. Completely retreat from the target market.
2. Create a new, secondary channel of distribution.
3. Build your credentials by entering less important geographic markets and attacking the primary market when your reputation is stronger.

Without a channel design plan, you'll probably choose the first approach above and throw in the towel. But with a plan, you can think through your options and choose one of the latter two approaches. Frequently, after you acquire credibility in the market via a secondary channel of distribution, the primary channel notices your success and becomes receptive to you.

If your channel structure is already in place, the Channel Design Sequence helps you evaluate whether it is satisfying all of your end user buying requirements. Proceeding through the Channel Design Sequence ensures that your channel marketing program is functioning as you and your customers want it to. Basically, what you're doing is reusing your initial plan as a form of channel insurance.

The positive end result? Your company, your channel members, and your end users will respect the care you used in selecting distributors. And your ability to conceptualize, implement, execute, and manage the eleven steps will earn you the coveted title of "channelmaster"—the gold braiding of your marketing rank!

## The Channel Design Sequence

There are eleven steps in the Channel Design Sequence, as shown in Exhibit 2-1. They are discussed below.

### *Step 1:* Identify the New Market You Want to Penetrate or New Product You Need to Launch

What product do you want to launch in your channel? What market segment do you want to reach?

Say you've been selling power protector products to the electronics and electrical markets. One day you realize that two new markets, the computer and medical segments, are emerging as significant new sales revenue possibilities. You also realize that they have different customer satisfaction requirements (product, pricing, promotion, service) that must be fulfilled through an appropriate channel of distribution. Proceed to Step 2, channelmaster.

### *Step 2:* Verify the Need for a New Channel of Distribution or Some Form of Channel Reorganization

There are many reasons why a channel should be created or modified. Any of these situations may justify the need for a channel change:

---

**Identify the new market you want to penetrate or new product you need to launch.**
**Verify the need for a new channel of distribution or some form of channel reorganization.**

---

**Exhibit 2-1.** The Channel Design Sequence.

1. Identify the new market you want to penetrate or new product you need to launch.

⇩

2. Verify the need for a new channel of distribution or some form of channel reorganization.

⇩

3. Evaluate all macro market conditions.

⇩

4. Conduct a competitive channel analysis.

⇩

5. Research and rank customer/end user satisfaction requirements.

⇩

6. Specify and rank the tasks you want your channel partner to perform.

⇩

7. Investigate all possible channel of distribution structures.

⇩

8. Decide upon eagle channel partners.

⇩

9. Obtain internal corporate recommitment.

⇩

10. Approach and sign the selected distributors.

⇩

11. Monitor and evaluate the channel structure.

❐ A lucrative new market emerges, but your present channel cannot effectively sell or is not interested in selling your products and/or services to it.

❐ A competitor utilizes an entirely new channel that is more efficient or profitable than your present channel structure. Case in point: While Tupperware chose to stay with its traditional channel of Tupperware parties, prime competitor Rubbermaid began selling its products through power retailers like Wal-Mart. This is an excellent example of a flanking market strategy.

❏ New products with new end user requirements cannot be effectively serviced by your existing channel. Thus, IBM turned to indirect channels to sell its microcomputer products to consumers and small businesses, bypassing the direct sales force that sold mainframe computers to companies.

❏ New, potentially lucrative CODs emerge that cannot be ignored or your sales and marketing performance will deteriorate. A prime example is the internet, whose influence as a real or potential channel of distribution is increasing every day.

❏ Macro environmental influences (sociocultural, economic, governmental, technological, or legal) force your adherence, conformity, or, at minimum, marketing attention. Witness health care products companies, which must certainly modify their COD strategy to meet the changes being instituted by HMOs, PPOs, and other channel influencers.

❏ A policy or procedure change, acquisition, or merger dramatically and quickly enforces new philosophies. For example, an indirect channel company acquires a company that sells its products via a direct sales organization. This may force a change in overall channel philosophy.

❏ Your channel security check detects a change in the way end users buy your products or services. An ongoing customer segmentation program is a must!

❏ Global influences and developments require an expanded international presence.

Once you have identified the need for a change, you need to decide whether you can modify an existing channel relationship or must create a new channel of distribution. Before you do anything, run your plans by your existing channels. Ask your present distributor organization whether it would like to partner-participate with you in your new venture. Chances are it won't—but it surely appreciates being asked. *Never* assume that your present COD doesn't want to be a part of your future marketing strategic direction. And *never* launch a new channel without communicating first with existing ones. Doing so isn't just tactless. It's dangerous. Imagine the damage created when your primary existing channel learns of your plans from a competitor first!

## *Step 3:* Evaluate All Macro Market Conditions

To consider macro market conditions, you must rise above the everyday, micro-channel world and very closely consider those macro influences that control your destiny. They include:

❏ End user buying behavior
❏ The economy

❏ Technology
❏ Target channel variables
❏ Competitive actions
❏ Political factors
❏ International factors
❏ Your company considerations
❏ Legalities

While most of these influences are out of your managerial or corporate control, they can very easily spell the difference between victory and defeat for your channel marketing efforts. You need to assess the effect any of these conditions could have on your ability to manage your distributors. Unless you evaluate their possible influence, you may end up facing an insurmountable obstacle that would prohibit you from forming the most efficient channel of distribution. These influences are discussed in detail in Chapter 3.

It's a good idea to evaluate internal company factors as well. For example, suppose a direct sales-oriented company decides to bring on indirect channels to sell into an emerging market. Clearly, the corporate culture leans toward the former and not the latter. What this means to you, the indirect channelmaster, is that there will most likely be a strong internal preference given to direct sales and not your area. If you understand this up front, you will be better prepared to cope with a political situation that is primarily out of your control.

## Step 4: Conduct a Competitive Channel Analysis

When you have determined that a new channel is necessary or desirable, conduct a complete study of all present and possible future channel opponents. (Chapter 4 shows how.) It is critical that you identify all competitive influences that could affect implementation of your Channel Design Sequence, so you can temper marketing strategies accordingly. For example, if you are not a dominant company and are also a late market entrant, it makes sense to assess the power that your competitors already possess. Evaluating your channel competition helps you understand your value to your distributor candidates and avoid making false assumptions about your appeal to them.

## Step 5: Research and Rank Customer/End User Satisfaction Requirements

You must assess what the customer or end user requires from the organization that sells your product or service. Canvas an adequate number of buyers to discover how well they know your product, whom they purchase your type of product from, what channel tasks their preferred supplier provides, and whether they intend to purchase any of your product from their distributor in the future. Pay special attention to satisfaction requirements that are mentioned often. For example, consumers may frequently state that the immediate availability of local inventory, responsive customer service, and a one-stop shop for all similar product needs are the primary reasons why they do business with their preferred supplier. This affirmation will determine their actual rank of importance to the end user. Chapter 5 covers these factors in detail.

## *Step 6:* Specify and Rank the Tasks You Want Your Channel Partner to Perform

Here, you define and rank what you and your company want your channel members to do for you. Combine these standards with the customer/ end user satisfaction requirements determined in Step 5, and you arrive at a list of master channel selection criteria. Chapter 6 helps you decide on those tasks and rank their relative importance to your company. Use these selection criteria to evaluate all future distributor candidates so that you bring only eagles into your channel of distribution.

## *Step 7:* Investigate All Possible Channel of Distribution Structures

Your next priority is to thoroughly research and determine what possible channel structures are available to you. Construct a matrix that illustrates the various structures through which you can reach your end users. (Exhibit 2-2 shows an example of such a matrix—this one specifically for the computer and peripheral manufacturer field.) Chapter 7 describes the process needed to accomplish this assignment. Then, you need to decide which channel structure opportunities should be brought on board first, second, third, and so on. It would be a grave mistake to assimilate several CODs at the same time. The priorities for channel introduction should specifically orient around channel sales revenue potential, profit possibilities, and whether or not you can adequately provide the internal support for the channel.

## *Step 8:* Decide Upon Eagle Channel Partners

Here, you make the final candidate decisions and decide the sequence in which you will bring them into your organization. (See Chapter 7.) The decision process is a rather simple one. Merely apply the critical mass selection criteria to each potential channel partner to determine whether or not it meets your standards. You will present your channel partnership

**Exhibit 2-2. Typical channel of distribution matrix for the computer/peripheral manufacturer industry.**

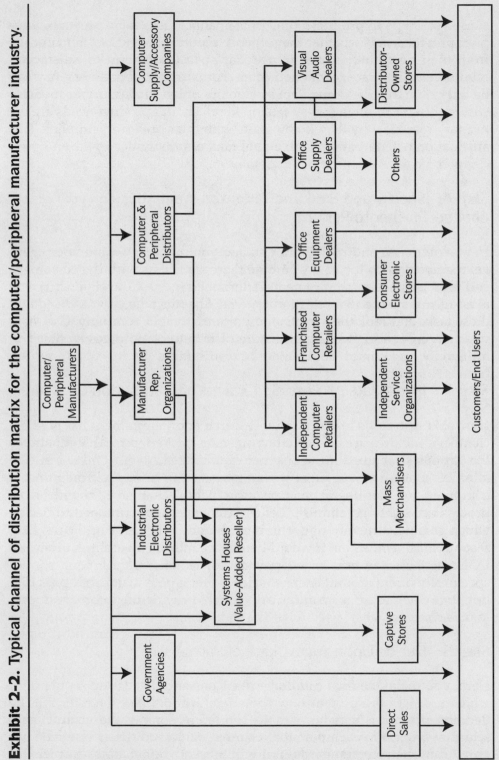

plan to those that pass. Keep the appropriate corporate managers in your company (general manager, comptroller, credit manager, sales manager) advised of your channel design action plans to avoid any misinterpretation of your actions. Honest and total company managerial buy-in must be given to the total channel plan prior to your implementing it. Enter Step 9.

## *Step 9:* Obtain Internal Corporate Recommitment

Change is easier when everyone is on board and prepared for it. That's why it's important to have a final, "jump start" meeting with your immediate superior and any other concerned managers before you execute the final phase of your channel design plan.

Let them know that the new channel will most likely create some anxiety among people in your existing channels and that they should be prepared to handle possibly heated discussions about the topic. It is also prudent to inform them about your new distributor sign-up efforts, so that these managers will know when these new faces will become part of your company's indirect sales organization. The better informed everyone is, the easier it is to make your new channel a success. The corporate recommitment meeting is covered in Chapter 8.

## *Step 10:* Approach and Sign the Selected Distributors

Next, present your channel marketing plan to your prospective targets. Don't be disappointed if the channel candidate allocates a mere thirty to sixty minutes for you to present your plan, which to you is a magnificent document. Real eagles are hotly pursued by dozens of other channel marketing managers and have limited time for meetings with new product line candidates. Therefore, you need to be completely prepared. Your ultimate goal is to walk away with a signed contract, a stocking order, an initial start-up plan, and an enthusiastic partnership.

Your main marketing tool to achieve this goal is a strategic plan that briefly lists the reasons why this eagle candidate should do business with you. In the document, use bullet-like statements to summarize your policies, business advantages, and procedures. Chapter 8 explains how to pull together this enticement plan.

## *Step 11:* Monitor and Evaluate the Channel Structure

Remember Reason Number 4 of the top ten reasons why a channel program fails (given in Chapter 1)? "Sticking with traditional channels too long" can be prevented by adhering to Step 11. Unless you're watching, market and end user changes may make your channels obsolete and leave your sales high and dry. So monitor your channel structure. Keep an eye out for ways to improve it.

Making a decision to change channel structure is a necessary but difficult task. Emotions can creep into the process. If your company has devoted decades to selling its product direct, adding new channels can be traumatic. If you have close relationships with distributors in your existing channels, it's not easy to inform them that the time has come to part ways.

Don't be afraid to make a channel change, but do it with sensitivity, foresight, and a keen concern for channel ethics and legalities. It's never a good idea to burn your channel bridges. The distributor you eliminate today may be a distributor you return to tomorrow. Times change, and you must be able to alter your channel strategies to maximize sales revenue and profits by always maintaining the best channel partners possible.

## Tying It All Together

To tie all of the eleven channel design steps neatly together, map out the key action items in a structured critical event chart that shows what you need to do and when you need to do it in order to successfully build your channel. Such a chart helps you track your progress and ensures that critical events are not forgotten. By assiduously following these eleven steps, you gain substantially on your competition.

The Channel Design Sequence described in this chapter is a living managerial tool that will guide you through the critical process of selecting and forming solid business relationships with the very best eagle distributors. Equally important, you will avoid those candidates that would drain away precious managerial energies and resources. This is the growth cornerstone of channel of distribution marketing.

### *CASE:* NEW PRODUCT = NEW MARKETS = NEW MARKETING CHANNELS

You are the seasoned channel marketing manager for a leading audiovisual hardware manufacturer (overhead projectors, slide projectors, filmstrip projectors) that has the fortunate advantage of representing from 40 percent to 50 percent of the total annual sales of 125 dealers. To date, your overall channel of distribution relationship has been a superior one. Even though your products generate a major share of your dealers' sales revenue, you have not abused your power position, which has gained you a great deal of field respect. Sales and profits are consistently increasing, and all three parts of the COD—manufacturer, distributor, and end user—are quite satisfied and content. But your channel world is about to change dramatically.

Your immediate superior—the division general manager—walks into your office, closes the door (not a good sign), and firmly informs you that the company president has, on her own, decided to purchase a sophisticated learning system of specialized educational hardware and software. You knew nothing about this new product acquisition. The GM goes on to say that the president expects you to start selling the system in the next two to three months. To complicate things further, you know in your channelmaster's heart that your existing dealers cannot provide you with the sales and marketing expertise the new product and new market will demand. You also believe that your present dealer organization probably will not be interested in pursuing this market. And by the way, you have some rather serious doubts about your company's internal support capability for this sophisticated educational system.

With all of this in mind, address the following key issues:

1. What will you do with your existing, loyal COD?
2. If you decide to create a new COD, then how will you go about doing it? What channel design plan will you follow?
3. What about your internal sales and marketing support?
4. How will you handle your present, internal new product development syndrome to avoid future marketing problems?

**Case interpretational points:**

❏ Do not ignore your present COD in your channel design plans. Let the members of your channel know what the strategy is going to be regarding this *new* product targeted for a *new* market.

❏ Discuss all eleven steps of channel design with everyone involved (internal managers).

❏ Personally meet with the 20 percent of your dealers that give you 80 percent of your business to reduce their anxiety levels and also use them as an informal conduit of information to the remainder of your dealer organization.

❏ Do not introduce this new product until your internal support system is fully in place.

❏ Tactfully establish your channelmaster rank with the company president so that all future new product plans include your input at the beginning of the development cycle.

# Chapter 3

# Marketing Channel Macroinfluences and Internal Variables

```
┌─────────────────────────────────────────────────────────────┐
│  √  Step 1:  Identify the new market you want to penetrate or new product you │
│              need to launch.                                                  │
│  √  Step 2:  Verify the need for a new channel of distribution or some form of │
│              channel reorganization.                                          │
│  √  Step 3:  Evaluate all macro market conditions.                            │
└─────────────────────────────────────────────────────────────┘
```

A channel can be a cozy place, especially when relationships with your distributors and customers are good, and your market is stable. It's easy to hide out in the confines of your channel structure, entranced with the way you do business—until an enormous wave roils down your channel, drowning everyone in sight!

Every channel is influenced by macro environmental forces that are beyond your control. End users may change the way they buy or demand new services your channel is not providing. New products begin to chip away at your market share. The economy goes into a tailspin.

If you do not keep a constant surveillance on these indirect channel influences, the results can be disastrous. You must always be on the lookout for any significant developments that could affect the way you do business with your channel. The dynamics of channel marketing are constantly changing, and you must change along with them or end up with a channel dinosaur on your hands. All too often a cooperation has stayed within its traditional channel too long and then fallen prey to a macro environmental force.

Channelmaster, be ever observant of these important changes and

**Exhibit 3-1.** Marketing channel macroinfluences.

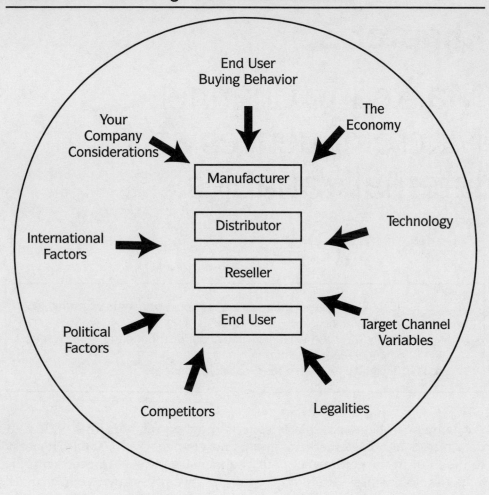

marketing channel macroinfluences, some of which are shown in Exhibit 3-1. Not only can they influence the way you do business with your channel, they are also essential to understand before you begin to design your channel. Step 3 in the Channel Design Sequence discussed in Chapter 2 is: *Evaluate all macro market conditions.* This chapter examines the following such variables:

- ❏ End user buying behavior
- ❏ The economy
- ❏ Technology
- ❏ Target channel variables
- ❏ Competitors

❐ Political factors
❐ International factors
❐ Your company considerations
❐ Legalities

# End User Buying Behavior

In a sense, each of us has a certain degree of influence over how products finally reach us. Collectively, we are *channel shapers.* Alert channel marketing managers watch for changes in the way end users procure their products or services and mold their channels to satisfy these up-to-date customer demands.

You must react to significant alterations in the way customers purchase your products or services. Watch for changes in:

❐ *Where* your customers buy your products
❐ *How* they buy your products
❐ *When* they purchase your products
❐ *Who* does the buying

You may need to alter your channel of distribution if you observe changes in any of these areas. That's what the computer industry recently did with its computer retailers, as this February 1, 1994 *Wall Street Journal* headline explained:

> **FORECASTS ASIDE, DEALERS OF PCS THRIVE AGAIN**
> *Barely a year after they were dismissed as retail's relics, old-time computer dealers are back.*

The article went on to say that the growing home computer market had led IBM, Compaq, and other major manufacturers to work once again with computer dealers, which were suddenly the dominant channel for consumers seeking home computers. Bottom line: You need to react to significant changes in the way customers purchase your products and services.

# The Economy

The economy affects all three parts of the Total Channel Equation. The performance of manufacturer, channel, and end user is controlled by their ability to borrow money for inventory acquisition, readily acquire raw materials to manufacture products, absorb labor expenses, and afford to purchase products or services in the first place. There are several indicators you should keep an eye on, channelmaster:

❑ *Interest rates* can substantially hamper the ability to borrow funds to conduct business effectively. High interest rates can slow spending, decreasing your sales commensurately.

❑ *Product and material shortages* can make it difficult to deliver product to the end user on time and in the desired quantity or volume. In poor economic times, material suppliers are reluctant to maintain adequate inventory level, and manufacturers are likewise hesitant to carry anything but bare minimum quantities of basic items. Both actions have a negative effect on the overall sales environment.

❑ *Inflation* may cause consumers to spend less on your product or service. When faced with an inflationary spiral, end users tend to hold on to their money and purchase only what is necessary to exist or operate their business.

❑ *Recession* can put pressure on you to decrease your cost of sales. Corporations facing a recession often decide that they cannot afford to continue to maintain their current channel structure. Direct sales channels are then often eliminated or blended into less costly indirect marketing channels.

Clearly, the economic environment affects how different channel members operate and efficiently function under these different influences. An alert channelmaster must always be observant for these retrenching pressures and must modify his or her strategies to cope with the economy.

# Technology

With the advent of computerized inventory control, teleshopping, telemarketing, on-line databases, and, of course, the internet, today's channel manager must constantly be on the watch for any new or revolutionary technological developments that can help or hinder all three parts of the Total Channel Equation:

---

**The Total Channel Equation**

Manufacturer = Channel = End User

---

For example, while most internet activity now involves exchanging information (with the end user requesting data, specifications, pricing, or availability of a product or service), it certainly makes marketing sense for a manufacturer to have a Web page to respond to these inquiries, which could very well evolve into sales.

As time goes on, the internet will play an important role in the completion of the sales cycle for an increasing number of products and services. Channelmasters must harness this sales power to the best of their advantage over the competition.

## Target Channel Variables

Two significant macroinfluences crop up the target channel: (1) availability of channel candidates, and (2) channel economics.

Often there are just not enough distributors available to provide you with adequate market coverage. Your competition may have locked you out by forming solid and powerful relationships with the best eagle distributors, or there may simply not be any in a particular territory. In this situation, you really have only three choices: (1) Form a business relationship with those distributors that are available, (2) employ the concept of synthetic channels to sell in areas without coverage (see Chapter 13 for details), or (3) walk away from the targeted marketplace. Obviously, if the end user audience is a very lucrative one, any alternative is better than a complete retreat. While the other two alternatives are not ideal, they may be necessary until you build up your channel strength and desirability and can attract eagles.

Channel economics play a role when the costs of doing business with the target channel are too high or you don't have sufficient profitability to afford certain channel economic requirements. It's rather elementary. If you cannot meet a distributor's profitability prerequisite, then the distributor simply will not form a business relationship with your company.

## Competitors

While you may have nothing to say about which direct and indirect competitors share your channel, and little or no control over their actions, you must still plan for and react to their tactics. You can do so by asking three basic questions:

1. Who are your main competitors?
2. How strong is their presence in the COD you desire?

3. Do you want to or are you compelled to use the same marketing channel as they do?

Your channel marketing plan has to include some counterstrategies to offset or improve your position in the marketplace that you mutually serve. You cannot afford to ignore competitive presence and must plan accordingly. (Chapter 4 shows you how.)

# Political Factors

The federal and state political arena is another area over which you have little or no command. For example, a channel marketing manager at a medical products company needs to be concerned about federal health care legislation that may require him or her to reorganize channels in order to meet new, more administratively demanding influencers such as HMOs and PPOs. These influencers must be included in this company's future channel marketing plans.

Environmental regulations could affect the way a company produces a product and therefore add to the total cost that is passed through the channel to the end user. In this case, the manufacturer must conform or risk a penalty or disqualification.

# International Factors

All of the aforementioned macroinfluences also apply in the global marketplace, along with many more. Managerial flexibility is a key factor in global success. The international channel manager must regard each country as culturally unique, and he or she must mold channel strategies to the established way of doing business in that part of the world. Chapter 13 explores international channel management and the many factors that play a role in global success.

---

**Ken's Words of Wisdom**

❏ Channel competition is not only external but also internal within a company.
❏ Fully comprehend your corporate culture prior to creating and implementing a channel of distribution program.

---

# Your Company Considerations

Company variables can be the most influential—and most frustrating—factors of all. Take, for example, conflicts with existing company channels. When a new marketing channel is created and starts to function positively, a predictable level of internal anxiety occurs in existing channel operations. The manager of the newborn COD is a *change agent.* Any altered business direction is always met with varying degrees of suspicion and sometimes envy. The most effective method of dealing with this political quandary is to clearly communicate total corporate commitment to the new channel of distribution, from the highest level of management to the foot soldiers in the field. Set up a communication check system to verify that the company's strategic channel message is reaching all senior, middle, and operational managers. Internal COD conflict should be addressed and dealt with in a quick and decisive fashion. Competitive channel warfare should happen outside the corporation—not internally.

Another company consideration are your credentials in the target market. Even if your company is well established and respected in your present market, it does not guarantee your acceptance in a new segment. A sixty-year-old corporation in the electrical industry can be a virtual unknown in the computer market—ego-deflating and frustrating to those who cannot understand why the distributors in your new market are not impressed by your reputation in the old market.

The level of marketing channel knowledge within your company is another factor. If knowledge is scant, you may be frustrated when you attempt to secure approval for a new distributor business policy. You may also be accosted with such dartlike questions as "Why can't you tell that distributor to keep its prices at the suggested list level?" or "Can't you stop the Chicago dealer from selling our products outside of its authorized territory in Dallas?" Statements like these are a clear indication that the other managers in the company don't know or care how a distributor lives and breathes and, more important, what the company can or cannot do to manage its channel partner.

Your company's internal channel support capability and attitude are another factor. Before you build any formal distributor relationships, ascertain your company's readiness to support the demands of your channel. Thoroughly discuss all distributor procedures with the appropriate managers and personnel in order entry, engineering, manufacturing, physical distribution, credit, finance, technical support, and, of course, senior management. Exhibit 3-2 illustrates the support elements that must be considered to guarantee a smoothly functioning total channel operation. Use this as a review vehicle to assess your company's channel sup-

**Exhibit 3-2.** The channel support elements that guarantee a smoothly functioning total channel operation.

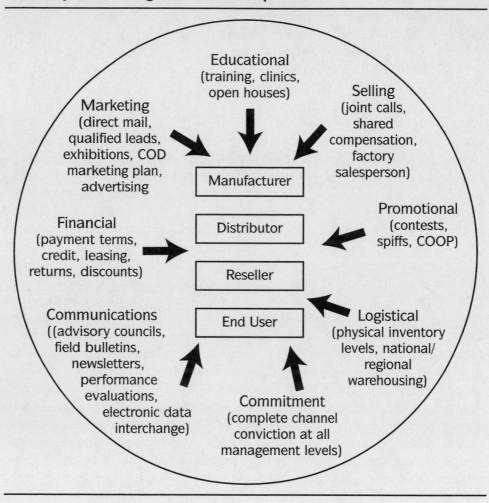

port system aptitude. If your company is unwilling or unable to perform all of these functions, then perhaps you need to look outside your company to fulfill these support tasks.

Time and again, corporations agree that indirect channels of distribution are an absolute must—but when it comes down to fair and equitable treatment, support fades and the employed, direct sales force once again dominates. Distributors quickly notice this second-class-citizen treatment and return the lack of apparent business commitment. The channel partnership that initially looked so good becomes questionable and, if nothing is done, eventually disintegrates over a period of time.

Our federal and state antitrust laws are constantly being altered with inadequate communication to corporate America, and, consequently, many channel marketing managers are not aware of regulations that may or may not have changed in their favor. The primary culprits are dynamic information technology development (i.e., the internet, etc.) and the global economic forces that influence the way we do business with our channels.

Before developing any channel strategy, the channelmaster must first be cognizant of the macro marketing channel forces that can affect the way business is conducted with distributors. Schedule a specific amount of your managerial time and energy to observe, record, and plan how these influences can be employed to your sales and marketing advantage. Bottom line: Always keep your channel peripheral vision open!

Chapter 4 discusses how to efficiently analyze, monitor, and plan against your primary channel competition.

## *Case:* The Enemy Within

You have just joined a consumer electronics company in the newly created position of director of new market development. One of your initial charges is to quickly investigate two vertical markets as possible channels of distribution: (1) the military/governmental market, and (2) national power retailers. Your company has another marketing director who manages the solidly established, twenty-year-old direct-mail catalog and manufacturer sales representative channels. Initially, you have been told that you will have no direct reports nor any staff to assist you in your COD investigation, creation, and implementation. Therefore, you must use the other marketing director's internal sales support areas (customer service, order entry/processing, and physical distribution) for all of your new channel needs and requirements. This seems, on the surface, to be a workable situation.

**Three months later . . .**

Your channel marketing plan is brilliant. You have achieved all your business objectives well ahead of schedule and have just reached formal business relationships (signed contracts, stocking orders, training schedule agreed to, and so on) with Kmart, Wal-Mart, and Target stores as your power retailer channel, as well as with six vertical market distributors that specialize in selling consumer products to the military/governmental markets. You have caused many managerial eyebrows to be positively raised.

But unbeknown to you, the other marketing director has developed a serious case of jealousy. In fact, he has secretly told his order department and customer service managers not to cooperate with you in any way. Mysteriously, priority purchase orders from your two new channels are being lost or shipped incorrectly. To add salt to the wound, you have overheard some very rude and uncalled-for telephone conversations between order entry and customer service personnel and your two new channels of distribution. You are at your wit's end, and you know that this politically dangerous situation must be corrected—as soon as possible.

What will your plan of action be? Be specific in terms of when, whom, and what tactics and strategies you will employ.

**Case interpretational points:**

❐ Whether you believe it or not, there will always be some degree of internal political conflict, especially when a new channelmaster is more successful than a senior channelmaster.
❐ Confront the insecure channelmaster. If that doesn't work, have a meeting with your immediate superior to resolve this conflict.
❐ No matter what you do, make sure that you have concrete facts to base your case on.
❐ Deal with this situation ASAP!

# Chapter 4

# Competitive Analysis and Strategy

---

√ *Step 1:* Identify the new market you want to penetrate or new product you need to launch.

√ *Step 2:* Verify the need for a new channel of distribution or some form of channel reorganization.

√ *Step 3:* Evaluate all macro market conditions.

√ ***Step 4:*** **Conduct a competitive channel analysis.**

---

Know thy enemy, channelmaster!

As Exhibit 4-1 shows, success today and in the future rests on achieving the highest possible level of sales and marketing superiority. It's hard to achieve and sustain this superiority without an intimate knowledge of your primary and secondary opponents and how their strengths and weaknesses compare with your own.

Your ultimate goal should not be to meet competition but to *beat competition* by monitoring its actions and anticipating its market moves. That's why Step 4 in the Channel Design Sequence (see Chapter 2) is to conduct a thorough analysis of your present competitors. Unless you do, you may not know exactly what you are up against. Without competitive information, you may not find out until you are implementing your channel marketing plans that your opponent's business policies (pricing, credit, payment terms) are vastly superior to your own. There should be *no* surprises.

This chapter shows how to compile and evaluate a profile of your competitors. It also shows you how to use it to formulate a competitive strategy and marketing plan that is easier and more effective to implement—because you will have removed any apprehension concerning your field opposition.

The need to gather competitive information does not end when your

**Exhibit 4-1.** The dependence of success on sales and marketing superiority.

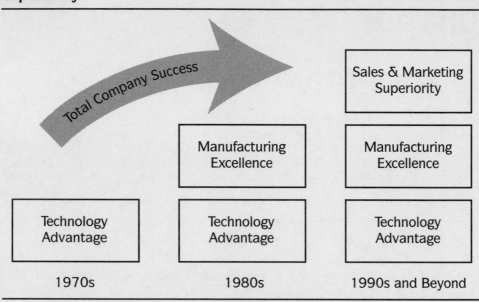

channel is up and running. You always need to know what your competition has up its sleeve. This chapter also examines ways you can gather and benefit from information from your existing channel.

## Uncovering Direct and Indirect Competition

Your channel environment is home to both direct and indirect competition. Direct competition is easy to define and recognize. These are companies that use the same channel to sell similar products to the same end user. Indirect competition consists of all other manufacturers' product lines carried by your channel members that are sold to the same target audience. Those other companies are vying with you for physical inventory, sales commitment, and marketing attention. When you are denied these resource investments, it is because your indirect rivals have secured them. Indirect competition frequently goes unnoticed, especially when your primary focus is on your direct competition.

Exhibit 4-2 shows the direct and indirect competitors of a company that manufactures power protection products. In this example, the innermost ring represents direct competition, or all other surge protector companies. In each successive ring, the level of competitive intensity

**Exhibit 4-2.** The direct and indirect competitors of a power protection products company.

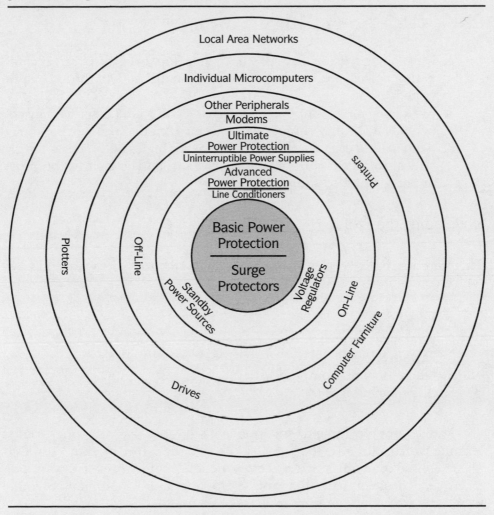

decreases—but these computer peripherals are still clamoring for marketing attention and resource investment.

Develop a set of rings for your own industry, and determine the importance your distributors place on each ring category. That will clearly indicate how much resource allocation they award. Combine your distributor's comments and its published product line listing (a category or line card), to list and position both your direct and indirect competition. Now you have a very good grasp on who your field opponents are and their commensurate channel status.

# The Three Steps of Direct Competition Analysis

Direct competition analysis focuses on three main activities:

1. Developing a descriptive profile of your top three to six direct competitors. This profile should be continually and faithfully maintained.
2. Evaluating each competitor's strengths and weaknesses as they accurately and fairly compare to your characteristics.
3. Anticipating each competitor's future strategies and tactics. This is critical to your future success or failure and is clearly the most important part of your study.

## Developing the Profile

There are five basic types of competitors to watch for. You want to know which competitors are:

1. Large
2. Profitable
3. Fast growing
4. Similar to your company
5. A combination of the above

Match your top three to six opponents to these five categories to determine which ones pose the greatest threat to the future of your business. These are the companies that deserve a detailed competitive analysis. For example, a rival company that is fast growing and also similar to yours would deserve an above average share of your attention.

You should also classify your competition into the following two groups:

1. *Direct competitors* to your company's products and marketing strategies
2. *Indirect competitors* that do business in the same marketplace through the identical channel of distribution

Now, build your profile of each of your competitors by securing the following information:

1. *Their short-range objectives, strategies, and tactics.* Where do they want to be in one, three, five, and ten years?
2. *Their long-range objectives, strategies, and tactics.* Where do they want to be in more than ten years and beyond?
3. *Their strengths.* What is their management prowess, image, quality, and reliability?
4. *Their weaknesses.* What deficiencies are worth noting?
5. *Their intentions toward you.* Are they point-blank attacking your company?
6. *Their particular mix of the four Ps of marketing.* How do they stand on product, price, promotion, and placement? (See Exhibit 4-3.)
7. *Their overall sales/marketing position in segments served.* How are they generally perceived by your customers?
8. *Their international market status.* Are they a global company?
9. *Their overall market position in other company areas.* How do they stand regarding operations, finance, research and development, and engineering? It is important to evaluate your opponent's market position in *all* functional aspects, not just sales and marketing.
10. *Their innovativeness/creativity.* Do they excel in state-of-the-art conceptual thinking?
11. *Their strategic intelligence (or lack thereof).* Are they more tactical than strategic in their management style?
12. *Their overall management capabilities.* What is their administrative expertise among operational, middle, and senior management?
13. *Their ethics.* Do they adhere to a professional set of standards?
14. *Their bureaucratic or entrepreneurial spirit.* Are they a well-established, highly bureaucratic company or a start-up company with a looser structure and spirit?
15. *Their customers' perceptions.* Why did your channel and end users choose your product over your competitors' products? Which competitors did they also consider, and why?

## Where to Find Information

There are many information sources available to you. Within your particular industry or market, you can find competitive information from:

❑ Customers
❑ Existing indirect channels (distributors, dealers, manufacturer reps, value-added resellers, and so on)
❑ Trade shows
❑ Seminars

**Exhibit 4-3.** The four Ps of marketing.

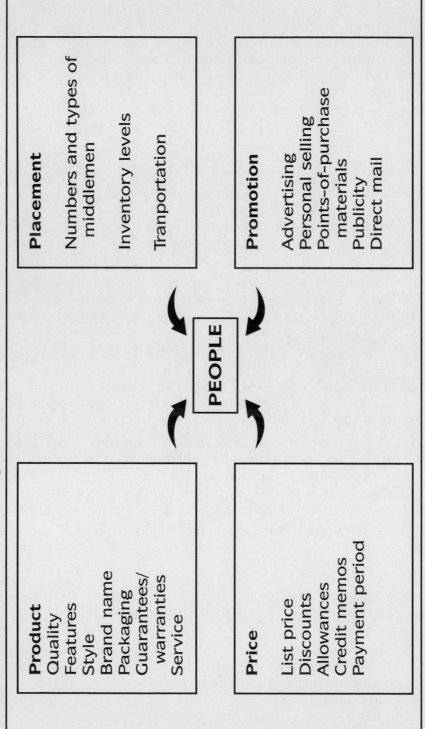

**Product**
Quality
Features
Style
Brand name
Packaging
Guarantees/
  warranties
Service

**Placement**
Numbers and types of
  middlemen
Inventory levels
Tranportation

**PEOPLE**

**Price**
List price
Discounts
Allowances
Credit memos
Payment period

**Promotion**
Advertising
Personal selling
Points-of-purchase
  materials
Publicity
Direct mail

❏ Suppliers
❏ Trade associations
❏ Consultants
❏ Competitors' employees
❏ Advertising agencies
❏ Other channel managers at noncompetitive companies in the same industry

You can also collect competitive information from within your company by harnessing the intellectual eyes and ears of all parts of your company.

Start with your direct sales force, and include a quarterly bonus for competitive feedback in the salespeople's compensation package. Develop and use standard competitive reporting forms to be submitted every three months. Exhibit 4-4 shows a simple such form that all levels of company personnel, including direct and indirect channel personnel, can easily use. In addition, have your direct salespeople present their competitive findings at scheduled regional and national sales meetings. Base their bonus award on the accuracy and importance of the data received, as verified by the senior channel marketing manager and appropriate staff members (engineering, finance, manufacturing).

Engineering, operations, and finance are oftentimes privy to valuable pieces of information. Make them active participants by letting them help develop your competitive reporting plan and including them in your internal rewards program. Other departments can also uncover important data. Be sure to include:

❏ Advertising
❏ Credit
❏ Customer service
❏ Legal
❏ Management information services
❏ Human resources
❏ Production
❏ Public relations
❏ Purchasing
❏ Research and development
❏ Sales
❏ Marketing
❏ Strategic planning
❏ Training
❏ Product management

**Exhibit 4-4.**  Competitive reporting form.

Name and Location of Competitor: _____

_____

_____

Rank importance of threat:  Primary _____   Secondary _____   Tertiary _____

Reporting Individual: _____

| Field Information Obtained | Source | Suggested Action to Be Taken |
|---|---|---|
| *Marketing 4 Ps* | | |
| Product | | |
| Price | | |
| Promotion | | |
| Placement (Channels) | | |
| *Other Functional Areas* | | |
| Financial | | |
| Operations | | |
| Engineering | | |
| Research & Development | | |
| Sales/Marketing | | |
| *Miscellaneous Field Intelligence* | | |

Signed: _____         Date: _____


Schedule and lead quarterly meetings at which competitive information is shared. Total marketing works if the entire company is truly involved.

Another source of competitive information is published data. Look for nuggets in:

❑ Competitors' annual reports
❑ Competitors' promotional materials
❑ Industry publications

◻ Competitors' 10K reports
◻ Financial periodicals
◻ Security analysts' reports
◻ Publications and speeches by competitors' managers
◻ National newspapers
◻ Local newspapers in cities where competitors have facilities
◻ Directories like *Standard & Poor's*
◻ State and federal government publications
◻ Want ads
◻ Press releases
◻ Advertisements
◻ Internet and other new technologies
◻ Lawsuit disclosures
◻ Chamber of Commerce reports

## Obtaining Competitive Information From Your Channel of Distribution

Once you have established your channel, one of your most frustrating challenges can be obtaining data about your competition from channel members, direct and indirect alike. While competitive field feedback is critical to your market planning process, it is not critical to your potential channel partners. Your creativity is thus put to the test as you try to extract valuable marketing data. Here are some results-proven approaches:

◻ *Offer rewards.* Offer travel incentives, merchandise, and other rewards to your indirect channels for submitting competitive information. Again, let an internal sales and marketing panel determine the information's value and the size of the award. The competitive reporting form shown in Exhibit 4-4 can be employed here as well.

◻ *Foster close relationships with those in the know.* Develop close relationships with eagle distributors that have an established pipeline to competitive information. These market leaders wield a great deal of political power in both the ranks of the COD and among the manufacturers they represent. An astute channelmaster expects to expend a great deal of effort to achieve a "business closeness" alliance with these informational gold mines.

## Evaluating the Competition and Anticipating Competitive Moves

Once you have accumulated competitive information, set up a file or database for each of your competitors. Update it as new information is discovered. Plan to perform detailed quarterly reviews of the files of your primary competitors, and review files of secondary opponents every six months. Ask your outside sales manager, customer service manager, and others with a stake in the channel to review and add to the files. Make seeking out information on your opponents part of your sales force's competition by paying them a quarterly bonus for submittal of the competitive reporting form (Exhibit 4-4). After all, they're the front line of your field marketing offense and "engage the enemy" more often than you have the opportunity.

Don't keep this valuable collection of data to yourself. Put it in some kind of quarterly or priority red report to all concerned parties.

## Basing Your Competitive Strategy on the Market Life Cycle

Your competitive strategy should complement the status of the life cycle of your market. The market life cycle shown in Exhibit 4-5 is a series of chronological stages or phases through which a marketplace naturally progresses as it reacts to changing customer demands. The level and intensity of competition—and how you should respond—vary during each of its five phases.

1. *Introduction:* A new market and its products emerge. Both the marketing channel and buying public often respond in a merely inquisitive way, and competitive presence is minor. Your embryonic sales and marketing plans are put on trial during this phase and revised to prepare for the growth stage.

2. *Growth:* Sales increase once customers start to recognize a market or product's value to their own individual business environment. New rivals appear, and you must classify the seriousness of their threats to your market position. Your promotional plans should maximize sales and revenue opportunities to further solidify your market position.

3. *Competitive Turbulence:* Success draws attention. More competition enters the market as others envision

**Exhibit 4-5.** The market life cycle.

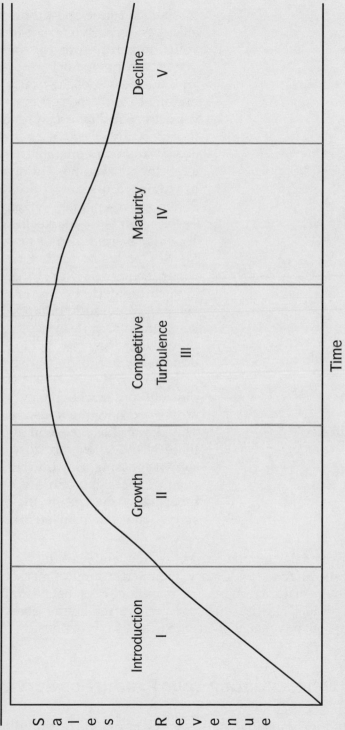

Sales

Revenue

| Introduction | Growth | Competitive Turbulence | Maturity | Decline |
|---|---|---|---|---|
| I | II | III | IV | V |

Time

*Source:* Frank Lynn and Associates, Chicago.

the sales revenue and profits they can realize. As an early entrant in the market, your competitive proactiveness pays dividends as your channel armor of strategies and business policies gains distributor preference and fends off most of these adversaries. Simultaneously, end users come to expect lower prices as a result of the proliferation of companies that have entered the market. Be cautious and do not be drawn into any price-deteriorating field combat—not just yet, anyway.

4. *Maturity:* The autumn of the market life cycle is here. Your rivals either depart or retrench their market tactics by further reducing their channel and end user pricing, or engaging in such life cycle extension efforts as developing previously untapped niche market segments. In this phase, end users are purchasing less and turning their attention to new, more innovative technologies or opportunities. Now is the time to implement any market life cycle–elongating tactics you have previously planned.

5. *Decline:* The market life cycle end is in sight, and there is little you can do to prohibit or slow its passing. However, thanks to your channel foresight, you are exploring another new market in the introductory stage. True channelmasters always win.

The personal computer market is an example of the market life cycle that all of us can relate to. Clearly, the microcomputer market is now venturing into the maturity phase. The manufacturers that have survived have had to continually revise their competitive marketing plans to take full sales and profit advantage of each market life cycle phase.

## Differentiating Your Product or Service

You can block competitive moves by positioning your product or service in a way that clearly shows its advantage over your competition in the eyes of your channel and your end users. There are a number of ways you can accomplish this objective:

❐ Achieve a higher product *quality* image in the eyes of your customers.
❐ Offer consistently superior *customer service* (end user and channel) that exceeds all marketplace satisfaction requirements.
❐ Forge formal and informal *business relationships* that build long-term loyalty.
❐ Employ the most efficient, state-of-the-art *business technology* to improve communication flow among all channel members.
❐ Implement *policies* that make it easy to do business with your company.

The more ways you can differentiate your product or service, the stronger your position will be. I recommend that at least twice a year you review all five of the above differentiators to evaluate how your company compares to your primary competitors. Above all, do not allow your opponents to outdifferentiate you.

It is especially important to compare your business policies (warranty, credit, payment, sales, and so on) to those of your primary competitors. Your rivals may make dramatic changes in their business procedures that would be to their advantage, especially when broadcast to your mutual channel members. Your policies can make it difficult or easy for your channel of distribution to do business with you. Make sure they make it easy!

## Rating Your Competitor Intelligence

How well do you know your competition? Answer these questions about your most significant competitors, and you'll get an accurate reading of your "Competitor Information IQ." If you have enough information to answer each question adequately, then you and your company have a high competitor IQ—a sustainable competitive advantage!

### The Competitor Information IQ Test

1. *Customers.* Who are your competitors' major customers? Where are their customers located? How much of a product or service does each customer buy from your competition?
2. *Distribution.* How does your competition get their products or services to markets?

3. *Marketing.* What pricing, product, or regional marketing strategies are your competitors using?
4. *Sales.* How large are your competitors' sales forces? What are their sales terms and conditions?
5. *Advertising.* Where does your competition advertise? How much do they spend on advertising?
6. *Finance.* Is your competition profitable? If so, by how much? What are their overhead costs?
7. *Operations.* What are the size, location, and capacity of their facilities? How efficiently do they produce their products or services?
8. *Organization.* What is their organizational structure? Are they very decentralized? Who makes the key decisions?
9. *Research and development.* What patents and trademarks do they own? What new products or services are they working on? How much do they spend on research and development?
10. *Strategic plans.* What are their long-term and short-term plans? Will they retain their core business or expand into other markets? Do they intend to acquire other businesses?

How did you do? Are you satisfied with the answers and how much you know about your company's competition? If not, then it's time to seriously assess and, as necessary, reorganize your internal and field intelligence-gathering abilities. A benchmark channel marketing effort!

In closing, I am reminded of an unknown author's Zenlike quote:

When standing, *stand.* When sitting, *sit.* But above all, *don't wobble.*

Channelmaster, when it comes to being an efficient and determined gatherer of competitive data, don't wobble!

## *CASE:* A NEW RENEGADE CHANNEL APPEARS

Your company is in the enviable and very fortunate position of being the market leader for your product line of market-specific law firm and financial management computer software. Your sales revenue increases 15 percent annually, and you have a stable and loyal-as-they-can-be group of value-added resellers (VARs).

**Enter "the enemy" . . .**

Your vertical market success has drawn the attention of an unknown competitor, which has chosen to sell through a select group of computer market-oriented manufacturer sales representative companies. You have been completely surprised by this competitor's aggressive appearance into the marketplace that you thought was entirely yours, and you have rightfully determined that a strong corrective course of action must be taken quickly. However, first you must gather as much competitive data and information about this new channel invader as you can—an invader that you know absolutely nothing about! Your mission is a clear one: Research and gather facts, then formulate an aggressive countercompetitive plan.

Describe the actions you would take and what competitive analysis and monitoring plan you would conceive and execute.

**Case interpretational points:**

□ Shame on you for being surprised! This should not have happened.
□ Conduct a thorough competitive analysis ASAP!
□ Establish a continual competitive monitoring program.
□ Anticipate the competitive reaction to your plan.
□ Are there other competitors lurking in the shadows?

# Chapter 5

# Discovering Customer Satisfaction Requirements

---

√ *Step 1:* Identify the new market you want to penetrate or new product you need to launch.

√ *Step 2:* Verify the need for new channel of distribution or some form of channel reorganization.

√ *Step 3:* Evaluate all macro market conditions.

√ *Step 4:* Conduct a competitive channel analysis.

√ **Step 5: Research and rank customer/end user satisfaction requirements.**

---

If you have faithfully executed the first four steps of the Channel Design Sequence, you know which market you want to penetrate and why a new channel is needed. You have also acquainted yourself with the macro variables that affect the market and your decision, and you have analyzed the competition you are likely to encounter.

Before you go any further, you need to know what your customer or end user wants. That's why every intelligent channel strategy begins with a customer segmentation analysis. Find out *who* your end users are and how they behave. How do they use the product? What are their needs? Are they loyal users? What is their lifestyle? Pinpoint their social class, and try to understand their opinions, activities, and attitudes. What are their demographics? Dig up data on their age, gender, income, education, ethnic origin, occupation, and location. Find these facts first—and then match the channel to those needs.

# Conducting a Segmentation Analysis

To conduct your segmentation analysis, compile a list of actual and potential end users from your target audience. Don't limit your focus to large end users or customers in one area of the country. Include customers of all sizes and types from several market and geographic areas. For a nominal price, you can obtain this customer list from industry/market directories, trade associations, and, most frequently, trade publications. Tell the editor, publisher, or executive director what data you need, and ask for either a subscriber or membership list of the appropriate size and characteristics. You can also get customer information from companies that are already selling to your target customers through an established channel of distribution. If you work for a multidivisional corporation, check your company for another business unit that sells its product mix to these end users.

To ensure an adequate sample size, try to contact about one hundred prequalified individuals, or fewer if your market is very small. When you feel there is a commonality of responses among your contacts, you will have compiled an accurate survey of your end user satisfaction requirements.

Canvas customers using one of five forms of market research: (1) in-person face-to-face interviews, (2) in-person focus groups, (3) mail surveys, (4) telephone surveys, and (5) telephone focus groups. I have found that the most effective research is made up of 80 percent telephone surveys and 20 percent personal interviews.

Ask the customers these questions:

❐ How well do they know your products or services? What do they know about them?
❐ What is their local or favorite supplier for your product or type of product? (This critical information helps form your eagle list.)
❐ What specific channel tasks do they want and require from their preferred supplier? Which of those tasks has the highest priority?
❐ Do they intend to purchase any of your product from their distributor in the future? If so, when, and in what quantity?

These questions help you uncover the channel structure that your end users prefer to patronize. You want to be a player in the dominant channel—the channel through which most end users do their purchasing. When you know which channel you'll be playing in, it is easier to pick your team of distributors.

Pay attention to those satisfaction requirements that are mentioned frequently. For example, customers may tell you that they do business with their current distributor because they like the immediate availability of local inventory, responsive customer service, and a one-stop shop for similar product needs. When your survey is complete, rank these reasons. Then by all means see to it that your channel strategy offers those factors important to your end user.

## Uncovering Other Marketing Nuggets

Once you strike up a conversation with an end user, listen carefully to everything he or she says. Besides answering your questions, the person may well reveal other "marketing nuggets." Take careful notes if you uncover such nuggets in the following areas:

❐ *Competitive information.* Listen for positive or negative comments that may help you formulate your marketing strategies to deal with your field opponents. Discontent with the quality or availability of a competitor's products may be a window of opportunity for you to improve your position in the marketplace.

---

**Conducting a Successful Telephone Survey**

Keep these guidelines in mind as you prepare your telephone survey:

❐ *The best time to reach an individual is either early in the day or late in the afternoon.* Midday hours are crowded with meetings, appointments, and project assignments.

❐ *Plan your opening statement to grab the person's attention.* You have only twenty seconds or so to get the person to commit to talk to you. Open with a simple appeal like "I wonder if you can help me? I'm Jill Smith, director of marketing for Lyricon. I'm establishing a channel of distribution to better serve end users like yourself. May I ask you a few important questions?" Don't mention specific products or services in your opening.

❐ *Don't be discouraged by rejection.* Even great opening statements won't always persuade people to talk to you. Don't take rejection personally. Consider every successful contact a significant victory for your research cause.

---

❒ *Product improvements.* A talkative end user may have ideas about improving a product by adding a few features, reducing the cost, or changing its appearance.

❒ *Marketplace health indicators.* Often the interviewee expresses an opinion on the overall health of the marketplace you are targeting. Comments that are repeated are worth considering before you form your channel.

❒ *Buying behavioral changes.* Listen carefully if end users tell you that they are beginning to purchase differently, so you can design the channel to satisfy these new buying behavioral requirements.

❒ *New technology.* Comments about how technology is used may tell you how you will do business in the near future. For example, end users may indicate they want to order via the internet instead of a traditional channel.

# Chapter 6
# Channel Selection Criteria

---

√ *Step 1:* Identify the new market you want to penetrate or new product you need to launch.

√ *Step 2:* Verify the need for a new channel of distribution or some form of channel reorganization

√ *Step 3:* Evaluate all macro market conditions.

√ *Step 4:* Conduct a competitive channel analysis.

√ *Step 5:* Research and rank customer/end user satisfaction requirements.

√ **Step 6: Specify and rank the tasks you want your channel partner to perform.**

---

In order to find the channel members that best serve your needs, you need to determine the selection criteria you will use to choose them. This is one of the most important steps in the total Channel Design Sequence, and it should not be rushed no matter *how* pressured you feel. Too often, channel managers rush into choosing a distributor for two basic but unacceptable reasons:

1. They want to establish a full complement of distributors for complete geographic and market coverage as soon as possible.
2. They are under internal pressure to fill territory vacancies with any distributor that's available.

Rush your decision, and you risk choosing second-rate distributors that produce second-rate results—placing you at risk for sales leakage, lost revenue, and eventually a traumatic decision to terminate the distributor and repair your mistake.

This underscores the importance of investing managerial time in compiling your channel selection criteria plan in an organized way. You owe it to yourself, your company, and the end user of your product to avoid unnecessary future channel reorganization and channel jumping because all parties involved in the channel equation are deprived of excellence. Take the time up front to pick the eagles, and forget about the rest.

## What Are Channel Selection Criteria?

Channel selection criteria are what you and your end user want your distributor to look like. The criteria help you know what kind of corporate personality you want to work with and how you want your distributors to operate. There are two steps to defining these criteria. First, you need to determine what *you* want. Second, you need to find out what various distributors offer. Seek the closest possible match between these two, so that your channel will satisfy as many end user requirements as possible.

Involve other managers in developing your criteria. Seek opinions from other internal managers, such as the comptroller, credit manager, engineering manager, and, naturally, your immediate superior. After all, total marketing is a corporate team effort, and their inputs are a valuable commitment to reaching that goal.

The number of selection criteria that you actually use is entirely up to you. You may have twenty or thirty criteria or as few as five. Regardless of the number, your criteria should cover your most important channel business issues combined with your end user satisfaction requirements.

Once you have chosen your list of prescriptives, rank them in order of your corporate *and* end user importance. If your end users want to purchase from a concern that carries local inventory, that should be listed in your critical mass of selection criteria. If price integrity is an important factor, then list it as well.

When your list is finished, use it. Measure each candidate you encounter against your list. You are looking for complementary business practices, as well as signs of an "oil and water" relationship it might be best to avoid. A close match between your criteria and the distributor's capabilities may indicate that a profitable and positive business partnership can be developed. Very little overlap indicates a poor fit.

## Critical Channel Selection Criteria

During my three decades as a channelmaster in many industries and marketplaces, I've applied lots of criteria to hundreds of potential distributors. The following list of forty-two channel selection criteria represent areas that are critical to the success of a good channel relationship. Exhibit 6-1 summarizes these selection criteria.

## Exhibit 6-1. List of channel selection criteria.

### Business and Operational Criteria

1. Business age of the candidate
2. Reputation

   - Among customers
   - Among other manufacturers the distributor currently represents
   - Among peers
   - Among trade publications
   - Among trade organizations
   - In the local community

3. Professional background of key executives
4. Business and managerial stability
5. Financial strength
6. Sales revenue performance

   - Overall sales
   - Complementary product line sales

7. Branch locations
8. Number of active customer accounts
9. Present territorial coverage
10. Complementary manufacturer product lines represented
11. Competitive product lines represented
12. Product variables

    - Technical expertise
    - Perishability
    - Bulk and weight
    - Individual unit value
    - Newness
    - Knowledge of existing product lines

13. Repair and service capabilities
14. Knowledge of local market conditions
15. Employee quality
16. Managerial ''chemistry''
17. Overall condition of facilities

### Sales and Marketing Criteria

18. Type of market coverage offered

    - Horizontal
    - Vertical
    - Both

*(continues)*

**Exhibit 6-1.** *(continued)*

19. Proportion of internal to external salespeople
20. Sales force compensation
21. Sales cycle performance requirements

   • Presale
   • Transaction
   • Postsale

22. Sales competency

   • Number and quality of salespeople
   • Technical competence of salespeople

23. Sales and marketing aggressiveness

   • Local marketing activities
   • Customer and order pursuit
   • Dealing with their competition

24. Internal sales and marketing support resources and capabilities
25. Ordering and payment policies
26. Customer order fulfillment performance

   • Typical time required for complete delivery of a customer's purchase order
   • Accuracy of shipment of order contents
   • Percentage of out-of-stock occurrences

27. Price integrity
28. Ability to develop new markets
29. Distributor advertising and sales promotional programs
30. Training programs
31. Consent to sign a contract
32. Agreement to accept a sales quota
33. Willingness to share data and local market information
34. Willingness to participate in joint sales and marketing programs
35. Inventory management expertise
36. Adequate inventory commitment
37. Future growth prospects

**''Coup de Grace'' Factors That Indicate a Motivated Candidate**

38. True desire for your product line
39. Willingness to share key customer list
40. Willingness to commit resources to your product line
41. Existence of a strategic business plan
42. Willingness to participate in strategic business planning with your company

## Business and Operational Criteria

The first seventeen criteria are the most basic facts you need to know about any distributor candidate.

1. *Business age of the candidate.* The newer your candidate, the less history you can investigate. In the case of a start-up distributor, you may have to evaluate *more* criteria to reach your partnership decision, while a seasoned company may have credentials and history that are easier to evaluate.

2. *Reputation.* Thoroughly check the candidate's reputation among its customers, other manufacturers it represents, and its peers. You should also check the candidate with regard to trade publications and organizations and the candidate's local community.

To discover the candidate's reputation among its customers, use the information gathered in Step 5 of the Channel Design Sequence (see Chapter 5). When you asked end users about their channel satisfaction requirements, you probably learned whom they purchased products from and why. Their comments provide an excellent base for evaluating each candidate's credentials.

To research the candidate's reputation among other manufacturers it represents, obtain a copy of the distributor's line card or catalog, and contact the channel marketing managers at manufacturers the distributor currently represents. Explain that you are considering the distributor candidate, and ask for their candid opinion of their business relationship. For the best informational fit, seek out companies whose products are similar to yours. Their concerns and criteria are also likely to be similar.

Reputation among peers is the easiest to establish. Eagles know each other. They belong to a special club whose entrance requirements include a high level of professionalism, price integrity, and above-average managerial capabilities. Thus, peer identification is one of the most significant credential verifications you can obtain. Once you form a relationship with an eagle, ask for recommendations in other geographic or market areas where you need representation. Don't forget to ask if you can use the eagle as a reference. In fact, ask to be introduced to other eagle candidates. This is basic eagle nesting strategy that really works!

It's also a good idea to verify how your candidate is regarded by trade publications, trade organizations, and the local community. Every leading trade magazine publishes at least one issue per year that ranks distributors in a given market by size of sales revenue, special marketing expertise, primary product lines carried, and geographic territory. These issues usually include the names of managers, officers, or owners you can contact.

Some of these publications examine the top fifty or one hundred large distributors; others cover the top one hundred small distributors. You want to see publications examining both. It's a good idea to blend distributors of different sizes to avoid concentrating a disproportionate share of channel power in any one group. Save these magazine issues!

Like trade publications, trade organizations also rank their membership. Trade directories are conveniently divided into sections that list and describe the manufacturers, distributors, dealers, VARs, and manufacturer sales representatives that belong to the organization.

An organization's reputation in its own community lets you verify another face of your candidate. If a candidate's values resemble yours, a cohesive business match may well be possible.

**3.** *Professional background of key executives.* Obtain or compose a profile of the distributor's mainline managers to further ensure channel compatibility. A gulf between the professional personalities of candidate managers and your staff could eventually be a tremendous source of irritation.

**4.** *Business and managerial stability.* Ask candidates to answer questions that reveal their business "fabric":

❐ Have there been several reorganizational changes in the past few years? Frequent changes may indicate a poor managerial environment and high turnover.

❐ How do the distributor's employees feel about their company? Pay attention to comments indicating internal dissatisfaction. Dissatisfied employees could treat your end users poorly.

❐ How do other channel managers feel about the candidate? This is important input—but watch out for problems that may be specific to only one manufacturer because of a personality conflict or communication disorder.

❐ Are the distributor's managers and employees co-owners? Key individuals who have equity positions will probably want to stay with the company—a positive sign of internal stability.

**5.** *Financial strength.* Examine financial documents that show the candidate's performance over a period of years. Look for danger signs that may indicate future payment problems. Other manufacturers whom the distributor represents are a good source for this information.

**6.** *Sales revenue performance.* Examine two aspects of your candidate's sales records: overall sales performance, and complementary product line sales. Have there been any fluctuations in overall sales performance in the last three to five years? If sales were negative for three years running, find out why. You should feel comfortable with the distributor's ability to manage its own business and assume revenue responsibility for your product lines. As for complementary product line sales, how complementary lines are sold is a good barometer of how your related products will be marketed.

**7. *Branch locations.*** Be sure to ask where the candidate's stocking branch operations are located. If they are outside the territory you intend to grant them, you risk unauthorized branch sales of your products into a different authorized dealer's area. Make sure that you clarify your business procedure on officially assigned territory.

**8. *Number of active customer accounts.*** This is a good barometer of service. Ask the candidate how many accounts it has, and then ask how many customers purchased products in the last twelve months. If the distributor says it has 2,000 customers but indicates that only 750 have made purchases in the last year, you'd better find out what happened to the other 1,250! Why haven't they purchased within the last year?

**9. *Present territorial coverage.*** Does the distributor cover a geographic area that matches the authorized sales territory you are offering? Serious mismatch could lead to conflict, not only between you and the distributor but, just as seriously, among other distributors in your organization. The authorized territory offered must be clearly understood and agreed to by both the distributor and the manufacturer prior to signing any contract.

**10. *Complementary manufacturer product lines represented.*** If your partner candidate represents similar product lines, it's almost a given that it sells to the customer base you want to reach. This can easily be confirmed by reviewing the candidate's line card or catalog.

**11. *Competitive product lines represented.*** What competing product lines does the candidate carry? Are they your primary, secondary, or tertiary opponents? Rule out candidates that carry lines from your primary opponents. To align yourself with such a distributor would simply be too compromising. But a candidate that sells a secondary competitor may or may not be a problem, depending on your point of view. If you have faith in your products and marketing ability, this category should not concern you. Basically, this is your call—but give it some serious channelistic thought prior to formalizing a contractual relationship.

Remember, however, that it is illegal to coerce a channel member to deemphasize or terminate a relationship with one of your rivals. You just cannot do that. (Chapter 12 tells you why.)

**12. *Product variables.*** Can your candidate handle your product or service? To avoid being saddled with a finished product that lacks a suitable channel of distribution, determine the product variables that your candidate will have to take into consideration. Closely compare these selection criteria to each nominee to make certain of their acceptance:

❐ *Technical expertise.* Is the candidate technically capable of selling your product? Can it be trained to sell it? Is it even interested in your product at all?

❐ *Perishability.* If perishability is a product issue for your company, then it is necessary to confirm that your candidate can perform to your standards so that product quality is not compromised. For instance, if your unit has a battery that could lose power over time, is the distributor willing to recharge it if necessary? This sounds simple, but some distributors are rigid about the functions they will or will not do.

❐ *Bulk and weight.* These two specifications affect how your product is transported through your channel to the end user, as well as how much physical inventory your channel partners are willing and able to sustain. Sometimes, a distributor deals only with United Parcel Service and not with a freight company. If your product weighs beyond the UPS limit, you may have a product variable mismatch.

❐ *Individual unit value.* It is always possible that your channel partner may not feel comfortable in supporting and selling a product with a substantial price. High prices may mean it is more difficult and time-consuming to sell, and your COD may not want to perform those lengthy sales tasks, which might not match your channel's overall way of doing business.

❐ *Newness.* Candidates do not always react positively to new products, often preferring manufacturers whose product lines are easy to sell. Frequently, new products require extra time, effort, training, and expense. Unless you represent a high percentage of a distributor's sales or profits, chances are it will take an uphill battle to convince your channel to actively sell your new products.

❐ *Knowledge of existing product lines.* Does the distributor have an elementary or advanced knowledge of your product—or none at all? Identifying the candidate's experience level lets you determine the size of the training task ahead. A candidate with some working knowledge of your products faces a shorter learning curve—a very definite channel selection criteria advantage.

**13.** *Repair and service capabilities.* If product repair and service are selection criteria considerations, then by all means take the time to evaluate the candidate's level of technical competence (including the competence of its personnel) and servicing equipment as it compares to your requirements.

**14.** *Knowledge of local market conditions.* A candidate should be able to intelligently discuss the overall condition of its surrounding geographic business environment. If it cannot, it may be a "surface feeder" that is interested only in selling your products to anyone at any price—with no concern for future sales and marketing commitment of your product line. This "live for today" attitude is a negative characteristic that you want to avoid.

**15.** *Employee quality.* This business yardstick further indicates the business compatibility that both of your companies need to experience. If your employees are professional and disciplined in all endeavors but the distributor's associates are disorganized free spirits who are like unguided missiles, I daresay an uncomfortable atmosphere would be created by this vast difference in environments.

**16.** *Managerial "chemistry."* Look for chemistry in your direct and indirect communications with the candidate. Friendly meetings, letters, and telephone calls indicate overall openness and point to a high-quality relationship. Are you and your staff comfortable or ill at ease with your counterparts at the distributor? If you do not have positive managerial chemistry, then your future business closeness is questionable.

**17.** *Overall condition of facilities.* Before you sign up a distributor, tour the candidate's operations to visually verify your feelings as to the "wellness" of the company. Walk through all departments and observe vital signs (or lack thereof), such as overall appearance of personnel, technology used, orderly office facilities, and the level of communication between office employees and outside individuals, including end users and manufacturers. This could be eye-opening, especially if you discover a serious deficiency, such as low physical inventory levels or sales records kept on matchbook covers.

## Sales and Marketing Criteria

**18.** *Type of market coverage offered.* What kind of market coverage does the candidate offer? If you are seeking a horizontal strategy and the distributor sells its product lines to all types of customers with no regard to any form of market specialization, you may have a match. But if you want to penetrate a vertical market, you need a distributor with a high degree of expertise in a specific marketplace. If you want to penetrate horizontal *and* vertical markets, you need to find candidates that can serve both. Be sure to determine exactly which type of market coverage fits your strategic plan, and then set out to find the class of distributor that offers it. It's just that simple.

**19.** *Proportion of internal to external salespeople.* Find out the proportion of internal salespeople and external, "feet on the street" reps. Every industry and market has an acceptable ratio. Does your potential channel partner follow the norm? If not, why not?

In the computer industry, for example, a distributor typically has 60 percent external salespeople and 40 percent internal salespeople. A distributor whose proportion runs 80 percent internal and 20 percent external may believe in telemarketing rather than customer demonstrations of the products it sells. Whether this is a problem depends on how you want your product to be sold to the eventual end user.

**20.** *Sales force compensation.* Are the distributor's salespeople on straight commissions (the golden carrot approach), straight salary (which might indicate a "9 to 5" attitude), or a combination remuneration plan (a comfortable base salary, an unlimited commission opportunity, and a quarterly bonus tied into the company's marketing strategies)? Find out so you'll know what kind of salesperson mentality you'll have to deal with and motivate.

**21.** *Sales cycle performance requirements.* What specific sales abilities do you want the channel candidate to have in each of the three phases of the sales cycle?

❐ *Presale.* Should the candidate demonstrate the product or conduct certain promotional activities, such as direct mail and advertising?
❐ *Transaction.* Should the candidate be able to administer a contract, process credit, and bill?
❐ *Postsale.* Should the candidate service, repair, or install products?

Be sure to ascertain whether the distributor is capable or even interested in performing the duties you require.

**22.** *Sales competency.* There are two issues to consider when evaluating sales competency: the number and quality of salespeople, and their technical competence.

It's always a good idea to meet some of the distributor's foot soldiers and, if possible, go along on a few customer calls. This way, you get a feeling for the company and as well as firsthand evidence of the salespeople's ability to sell to end users.

If your product requires a certain level of technical competence, it's even more important to meet salespeople face-to-face. You may also want them to go through a product certification program to ensure that they meet your technical standards.

**23.** *Sales and marketing aggressiveness.* How creative and organized is the candidate about local marketing activities? See how it handles direct mail, exhibits, telemarketing, customer open houses, contests, cooperative advertising, and such. How do its marketing activities compare to your marketing programs?

How does the candidate pursue an order in all three phases of the sales cycle? Are your approaches similar or vastly different? Are you aggressive about securing an order, and are they laid-back?

Look at the way the candidate deals with competition. Does the candidate share the local market business, or does it want to be the dominant distributor in the area? This is a key question to ask, because some distributors are complacent and not at all interested in growing their business.

**24.** *Internal sales and marketing support resources and capabilities.* Does the candidate's internal sales and marketing support (customer service, technical support, physical distribution, internal sales, and so on) meet your requirements? If it doesn't, what will it take to bring it up to your standards? Serious nonconformity could be a bellwether of future problems.

**25.** *Ordering and payment policies.* Are the candidate's ordering and payment policies in concert with your terms? A striking difference may very well reflect a major dissimilarity in the way your two companies conduct business. That dissimilarity may in turn cause operational conflict in the way you communicate financially. Case in point: Your company does not allow model mixing to gain maximum discount, and the distributor is used to this type of ordering policy. Here is where a business conflict erupts.

**26.** *Customer order fulfillment performance.* Locate these very important statistics:

- ❏ Typical time required for complete delivery of a customer's purchase order
- ❏ Accuracy of shipment of order contents
- ❏ Percentage of out-of-stock occurrences

Where do you go to obtain these data? Ask the distributor candidate or other product manufacturers carried by that distributor. A little investigative work on your part can determine whether the candidate's level of achievement meets your performance standards.

**27.** *Price integrity.* A distributor with price integrity sells your product for the highest possible price and does not give away your product by pursuing an unnecessarily low pricing strategy. Whether the candidate has price integrity emerges when you talk with other manufacturers about the marketplace pricing practices of your channel candidates. In addition, reputable distributors ask, before they sign a contract, whether you are considering certain price-degenerating distributors. If you are, they won't want to belong to your COD. There is no question that you should put a high ranking on this criterion to steer clear of the tragedy caused by unnecessary price and customer service deterioration.

**28.** *Ability to develop new markets.* New market development is a key factor for many companies choosing a channel partner. If you plan to rely heavily on your channel to penetrate new markets, make sure the candidate knows it up front. Quite frankly, distributors as a whole are not enthusiastic about venturing outside their comfort zone or everyday marketplace to exert missionary sales effort in a new market. But a forward-thinking distributor is always on the lookout for new market opportunities and plans its marketing strategies accordingly.

**29.** *Distributor advertising and sales promotional programs.* It's a plus when a distributor's media communication efforts are similar to your own. Complementary marketing characteristics can form a very powerful strategic alliance that carries through from a national to local market image. When a distributor's advertising philosophy dovetails with yours, a win-win situation and increased sales revenue can are ensured, because the same target audience will be reached by a two-pronged coordinated media effort.

**30.** *Training programs.* This selection criterion should be close to the top of your most-wanted list. Find out the details of the distributor's internal training program. How frequently do personnel meet? What subjects are covered in the training? How important are those topics? Who conducts the training? How much time will they devote to training that you supply? Will they allow you to train personnel? How much time will they allocate to your products in their training? How much time do you desire? These questions are significant, because product and sales training are key elements in the comfort level you eventually achieve. Always strive for the maximum amount of training commitment.

**31.** *Consent to sign a contract.* Many candidates are family-owned, entrepreneurial businesses that occasionally operate on a handshake. While it is preferable to have a signed contract, on occasion you may have to operate without one.

If a distributor won't consent to signing a contract, first verify with other manufacturers that this nonsigned agreement is the distributor's usual way of conducting business. In this way, you can confirm that you're being treated like everyone else. However, if the distributor does sign contracts with others, its refusal to sign a contract with you may indicate that the distributor places a low level of importance on your product line. If that is the case, ask yourself whether you want this type of indefinite relationship.

If you choose to proceed without a signed agreement, then insist on an initial meeting to set ground rules and discuss key elements of your relationship. These include:

❏ Primary sales and service geographic area
❏ Markets assigned
❏ Products
❏ A mutually agreed-upon quota
❏ All other important business policies (credit, payment, warranty, and so on)

Follow up your meeting with a letter outlining what was discussed. In this way, you'll have unilaterally stated how your companies will progress with the relationship. Makes sense, doesn't it?

**32.** *Agreement to accept a sales quota.* Both of you should agree to strive toward an annual sales target that is measured and discussed over the year in your business review meetings. The distributor should exhibit a sincere belief that it can and will do everything possible to attain this goal.

**33.** *Willingness to share data and local market information.* The distributor is the last link in the channel of distribution. It makes the final sales contact with the end user. Distributors know that this information about the sales contact is valuable, and they often try to keep it secret. While there are ways to improve the channel relationship and communication flow even when the distributor does not give you this information, it's a plus when a distributor openly provides information about whom it sells to, at what price, and any other special marketing intelligence (competition, special product application, emerging markets) that is available to the distributor and not you. Openness at the outset prevents problems later on.

**34.** *Willingness to participate in joint sales and marketing programs.* Channel partnerships are based on a give-and-take relationship. The distributor's receptiveness to your sales and marketing programs is a clear indication of the solidarity of the relationship. An "oil and water" attitude toward your overall marketing direction may presage a mismatch in channel partners.

**35.** *Inventory management expertise.* How many inventory turns does the distributor expect from a product line within a year? Is it overstocked with other manufacturers' products? If so, which ones and why?

What do other inventory managers have to say about the candidate's inventory management capability?

**36.** ***Adequate inventory commitment.*** Does the candidate's inventory philosophy match yours? Will it commit to an adequate inventory, or does it want only to broker your product line? To avoid channel conflict, your physical inventory philosophies should mesh.

**37.** ***Future growth prospects.*** Look into the future and judge whether or not the channel candidate will or could be a viable fit in your strategic marketing plan. Based on what you have learned, is the candidate capable of launching your new products and penetrating new, emerging markets and market segments? Look for channel partners who can and will grow with you.

## "Coup de Grace" Factors That Indicate a Motivated Candidate

**38.** ***True desire for your product line.*** It is certainly motivational for both parties to be enthusiastic about the new partnership and to openly communicate their positive business feelings. Are the distributor's customers "calling out" for your product line? If so, desire for your company's products already exists with the distributor's customers. This is a very good sign and one that you don't often hear in the course of your initial contacts. Feel fortunate if you hear this type of comment, and pursue the candidate to continue the euphoria.

**39.** ***Willingness to share key customer list.*** Because you don't know the candidate, you will probably be refused this information, but it doesn't hurt to ask. If you do get to see this information, it will help you compare the distributor's customers to your target audience. The candidate's willingness to share this information is further evidence of potential business harmony.

**40.** ***Willingness to commit resources to your product line.*** Get excited when a distributor candidate voluntarily approaches you and suggests that your companies engage in and share the commensurate costs of a local marketing event (open house, direct mail, advertising). This willingness to commit financial and personnel resources is rare, because many entrepreneurial organizations play it close to the vest. Remember that other manufacturers compete with you for these same resources. A favorable commitment to your company is further proof of a workable partnership.

**41.** Existence of a strategic business plan. A very definite plus—feel fortunate if such a document exists! Because of their entrepreneurial nature, very few distributors actually have a business plan. If a candidate has one, see if it coincides with your plan's objectives, strategies, and tactics. Doing this can ensure a directional match between the businesses.

**42.** *Willingness to participate in strategic business planning with your company.* The candidate's willingness to participate in future strategic business planning activities (new products and markets, advisory council participation) is a clear sign of your importance, or lack thereof, to the candidate.

# Composing Your "Wish List"

No distributor can meet every one of these forty-two criteria. That is why you need to decide which tasks and qualities are most important to you. Develop a list of criteria that express what *you* and your *end users* want from the channel, and apply it to each distributor you meet during the location and selection process.

Begin by revisiting your marketing plan to review what you want to accomplish in your target marketplaces. Do you want to increase sales revenue by 15 percent or to enter two new, undeveloped markets? These objectives and strategies need to be translated into your channel selection criteria.

Next, find out what others in your company want your distributors to do. Survey other internal managers to ascertain the tasks they want your distributors to achieve. Ask your credit manager for credit and payment terms, your engineering manager for technical expertise required, your direct sales force manager to address compatibility issues between direct and indirect channels, and so on. Add your personal channelmaster wishes to the growing list.

Finally, add the end user satisfaction requirements to the total channel selection criteria list. At this point, you'll probably have between twenty and thirty criteria that you now need to rank. To rank them, form an internal channel selection criteria committee that includes your general manager, indirect channel sales manager, customer service manager, and you—the channelmaster. At your meeting, discuss and vote separately on the importance of each selection criterion. To arrive at your priorities, use a scale of 1 to 10 or A, B, C.

Finally, summarize all of these opinions and blend them into a final list. Some criteria will clearly be important to you and other managers; others may matter more to you than to the others. It's up to you to make the final call. When the list is complete, you can begin to apply it to candidates as you locate them.

In summary, you should spend a major part of your managerial time in this critical phase of sculpting the relationship. Not only is it important for you to compose and rank your channel selection criteria in a list that you apply equally to each candidate, but it is important that you properly and completely communicate your criteria desires to each potential candidate. In turn, candidates can then make an intelligent decision that fits their own business culture and capabilities. A sound business partnership begins.

## *Case:* A Channel Change of the Highest Order

Your company, a manufacturer of computer hardware peripherals, has just acquired a specialized computer peripheral company whose software programs are designed for the CAD/CAM/CAE (Computer-Aided Design, Computer-Aided Manufacturing, Computer-Aided Engineering) marketplaces. Because of the acquisition's more general hardware focus, your existing channels of distribution—regional and national computer distributors and large volume value-added resellers—are probably not capable of or interested in reaching this very well-defined marketplace. In the acquisition package, your company has also assumed full ownership of $750,000 of product inventory. Consequently, your immediate superior has issued an edict to you to immediately find another channel of distribution to move this inventory burden and thus create sales revenue profits. Describe how you would proceed and what new COD selection criteria you would use. Answer these questions:

- ❐ Why wasn't any marketing channel strategy considered prior to acquiring the software company?
- ❐ Should you give your existing channel ''right of first option'' to market the software programs?

**Case interpretational points:**

- ❐ Channel of distribution strategy should always be included at the very beginning of any marketing program.
- ❐ Company politics sometimes play an unfortunately influential role in channel management decisions.

❏ Employ the entire Channel Design Sequence (all eleven steps) from Chapter 2.

❏ Use a critical mass listing of selection criteria that adequately represents both end user satisfaction requirements and also what business tasks you want the channel candidates to perform.

❏ Proceed as soon as possible.

# Chapter 7

# Eagles Don't Flock: Locating Channel Member Candidates

√ *Step 1:* Identify the new market you want to penetrate or new product you need to launch.

√ *Step 2:* Verify the need for a new channel of distribution or some form of channel reorganization

√ *Step 3:* Evaluate all macro market conditions.

√ *Step 4:* Conduct a competitive channel analysis.

√ *Step 5:* Research and rank customer/end user satisfaction requirements.

√ *Step 6:* SpecIfy and rank the tasks you want your channel partner to perform.

√ **Step 7: Investigate all possible channel of distribution structures.**

√ **Step 8: Decide upon eagle channel partners.**

Although you can't check the Yellow Pages under *D* for *distributor*, locating eagle distributors is not an insurmountable chore. It consists of two primary tasks:

1. Choosing the channel structure that best meets your needs
2. Finding the best candidates in your chosen channel

**Ken's Words of Wisdom**

❐ The major markets aren't necessarily the targets you first attempt to penetrate.

❐ Go regional first, then national.

Like an intellectual jigsaw puzzle, you piece together the channel that will maximize your sales revenue and profits in your target market.

## Locating Channel Candidates

There are many, many channel types and structures. (Look back at Exhibit 1-4, in Chapter 1, for proof.) Your task is to find the channel structure that will give you the "biggest bang for the buck"—i.e., the one that meets all end user requirements and provides you with the best return on your investment. By making a matrix for your industry or marketplace, you will have a road map that will guide you through your investigation.

In most instances, your end user research will identify the best structure to pursue. If research shows that end users prefer to buy your category of product through local value-added resellers that in turn purchase your products through regional and national distributors, then you have identified your primary channel structure.

To determine whether a channel structure meets your end users' needs, compare it with the factors you discovered in your end user research. Pay particular attention to the dominant channel in your industry. This, the most powerful and best-established channel, is the one that sells the most product and generates the most sales revenue and profit for the manufacturer. For example, 60 percent of all products in the computer industry pass through the channel shown in Exhibit 7-1. If the dominant channel works for you, go with it. There's no need to reinvent the wheel!

On the other hand, 40 percent of all computer products pass through other channel structures, which are illustrated in Chapter 2 in Exhibit 2-2. You may need to sell through several channel structures to reach the maximum number of end users. Thoroughly evaluate *all* of the forms of marketing channels within your target marketplace. Remember, too, that your channel must fit your product line and meet your company's business objectives. Prioritize your channel structure choices by potential revenue payback opportunity to determine which ones meet your criteria.

## Choosing a Market Coverage Strategy

Before you begin finding potential channel partners, decide how many you want in a given geographic territory or market area. As Exhibit 7-2 illustrates, there are three types of market coverage:

1. *Intensive coverage* means authorizing as many distributors as possible to sell products in a given geographic area or market segment. An

**Exhibit 7-1.** The dominant channel in the microcomputer industry.

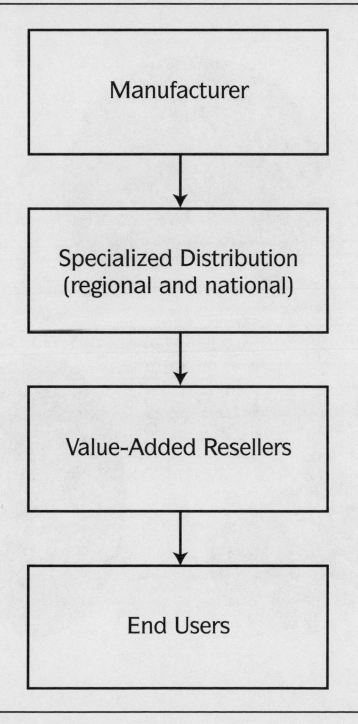

**Exhibit 7-2.** The three types of market coverage.

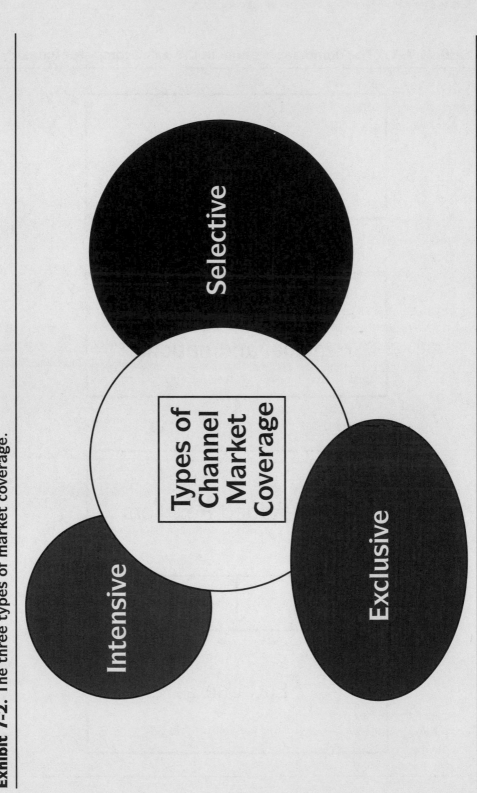

example of this "shotgun approach" would be commodity-type products sold during certain seasonal periods of the year, such as Christmas decorations in October, November, and December. An intensive coverage approach ought to be appropriate.

2. *Selective coverage* means choosing only those distributors that meet certain channel selection criteria to sell products in a given market. For instance, certain designer label clothes can be sold only at sophisticated retailers like Nieman Marcus or Bloomingdale's.

3. *Exclusive coverage* means authorizing only one distributor per geographic area or market. Specialty products lend themselves to this kind of channel coverage, like those products sold through The Container Store, which sells home organizing items.

The geographic dispersion of your end users and markets plays an important role in your selection of a channel sales organizational format. So does the supply of top-notch distributors in your market. There aren't that many eagle distributors—distributors whose competence is unquestioned and whose integrity is unblemished. The availability of these distributors greatly influences your market coverage decision.

## Is Bigger Always Best?

Does size matter in choosing your channel partners? Actually, it's a good idea to mix small, medium, and large sales volume distributors and regional and national partners in your channel. Working with different kinds of distributors lets you benefit from a variety of sales and marketing expertise. For instance, a small or medium-size regional distributor can provide you with tight, local-market sales coverage because of its proximity to its customers. Conversely, a large national distributor may lack this local advantage but use more advanced and powerful sales and marketing resources to support your product line. Therefore, both channel types may have their place in your marketing strategy plans.

Channel power is another reason to stick with a variety of partners. If you do business only with national distributors, then those distributors end up with most of the channel power. Don't put all of your channel eggs in one basket. Entrust a few to small and medium-size distributors. Channel power is covered in Chapter 10, but it's an important factor to keep in mind now as you locate your channel candidates.

When mixing partners of different sizes and capabilities, it's a good idea to sign up regional partners before soliciting national distributors. Fill your dance card first with national power distributors, and then regionals won't even bother to sign up. If you are to new channel marketing, you might want to build your credentials in smaller regional markets before tackling large markets and national distributors.

# Finding the Eagles

Once you have determined the channel (or channels) with the highest appeal to you and your end users, you are ready to search for specific, high-quality members. Fortunately, some of the same sources you used to conduct your competitive channel analysis can also help you locate these eagle distributors. Use them to accumulate the meaningful data you need to reach clearcut decisions about the candidates you want to approach.

## Trade Publications

As Chapter 6 pointed out, the leading industry magazines offer a wealth of marketing channel information and data. Look for special annual editions that list "The Top 100 Distributors," "Academy Award–Winning Systems Integrators," "Wholesalers of the Year," "The 100 Best Manufacturer Representative Companies," "100 Dealers of Distinction," "The VAR 500," "The 50 Best Small Distributors," "The Top 100 Systems Integrators," "The Top 50 Retailers of the Year," and so on. You may already have scanned magazine rankings to find competitive information about your channel and its members. Now you can use them to find out everything from the distributor's name and location to its sales revenue, names and titles of key managers, and number of employees. Save these gold mines. They point you straight to the eagles you are looking for.

## Trade Organizations

Check the membership directory of the major trade organizations in your industry. These comprehensive directories are subdivided into sections covering distributors, value-added resellers, dealers, manufacturer reps, and so forth. They offer neat, descriptive profiles of each company in a particular category. The only drawback? They do not include distributors that are not members of the organization.

## End User/Customer Testimonials

If you conducted a customer segmentation analysis, you've heard an earful on the preferred distributors in the markets you researched. For more comments and recommendations, simply place a call to additional end users.

## Advertising by Manufacturers

Study those full-page ads that devote the upper portion of the page to the product message and the remainder of the ad to a list of authorized dealers. Pay special attention to ads from competitors or respected companies that manufacture complementary product lines. Use them to cross-check the information you are gathering on your channel of distribution.

## Advertising by Distributors

Space ads placed by distributors are a very important piece of channel location evidence to consider. These ads usually reflect a company's managerial and business direction and can give you a sense of whether its sales and marketing approach fits yours. Attention-getting advertising efforts are also proof of sales and marketing prowess—especially important when a distributor isn't a member of a trade organization or is too "young" to make a "Top 100" list.

## Trade Shows/Seminars

Because it gathers all of your potential channel members in one location, a trade show can save you travel, expenses, and time. For best results, devote a great deal of time to preshow preparation. Secure the trade show directory at least two weeks' ahead to set up appointments with those attending and exhibiting. Take advantage of distributor hospitality suites and trade show receptions. These events offer an atmosphere that is conducive to casual, off-the-cuff conversations that can eventually lead to a formal business relationship.

## Your Direct Field Sales Force

Ask your direct sales force for its recommendations. Your direct salespeople are in frequent field contact with all varieties of distributors and certainly have heard of the reputation of each company. Also, involving your direct sales force in the channel selection process helps minimize conflict. If you eventually choose the distributor that your direct salesperson recommended, then a credible relationship can start to materialize between these two parties.

## VIP Business Contacts

Every marketplace has its experts—people who know the industry inside and out and are respected by the channel members within it. Seek out their opinions about distributors they hold in high regard. Talking with these experts also serves as an influential, door-opening credential when you contact potential channel partners.

## Complementary Manufacturers' Catalogs and Literature

Check the catalogs and literature of complementary manufacturers for state-by-state, country-by-country listings of every distributor authorized to sell and service their product lines. To find the eagles, contact the channel sales and marketing managers. Explain that you are creating a new channel of distribution, and ask them for their managerial opinion of certain distributors and, if possible, a reference to open communication with these companies.

## Other Distributor Referrals

Eagles know each other. They belong to the same "club." After you sign one eagle, ask to be introduced to others. This is the most potent way of gaining an audience with these hotly pursued distributors. Use this approach, and you will be able to form business partnerships with at least 90 percent of your contacts. Incredible, but true! It can and will work for you!

## Your Competitor's Channels of Distribution

If no other choice is feasible, there is nothing wrong with replicating your competitor's channel. Expect rough times, as your rival will flex its marketing muscle in an attempt to block your entrance into its precious channel. While it is legally dangerous to prohibit competition in the channel, quite frankly, it happens all the time. Be aware of any action taken against you, and deal with it accordingly.

Be on the lookout for storm clouds hovering over your competitors. If you hear complaints about poor product quality, lack of support, or poor delivery performance on the part of a competitor, get a list of its distributors and give them a call. Distributors temporarily dissatisfied with your competition are very receptive targets to your positive marketing program approach. But don't misuse or abuse a temporarily advantageous competitive position. Unethical or potentially illegal behavior injures your industry reputation and damages channel partner relationships.

## Special Industry Surveys

Market research companies frequently compose and sell special industry directories, which you see advertised in the leading trade publications and at the major trade shows. Before you purchase, scan the contents or ask for a sample set of distributor profiles. It's possible that the same information may be available elsewhere at little or no cost.

## Your Local Library's Business Reference Section

One obvious source of information is your local library's business reference section. Explain what you're trying to do, and your librarian can uncover and show you government reports, magazine articles, specialized directories, and other information nuggets that you may never have found otherwise.

## Channel Search Firms

A handful of companies serve as "executive recruiters" in the COD business. Ask your industry trade organization what they are and where to find them. However, these companies can be quite expensive and may not be necessary once you have mastered the information in this book. You'll also see them advertising their services in the leading trade magazines.

## Marketing Channel Consultants

If time is of the essence and you have no time for research, retain a consultant with extensive channel experience. A qualified consultant can take you from ground zero to a fully implemented channel structure and program in an accelerated period of time. Check to make sure that he or she has experience in your specific business or product area before retaining such a person.

   With your selection criteria list and candidate location source information in hand, you are ready to contact and set up a channel enticement summit meeting with your clearly identified eagle distributor targets. Your intellectual jigsaw puzzle has been solved!

## *Case:* Where Do the Eagles Nest?

You have just been promoted from manager of technical sales support to director of marketing for a manufacturer of electronic components. Further, you have two existing channels of distribution: 175 electrical and 130 electronic distributors throughout North America. In your previous managerial capacity, you observed a major shift in the way your end users purchased your products over the last four years. You rightfully suspect that, because of this nonconfirmed buying behavioral change, your annual sales revenue performance has been negatively affected. In fact, you feel that's why you were promoted in the first place: to reorganize, if you must, and turn this situation around to produce positive results. This is an interesting position to be in, and you sense that some investigative—and, most likely, corrective—action has to be taken as soon as possible. You are confident that you have an adequate channel design plan ready for implementation. Now it's time to find and fix the new channel eagle targets.

Discuss in detail your action plan for locating the new distributors.

**Case interpretational points:**

❒ First, verify that a channel buying behavioral change is actually happening before you take any corrective action.

❒ Conduct a thorough customer segmentation analysis to identify any end user purchasing changes.

❒ Discuss your observations with other channel marketing managers selling complementary products in the same marketplace to see if they are experiencing the same transition in buying power.

❒ Involve your present distributors in your research efforts to enlist their local market expertise.

❒ Then, if you decide that corrective action is necessary, use as many locational sources as possible to ascertain that your final channel choices are the correct ones.

# Chapter 8

# Channel Candidate Enticements and Inducements: Business Policies That Bond Your Channel To You

---

√ *Step 1:* Identify the new market you want to penetrate or new product you need to launch.

√ *Step 2:* Verify the need for a new channel of distribution or some form of channel reorganization.

√ *Step 3:* Evaluate all macro market conditions.

√ *Step 4:* Conduct a competitive channel analysis.

√ *Step 5:* Research and rank customer/end user satisfaction requirements.

√ *Step 6:* Specify and rank the tasks you want your channel partner to perform.

√ *Step 7:* Investigate all possible channel of distribution structures.

√ *Step 8:* Decide upon eagle channel partners.

√ **Step 9:** **Obtain internal corporate recommitment.**

√ **Step 10:** **Approach and sign the selected distributors.**

---

Having accomplished Steps 1 through 8 of the Channel Design Sequence, you are ready to sign up the distributors you have targeted. This is one of the last steps involved in creating a new channel. The time you invested in researching your customer base, evaluating environmental issues, and determining your selection criteria is about to pay off. For you now *know* what kind of channel you need to set up and which distributors you want to sign. That knowledge has prepared you to meet face-to-face with your eagle distributor candidates. You are ready for the ultimate channel challenge, shown in Exhibit 8-1.

There are five steps involved in successfully signing up an eagle distributor:

1. Finding out and confirming what the distributor is looking for from a manufacturer
2. Compiling your channel policies, procedures, and support systems into an unbeatable package of "enticements" that will motivate the distributor to do business with your company
3. Reconfirming your company's commitment to the new channel
4. Making a convincing presentation to the distributor
5. Signing a channel agreement and commencing a successful business relationship

Notice that the third step above—reconfirming your company's commitment to the new channel—is actually Step 9 of the overall Channel Design Sequence.

Do not take the phases covered in this chapter casually. As Winston Churchill once said, "This must be your finest hour."

**Exhibit 8-1.** The goal of channel candidate enticement.

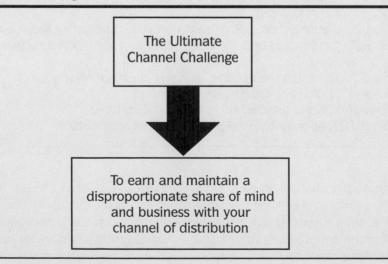

# Finding Out and Confirming What the Distributor Needs

No distributor can resist a package of enticements that delivers *exactly* what it is looking for. During your competitive channel analysis, you learned about the kinds of business policies your competitors offer. Before you approach distributors with your own package of enticements, check to make sure that your policies make the grade. This chapter lists dozens of policies and incentives you can use as enticements, but the following items are virtual must-haves to any distributor. Distributors evaluate your request based on these core concerns. To attract and retain good distributors, be sure to offer:

❑ Quality products that reflect well on the distributor's entire product mix

❑ Adequate compensation that meets the distributor's margin demands

❑ Committed manufacturer field salespeople who work to achieve satisfaction for the distributor, stand up for the distributor during conflicts, and coach the distributor's staff in how to proficiently sell products

❑ Competent internal support systems that provide top-quality customer service, technical support, training, and marketing services

❑ A company image of quality and respect that reflects well on the distributor in the eyes of its channel peers and its customers

❑ A deep reservoir of channel trust

## Building Channel Trust

The last item on the above list is channel trust, and it is a key element. Your distributors want to believe you. They want to know that you mean what you say. Doing your homework before you meet with a distributor can lay the foundation for this key quality, which will take many years to build. Even though it takes so long, you create a favorable first impression at your meeting if you show that you know what the distributor's business looks like and offer business policies that make sense. Follow through on your promises, and you'll be on your way to a solid, mutually trusting relationship with your key business partners.

Channel trust exists when:

❑ Channel power is proportionately balanced between the manufacturer and distributor, thereby creating a level playing field for all channel members.

❏ All parties are equitably treated.
❏ Business goals are similar or identical, so the manufacturer and distributor move in the same business direction instead of constantly butting heads.
❏ Reliable communication flows from the manufacturer to the distributor.

A gifted channel manager truly feels the business pain and pleasure of the channel and can thus accurately relate to his or her distributor's business requirements. That channelmaster wields the most trust-building tool of all: a market-meaningful combination of channel policies, procedures, and support systems that convince the distributor to do business with his or her company.

## Knowing What Your Competition's Channel Program Contains

Before you present your package, closely research your primary competitor's channel enticement lists to ensure that your offerings are as or more appealing and seductive. This information is quite easy to accumulate and evaluate. Your distributor candidate will be more than happy to tell you about your competition's policies and procedures and how yours stack up. The reason? Your distributor wants you to provide a much improved and more profitable group of channel inducements! By playing off each other, you can garner the necessary competitive field intelligence and arrive at a list of channel inducements that is acceptable to both parties.

As you uncover your competition's policies, you can conduct a SWOT (Strength, Weakness, Opportunity, Threat) analysis to identify those business policy issues that can make your company stand out from its opponents.

## Preparing Your Package of Enticements

Your meeting with a distributor candidate will be short—between thirty and sixty minutes. That is why it is imperative that your list of enticements should be firm and ready for rapid-fire negotiations. In this section, there are twenty-eight different enticements that you can package into your own program.

But remember: Don't offer *everything*! Like poker, the policies should be divided into *antes* and *pluses*:

❏ *Antes* are policies that are necessary to get you into the COD business. They are what you have to put into the pot in order to play. They include basics like meeting the channel's economic demands for profitability, quality, and physical distribution.

❏ *Pluses* are policies that strengthen your position and make an advantageous difference between your company and your main competition. Lucrative payment terms, an increased warranty period, or a higher standard of quality are all good examples.

By grouping your business policies and procedures in this way, you can present your channel marketing program more enticingly during the meeting. You are able to spotlight the policies and procedures that are critical to your candidate's business, thereby inducing the distributor to form a business partnership with your company. Keep in mind that the primary objective of your meeting is to walk away with a signed contract, an initial stocking order, and a mutually enthusiastic business alliance. Starting and ending the meeting with your strongest enticements helps achieve that aim.

Here are the different enticements you can use when crafting your package.

## 1. Adequate or Superior Discounts/Margins

The very first thing an eagle distributor asks is, "How much money am I going to make with your product line?" If you can't meet the distributor's requirements, the candidate will call an abrupt end to your meeting. Most of the time, a distributor candidate asks about your channel profit margins in your first telephone contact. If they are unacceptable, the conversation quickly ceases. If they are acceptable, then you may be granted a face-to-face meeting, depending on the distributor's time availability and the overall appeal of your product line/mix.

## 2. Quality Product

Always be prepared to specifically discuss your product line's quality—an issue that your prospective candidate is vitally concerned about. Superior or inferior quality not only reflects on the candidate's company but on the rest of the product lines it markets. Quality breeds quality. Distributors don't want part of a "bad apple" syndrome.

Put some serious thought into this part of your meeting agenda. Prepare some statistical proof of your product line's quality standards or other verifiable information that substantiates your grade of excellence. Take along the latest quality assurance and quality control data from your operations manager. A high-quality product is a real enticement. If your product is of high quality, tell the candidate why.

### 3. Full Product Line/Mix

Just as customers want one stop shopping from distributors, your distributors look to you for a full array of products. Before you approach distributors, make sure you offer a complete assortment of products. If a review of your product mix turns up important voids, take immediate action. If the missing products cannot be manufactured internally, use outside acquisition in the form of complete production or private labeling.

Product accessories also fill out your product line and offer distinct benefits to distributors. Sometimes, to win business, a distributor must reduce the price and profits of your main model. High-profit accessory sales can help absorb some of that lost revenue and margin. For example, a distributor that gives a 20-percent discount on an overhead projector can recoup profits by selling that same customer a dust cover, roll feed attachment, or spare projection lamp at full list price. Because the end user has already purchased your primary product, add-on accessories can be an easy second-effort sell.

### 4. Consistent and Responsive Sales and Marketing Support

This is really rather elementary. If channel partners do not receive quick, accurate, consistent, and honest responses to requests for information, they simply cease contacting your company. Quite frankly, they have better things to do than waste time with a manufacturer that does not quickly or correctly supply technical information, warranty claim processing, purchase order fulfillment, and product and sales training.

### 5. Rapid or Timely Delivery

Every marketplace has its own set of product delivery standards. Find out what they are and then decide how you can meet or beat the time required to fulfill the channel shipment needs. Imagine proudly telling an eagle distributor that your average order processing and shipping time is somewhere between two and three weeks—and then learning that the distributor ships 90 percent of all customer orders within twenty-four hours. Two to three weeks versus twenty-four hours is a definite policy mismatch. Be prepared to deal with this important inventory procedure or risk managerial embarrassment, noncompatibility, and a quick end to your long-awaited channel enticement meeting.

## 6. Drop Shipment Capability

Make drop shipments an exception, not the rule, but be prepared to tell the candidate they can be done if absolutely necessary. You don't want to do a lot of drop shipments: Interrupting your regular order flow costs you some additional processing expense, time, and effort. On the other hand, a drop shipment could save a distributor's order. Frequently, a distributor's customer will not pay an invoice unless the shipment is 100 percent complete. Imagine your distributor's anxiety level if your $5,000 product is holding up payment on a $500,000 order. Quite a problem, for all three parts of the COD! Let your distributor call or fax you, explain the emergency situation, and request a drop shipment to the customer's location. You ship, the distributor collects the full $500,000—and your business partnership continues to bloom. A veritable win-win-win conclusion!

One other point: By drop shipping to your distributor's customer, you learn the name, location, business type, and market of your distributor's customer. This is rather important information that is often unavailable to you.

## 7. Price Protection

Depending on the industry, price protection can be a major channel policy consideration. In a fast-moving, dynamic marketplace like cellular products, pricing fluctuations can be sporadic and significant. Channel and end user pricing can deteriorate as a product approaches a commodity classification while a great deal of units are available for purchase. With price protection, the distributor is protected when the manufacturer decides, for competitive reasons, to lower its entire pricing schedule. Let's say the distributor has $100,000 of your products in inventory, and you decide to reduce that inventory value to $90,000 by lowering end user pricing. Under price protection, you give the distributor a credit of $10,000 to its account. You've moved inventory, and your distributor has a credit of $10,000 to purchase more product. Another win-win outcome.

## 8. Product Warranty

Take a look at your primary competitor's warranty policy, and top it. If your competitor has a one-year warranty for full parts and labor, consider offering a two- or three-year warranty. This is a real advantage that can help build your reputation for quality and channel commitment. But before you change your warranties, find out what an extended warranty would cost. Consult with your quality assurance and product repair managers for costing data that enables you to reach a logical, financially responsible decision.

## 9. Dead on Arrival Priority Order Replacement

As with a drop shipment, this enticement could also solve a distributor's emergency. A product that comes to the purchaser dead on arrival (DOA) can create a high-priority channel problem for your distributor and its extremely irritated customer! Organize your procedures so that all the distributor need do is explain the situation to a specially assigned individual at your company. Your DOA order replacement specialist should then walk a priority replacement order through your system to quickly alleviate this dilemma.

## 10. Comprehensive Cooperative (COOP) Advertising

Cooperative advertising allows the distributor to perform, on a manufacturer preapproved basis, certain local market sales promotional activities such as direct mail, exhibitions, advertising (publications, radio, television), and open houses. The distributor is then reimbursed from an accrued percentage of total purchases from the respective manufacturer. This amount differs from industry to industry but normally is in the 2 percent to 5 percent range. You keep the funds in a designated account, and disburse them as you approve the distributor's promotional activities. Distributors must use the funds by the end of the year or lose them.

Investigate COOP programs in your target marketplace, and match or better others' reimbursement packages. Administered properly, this channel policy is a true win-win sales and marketing opportunity that can help promote your product line.

## 11. Competitive End User/List Pricing

Conduct a thorough end user market survey of the "street pricing" for products that are similar to your offerings, and position your pricing strategy so that it entices the highest number of end users while generating acceptable profits for your company and COD. Analyze your market frequently for pricing patterns and competitive threats that may influence or even force you to change your prices. For example, you may have to consider lowering your prices if the market leader does. While this is not desirable, it may be required in order to strategically stay in business.

## 12. Free Product Literature

Creative and interest-generating literature is a sales vehicle for your channel members to use to sell your product line to their customers. A word of caution: Limit the total number of pieces a distributor can have free of charge. Base that number on how much it costs you to create and print each piece. List the prices of your product pieces on a literature summary sheet that tells how many are available free. For instance, if a piece of literature costs one dollar to produce, then it is reasonable to provide one hundred copies free. Conversely, if it costs only five cents per piece, then perhaps 500 free copies would be appropriate. Requests exceeding the published limit can be applied to the distributor's COOP account. In that way, you do not discourage your enthusiastic channel partner's support of your product mix in its local markets.

## 13. No-Penalty Stock Rotation

No-penalty stock rotation motivates channel members to carry adequate physical inventory levels of your product line by allowing distributors to return slower, nonmoving units. Generally, product returns are allowed only once or twice during a twelve-month calendar period—the first two weeks in December, for example. The returns must receive an advance return authorization (RA) from the appropriate level of manufacturer sales and marketing management, usually the channelmaster.

After requesting permission to return products, the distributor must give the manufacturer at least a week to find another home in the channel for the products. Often, there are other distributors that, for their own local market reasons, are actively selling those models. Usually, only factory-sealed cartons can be returned. Nicked, damaged, or used products are not returnable.

It's a good idea to limit the amount of nonmoving stock a distributor can send back. This limit is normally based on a specified percentage of purchases during the period of time. These amounts vary but usually top out at 10 percent of total annual purchases.

To soften the expense of processing and reinventorying, request that the product return be accompanied by a purchase order of an equivalent amount. For example, if the return is for $10,000 worth of products, then the new order would have to equal the same dollar amount. While some manufacturers also charge a 10 percent restocking fee, it is perceived as a penalty and discourages the distributor from carrying an adequate inventory level.

In the final analysis, a no-penalty stock rotation plan encourages a distributor to actively maintain an adequate amount of your inventory by reducing the risk that it will lose its street value. Not having such a plan actually discourages distributors from carrying a complete, local market physical inventory.

## 14. Market-Knowledgeable Manufacturer Management

Nothing turns off a channel partner quicker than dealing with manufacturers that do not know or care about the distributor's marketplace, business challenges, and customers. A lack of experience and sensitivity can easily create an arcticlike atmosphere between the two channel parties. Do *not* place a naive, inexperienced manager in charge of an indirect channel of distribution. Hire a perceptive marketing manager, or pay the price in reduced distributor commitment revenues and commensurate profits.

## 15. New Product Development Plans

Let your channel know about new products. The more your distributors feel they're part of the manufacturer's inner circle, the more they'll commit to your new product marketing efforts when called upon to do so. But be careful. Keep in mind that, like you, other channel managers are constantly seeking out competitive product information. Share too much with your channel, and you risk a breach of confidentiality to the competitors that your distributors represent.

## 16. U.S. Manufacture

In some situations, a product manufactured in the United States can be a real plus. Wal-Mart, for example, prefers to buy and sell products made in the United States. Its procurement management is even paid a bonus for purchasing U.S. products. If domestic labeling makes a difference in your channel, by all means tout this advantage.

## 17. Major Account Sales Support

Major account sales support is a significant inducement in market areas that are home to national or international customers. By partnering with a distributor, the manufacturer presents a cohesive team that can be a valuable asset in cementing a national account relationship. Involving the manufacturer management in the national account's relationship with the distributor tells the national account that it can rely on a great depth of support. But there are dangers. The national account might ask to deal directly with you—and might even bring this up in front of your distributor. You also have to tackle the sensitive matter of split commissions and profits. To determine how sales credit should be split, pinpoint the services the national account desires at both corporate and local destination areas. For example, if the customer desires local installation and support, then you split the compensation in some appropriate proportion depending upon how much effort is exerted by each party. It could be fifty-fifty or perhaps 80 percent to the corporate distributor and 20 percent to the local market company.

## 18. Equitable and Swiftly Enforced Policy Decisions

Never try to wish away a tough policy decision. The longer you languish over a sensitive administrative question, the less confidence your channel will have. Correct, fair, and quick decisions are best. Because sensitive situations arise all the time, be prepared to respond appropriately to any procedural situation. And remember, when conflicts arise, all of your distributors are watching. Based on how deftly you handle conflicts, these observers form either a positive or negative opinion of your channel marketing programs and pass along their impressions to others along the "channel telegraph."

## 19. Payment Terms

Make sure your payment term policy complies with industry standards. Eagle distributors frequently favor those suppliers that have above-average payment policies. Try offering a 4 percent net thirty-day payment discount when the marketplace norm is only 2 percent. Better-than-average payment terms are another enticement that can positively impress your channel candidates.

## 20. Product Customization/Private Label Capability

This special possibility may appeal to large, national distributors that want to promote and market their tremendous size as a competitive advantage to their customers. Let such distributors know that you are receptive to changing product features to meet a distributor's customer requirement or affixing their corporate logo to your product to complement their business plans.

## 21. Your Corporate International Expertise

International expertise can entice multinational distributors that want to draw on a manufacturer for international business support. NAFTA and other similar trade agreements are opening doors that were previously closed and not accessible to these more sophisticated, international distributors. Identify channel members that would be attracted to manufacturer partners possessing this global advantage, and then show how you can assist them.

## 22. A Media Communications Program That Generates Qualified Sales Leads

Be prepared to discuss and show actual examples of all elements of your media communications program, including direct mail, space advertisements, public relations releases, telemarketing, your exhibit schedule, and product literature. Make sure you can explain the rationale behind each media program effort, and be prepared to state the number of *qualified* sales leads you intend to provide. Depending on how many manufacturers they represent, distributors receive hundreds—even thousands—of leads a week. They simply don't pursue those that have not been qualified by the manufacturer.

## 23. Special Pricing Assistance

A stark reality is that very few industries escape having to engage in special pricing. It is prudent to treat special pricing as a possible channel advantage that must be constantly and fairly administered. While you may indicate that special pricing assistance is available, *always* document and justify the issuance of any special pricing. Use a multipart special price form (see Chapter 12). Give one copy to the distributor, place a second in your permanent file, and place a third in an open, follow-up file. This form should list your product, the sales volume potential, and competitive information that warrants the issuance of special pricing. Above all, watch your legalities! Pricing violations are the most frequently prosecuted antitrust laws.

## 24. Regional Warehousing

While product variables sometimes necessitate it, experience has clearly shown that regional warehousing is extremely expensive and often difficult to administer. Before you make any promises, fully investigate the total cost of carrying regional inventory. Don't be persuaded by your distributors to put in a regional warehouse until you have completely investigated all of the facts, including the satisfaction requirements of end users. After all, one of the primary channel tasks of a distributor should be to carry a proper level of local inventory. If you perform the responsibility, you incur additional marketing costs.

## 25. An Effective and Frequent Channel Communications Program

Your distributor wants to know how pertinent information will be conveyed. During your meeting, show examples of newsletters, testimonials, and other communications vehicles. Chapter 9 can help you plan a credible communications program to support your channel marketing efforts.

## 26. Meaningful Product and Sales Training

Manufacturers are constantly pursuing distributors to take their product sales training. Realistically, distributors can accommodate only a chosen few companies. If you use sales training as an enticement, stress that its purpose is to show the distributor's salespeople how to sell your product line. Then make sure that your training program's quality and value are superior. Distributors don't want to waste their time. If your sales training is not meaningful, quite frankly, you'll never be invited back again. One such case comes to mind, when, as a young, inexperienced regional sales manager, I allowed a corporate-type product manager to conduct a one-day seminar on a new product we were launching. All he did was restate the features and benefits (FAB) from a literature sheet. My dealer's salespeople were justifiably disturbed over the waste of their time. They could read and understand FAB about a product themselves. What they really needed was hands-on demonstration, on-the-job training, to see how other dealers saw themselves successfully selling this product, and to understand what kind of new product launch incentive would be presented to them. That never happened to me again!

## 27. Territorial Integrity

As convincingly as possible, inform the potential channel partner that you do not intend to overdistribute your product line. If an exclusive market coverage strategy matches your channel marketing plan, tell the distributor that it will be the only authorized representative in its geographical marketplace. No distributor in his or her right managerial mind wants to have several other same-market, same-customer counterparts serving common geographic markets.

## 28. Demonstration Equipment at a Reduced Cost

If it's necessary to demonstrate your product to sell it effectively, then it behooves you to have a policy where, once a year, your distributor can purchase a limited number of demonstration models at just over your cost with the clear understanding that these units are for customer presentations only. You might also allow the expense of these demonstrator models to be applied to the distributor's cooperative advertising account.

# Preparing a Business Policy Statement

Prepare and print a clearly stated summary of your most important business policies, and give it to your distributor candidates. Such a document indicates that it is easy to do business with your company. A clear, concise policy statement—one that summarizes what the distributor can expect of you and what you can expect of the distributor—can prevent misunderstandings and head off most of the conflicts described in Chapter 10. It organizes your business procedures into a meaningful, easy-to-understand document. And when circulated internally, it also helps everyone in your company enforce these policies consistently.

The policy statement should take the form of a two- to four-page folder that is easy to read and use and can be updated inexpensively as policies change. Follow the outline format shown in Exhibit 8-2.

Before you commit your policies to paper, make sure they will be acceptable to the marketplace by evaluating them against policies of other companies in your industry using the same channel of distribution. Your

**Exhibit 8-2.** A format for a business policy statement.

### XYZ Company

| What XYZ expects of its distributors | What XYZ's distributors can expect of XYZ |
|---|---|
| Appropriate policy statements | Appropriate policy statements |
|  |  |
|  |  |
|  |  |

policies should not make it difficult to do business with your company, and they should take into consideration all three parts of the Total Channel Equation: manufacturer = channel = end user. Of course, if you have developed your enticements with care, then your business policy statement probably cuts the Grey Poupon. But it's a good idea to compare it with other companies' procedures circulating in the field.

Your business policy statement should describe policies regarding the presale, postsale, and transaction phases of channel business, including:

☐ Contracts and agreements
☐ Authorized primary area of sales and service responsibility
☐ Penalties for selling outside the authorized sales territory
☐ Company marketing plans, including space advertisements, public relations releases, direct mail, national and local exhibits, and cooperative advertising
☐ Pricing, pricing assistance, and price protection
☐ Product quality and warranties
☐ Required inventory levels
☐ Order size in units or total dollars
☐ National house or special accounts
☐ Major account support
☐ Compensation for time spent developing technical proposals and requests for proposals (RFPs)
☐ Product customization, private labels, and original equipment manufacturer (OEM)
☐ New product launches
☐ Discontinued products
☐ Dead on arrival priority replacement
☐ Billing and payment terms, credit procedures
☐ Freight and shipment, including drop shipment
☐ Delivery guarantees
☐ How performance will be evaluated
☐ Grounds for termination

## Reconfirming Your Company's Commitment

Your company's commitment—or lack thereof—can make or break your channel program. If you've followed the Channel Design Sequence, you have invested some time in building commitment for your new channel. But before you sign distributors and take stocking orders—before you turn your channel strategy into action—you should reconfirm that commitment.

Once, nearing the successful completion of a channel design, I returned from a trip to the West Coast with five eager new distributors and five generous stocking orders. No sooner was I back in my office than my immediate superior came in and closed the door. Not a good sign! "Ken," he said, "I don't know about these new computer distributors. I think we should hold off." It turned out that in my absence, he had fielded phone calls from internal salespeople who weren't sure what I was up to. Because I was a channel change agent, I was making them nervous. Fortunately, I was able to reassure him and forge ahead with our plans.

There are plenty of reasons for these last-minute nerves. For one thing, venturing into new territories and markets can cause one's anxiety level to rise. Existing direct channels fit like a comfortable old shoe—so why move into unknown indirect channels? Senior managers may become politically envious and withdraw their support. Or existing indirect channels may begin to try to slow progress toward a new channel. Before you formalize any distributor relationship, check for wavering commitment—and hold what I call a corporate recommitment meeting.

In the corporate recommitment meeting, convene in one room *everyone* who has contact with existing salespeople, distributors, or customers. Include your president or general manager, comptroller, customer service manager, engineering manager, credit manager, and any sales and marketing managers who may be contacted by existing channels of distribution and other concerned parties. Update them on your progress, and let them know you are about to sign up distributors. Tell them it is important that everyone stand behind the new channel plan because action is about to start by forming new, formal relationships. Let them know they can expect to field two kinds of calls: (1) anxious calls from members of the existing channels, and (2) calls from new distributors testing the relationship. Give them the information they need to answer questions, make policy statements consistently, and reassure existing channel members about their future with your company.

Making the plunge into the new channel is somewhat apprehensive business. A recommitment meeting calms last-minute fears and provides important reassurance for those who are anxious about the change.

## Making a Convincing Presentation to the Distributor

After months of preparation, you may disappointed to secure a mere thirty-minute meeting with your channel candidate. Don't take it personally. Eagle distributors are in high demand. The channel of choice is hotly pursued by dozens if not hundreds of other channel marketing managers pleading with them to carry their product lines. Often, these candidates receive six to ten telephone and mail contacts per day and grant a face-to-face meeting only to the chosen few they consider to be potentially profitable for their company.

So instead of despairing, rejoice—and organize. Short meetings are a way of life, and you must make every moment count. Organize your presentation to cover your most important enticements. And be humble. Don't overestimate your product line's real rank of importance to the distributor. Don't expect to be given the respect and distinction you are accustomed to receiving within your present, comfort-zone business environment (and, most likely, deserve).

Remember, distributors are a very different breed of business organization. Even if your product line is important to them, quite frankly, they can live without you. Don't let your ego make you think the channel lusts for your product line. Understand and accept your assigned channel rank. Remember, your potential eagles closely measure you and your company as you similarly evaluate them. If you do not fit their own set of selection criteria, the dialogue will go no further.

I like to organize my presentations around a "one-sheeter"—a sheet of paper that lists in one or two words the enticements I plan to discuss. I tailor the order of the enticements to the desires of the distributor, making sure to start off and end with the enticements it wants most. Then I build the momentum throughout my talk, so after thirty to sixty minutes the distributor *wants* to join my organization. I also make sure to make my pitch to the inner circle that holds my channel future in its hands.

## Hidden Authority and the Inner Circle

The inner circle is the power behind the throne—those individuals at all levels of management who form the true decision-making authority within a distributorship. These people have acquired power and influence and are respected for the roles they perform. They are the ones who decide whether or not to take on your product line.

As Exhibit 8-3 shows, managers who are outside of the inner circle are merely empty suits who have little or no authority in the overall direction of the company. They may have been promoted upstairs because of family ties or seniority. For example, the distributor's president/general manager who inherited the business from his or her parents may just be a "country club" rubber stamp in the company, while real authority resides with the chief financial officer. Whimsically, you can categorize different managers into four groups:

**Exhibit 8-3.** The inner circle of a company.

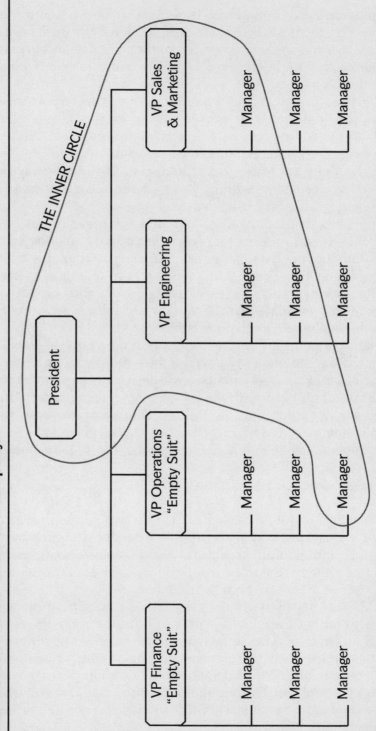

### The Inner Circle

1. Those who *control* what happens
2. Those who *make* things happen
3. Those who *watch* things happen
4. Those who *wonder* what happened

When you approach a potential distributor, be on the alert for the inner circle and for other hidden authorities. Authority isn't always found at the top. Often, it's the frontline employees who have the greatest say in deciding the rank and importance of your product lines—and who can also convey information from your company to the rest of the distributor's organization. Look in the ranks of sales personnel, technical support people, warehouse workers, and procurement employees for people who seem to wield an inordinate amount of informal power and influence among their peers and superiors.

Identify these hidden authorities and members of the inner circle by listening carefully to remarks that indicate the importance of certain individuals. Listen when the general manager says, "I've got to run this by so and so." "So and so" may be a twenty-year employee whose opinion carries major weight. Make sure these influences are included in your enticement presentation—and once you have signed up the distributor, develop a special program to create a positive relationship with these key personnel. Use special recognition and attention to persuade them to believe in and support your sales and marketing objectives, strategies, and tactics. Once the hidden authorities are on your side, you'll have an easier time passing along information about your products and programs—and you'll garner some valuable feedback in return.

---

**Ken's Words of Wisdom**

Watch for "hidden authority" in all channel of distribution environments.

---

## Signing the Channel Agreement

If you want to sign up the distributor at the end of your enticement meeting, wrap up the meeting by presenting your contract. Remember, your goal is to walk away with a contract and a stocking order. Take the time to explain the contract's contents, stressing clauses that relate to your enticements and reviewing anything that confuses the distributor. Before you leave, give the distributor a time frame for responding—perhaps one or two weeks.

A channel agreement should clearly and concisely list the business expectations of both parties. It should discuss issues that are important to both manufacturer and distributor and describe how both parties will do business.

Keep your contract short and easy to read and understand. A long contract oozing with legalese tells your distributors that it will probably be difficult to do business with your company—and maybe they should rethink their decision to enter into partnership. Four to six pages, excluding appropriate addenda or exhibits, is more than adequate. To keep it from being bloated with unnecessary clauses, *don't* let your attorneys draft your contract. You draft it first and submit it to lawyers for their review.

As Exhibit 8-4 shows, a basic contract consists of two sections: (1) ongoing business policies, like sales, marketing, and business policies that are not likely to change in a year; and (2) business policies that are likely to change from year to year. The ongoing business policies section includes:

- The terms of the agreement
- Contractual parties involved
- Contract renewal statement (automatic, or to be renewed every twelve to twenty-four months)
- Payment terms
- Delivery, installation, and shipping policies
- Sales promotion and advertising policies
- Termination for convenience clause
- Other termination procedures
- Product guarantees and warranties
- Patent, logo, trademark, and corporate protection statements
- Pricing information and policies
- Services and support required of the distributor
- Services and support provided by the manufacturer
- Order and return policies
- Credit policies
- Confidentiality statement
- Other pertinent business policies

Business policies that may change from year to year include:

- Authorized geographic territory
- Assigned markets
- Assigned products (main models and accessories)
- A mutually agreed-upon quota (in total sales dollars and, if possible, broken down in units over months or quarters of the contract year)

**Exhibit 8-4.** A basic COD contract.

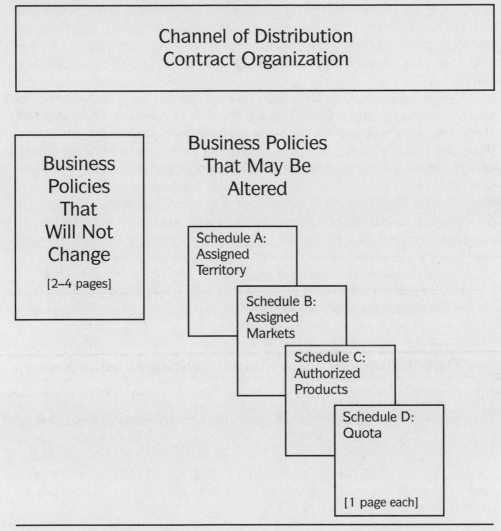

Source: Richard O. Beckert, Attorney-at-Law.

&#9633; Sales exceptions (national accounts, government contracts, and so on)
&#9633; Inventory requirements

By now, these items should sound familiar—because by and large, they are the very same issues you discussed in your enticement meeting. Your enticements, your business policies, and your contract should be compatible, if not identical!

Before you prepare your contract, try to review contracts from other companies in your industry. They may contain some legal or business advantages that merit inclusion in yours. Also, note that international channel contracts are dramatically different from domestic versions. Watch out for international laws that clash with your corporate philosophies.

One of the items in the ongoing business policies section that deserves special mention is the termination for convenience clause. *Every* contract should contain such a clause. This important little paragraph gives each party the right to terminate without offering a reason—a very important escape clause if you run into trouble with a distributor. Here is a sample clause:

> *This Agreement may be terminated without cause by either party by and upon sixty (60) days' prior written notice given to the other party by registered or certified mail, in which event this Agreement shall terminate on the date set forth in such notice. The date of mailing said written notice shall be deemed the date on which notice of termination of this Agreement shall have been given.*

## Proceeding With the Channel Design Sequence

When you have completed Step 10 (approaching and signing the selected distributors), you have completed every step of the initial Channel Design Sequence. When your distributors are in place, you can begin to focus more on matters of management, discussed in the chapters to come. Note, though, that there is still one more step in the Channel Design Sequence—Step 11 (monitoring and evaluating the channel structure). This is one of the issues addressed in Chapter 9.

### *CASE:* THE CHANNEL SEDUCTION

Your company, a thirty-year-old midtechnology test instrument manufacturer, has designed a totally new-to-the-world high-technology line of printed circuit board logic and signature analyzers. Because you are a seasoned channelmaster, you have been proactive in your strategic channel planning and have, from the start, recognized the need to create a new, specialized COD—namely, test instrumentation manufacturer sales representatives, more commonly called instrument reps. You have just completed your Channel Design Sequence through Step 7 and have formulated your criteria and located instrument rep candidates.

Now you need to compose a list of potent channel enticements to incite your candidates to enthusiastically sell your new product line. You realize that because your product is new to the world, you do not have any brand power, and your company is not positioned as a market leader. Your task is not unique, but it certainly is most challenging.

Compose an enticement list for the new channel candidates, and discuss other channel design implementation strategies you would employ.

## Case interpretational points:

❏ It is important to prioritize the enticements so that in an actual presentation, the distributor will be enticed to form an enthusiastic relationheswcwship with your company.

❏ As you communicate with your potential partners, the importance of your enticements will become very clear. The distributors will not be bashful about informing you of business requirements.

❏ Therefore, make sure that all enticements placed on the final presentation list can be achieved by your company. Do not make any assumptions that could later be embarrassing if you cannot provide the inducements.

# Part II
# Managing Your Channels

# Chapter 9

# Channel Management and Communication

---

√ *Step 1:* Identify the new market you want to penetrate or new product you need to launch.

√ *Step 2:* Verify the need for a new channel of distribution or some form of channel reorganization.

√ *Step 3:* Evaluate all macro market conditions.

√ *Step 4:* Conduct a competitive channel analysis.

√ *Step 5:* Research and rank customer/end user satisfaction requirements.

√ *Step 6:* Specify and rank the tasks you want your channel partner to perform.

√ *Step 7:* Investigate all possible channel of distribution structures.

√ *Step 8:* Decide upon eagle channel partners.

√ *Step 9:* Obtain internal corporate recommitment.

√ *Step 10:* Approach and sign the selected distributors.

√ **Step 11: Monitor and evaluate the channel structure.**

---

At the beginning of this book, I noted that the essence of channel distribution success is the ability to achieve a disproportionate share of your channel of distribution's resource commitment. In other words, your channel is willing to invest its time, money, and staff in your product line because it *prefers* your products over others it represents.

Management and communication have a lot to do with securing these hotly competed-for resources. Your business policies enticed the distributor into a relationship with your company. Now your management philosophy tells the distributor just how heavily it is prepared to invest in you. It's up to you to manage your channel in a way that makes the members of your COD want to increase their commitment.

Remember, you do not own your channel. Your distributors do. Therefore, you cannot control your channel. The best you can do is *manage* it—and that is a full-time job! In my view, the essence of management is communication. Channelmasters communicate with distributors in two basic ways:

1. Through formal management, such as contracts and policies
2. Through informal management of relationships

While the content of contracts and policies has already been covered, it's important to note that how those policies are enforced is an act of communication. As for relationships, suffice it to say that the more thoroughly you communicate with your channel members, the better your working relationship will be. And the better the relationship, the more business closeness you achieve. The need for clear communication never diminishes and is strongest of all in the first months of your partnership with a new distributor.

Before going on to that topic, note that an important part of channel management involves monitoring and evaluating the channel structure—Step 11 of the Channel Design Sequence—and changing channels should it prove necessary. This important subject is also covered in this chapter.

---

**Ken's Words of Wisdom**

❏ As a channel marketing manager, you do not *control* your channel, you *manage* it.
❏ Successful channel managers see themselves as true partners with their distributors.
❏ Develop as much "business closeness" as possible with your primary channel members.

---

# Ramping Up a New Distributor

A pleasant state of euphoria permeates the beginning of every new business alliance. Both parties are excited about the future and eager to collaborate in making business visions come true. But now is not the time to rest on your laurels, channelmaster! These early months are critical to the long-term success of your relationship. To build the greatest possible comfort and highest possible commitment throughout your distributor's management and personnel, make it a priority to extend this enthusiasm and positive spirit as long as possible.

Start by declaring a ramp-up period of three to six months. Let everyone in your company know the importance of treating new distributors like royalty. A little special treatment goes a long way! Consider assigning a mentor to the new distributor, perhaps a customer support person who can show the distributor the ropes and check in now and then to see how things are going. Your new distributor will be testing your support system, so everyone should respond to its requests in an extraordinary manner.

Look for and cultivate a "champion"—a salesperson on the distributor's staff who will eagerly support, sell, and communicate the attributes of your product line to others in the company. There's always somebody who favors your product line or your sales and marketing strategies over those of other companies represented. Strengthen his or her preference with special treatment, and you'll have an excellent conduit for passing along information.

Here are a few more ways to give your new relationship a positive foundation:

❏ Introduce the new distributor to your customers. Use press releases and other publicity vehicles to let the world know that your products can now be purchased from this source.

❏ Help the distributor take over existing accounts. Go along on sales calls to your biggest end user accounts to help establish the new distributor as the new source for your product or service. Turn over any contracts or leads from the previous distributor to the new one.

❏ Build confidence with easy assignments. Let new distributors start by selling products that are easy to sell and accounts that are easy to close. As they succeed, add in more complex products and accounts.

❏ Provide enough product samples, product literature, price sheets, and other collateral material for all of the distributor's sales personnel. Set aside your normal policies and be liberal. After all, you need to fill the distributor's information pipeline. Save restrictions for later in the relationship.

❏ Schedule factory visits and joint sales calls to build enthusiasm among the ranks.

❏ Conduct as much intensive, on-site and customer-call product training as the distributor allows.

❏ Give new distributors plenty of positive feedback on their work. No one can resist a compliment.

**Rest assured, you *will* be tested** by your distributors during this ramp-up period. All new distributors test the relationship to see just how solid it is. They present challenging situations for your reaction. If you say you can modify a product a certain way, they will deliver a purchase order requesting those modifications to see if you can come through. They listen carefully to your promises and watch how you follow through. If you say you'll ship a product within a week of receiving an order, do it. If they give you negative feedback, they will watch your reaction. If they lodge a complaint, they will see how quickly you respond. Every one of your policies will be tested. If you pass the test, your credibility and believability will be established in the eyes of your channel.

High credibility coupled with a profitable profit line is the recipe for your continued and lasting channel success. If your credibility is high enough, and your product is important enough, your distributor will increase its resource commitment to you.

## Guidelines for a Great Channel Partnership

*Regard your relationship as a strategic alliance.* Listen to your distributor partners. Learn about the pains and pleasures of their business. When you do so, you can translate the desires of your channel into company policies and procedures that work. By cultivating your relationships—especially with the 20 percent of your distributors that account for 80 percent of your business—you also achieve something I call business closeness, a very important ingredient when there are problems to be solved.

If you have good relationships with your distributors, you profit. Distributors that consider themselves partners in your success are happy to protect prices, promote old and new products, and participate in mutual sales forecasting. They also lend a hand when problems occur in your channel. You *can't* solve problems in the channel on your own. To tackle a problem or make the most of a sudden opportunity, you need channel members who respond quickly to your appeal for help.

Good relationships do not grow overnight. They are the result of careful tending and communication. Follow these guiding principles—''Ken's Rules for a Great Channel Partnership''—and you will earn your distributors' trust and loyalty. These are, after all, essential ingredients for any good relationship.

---

**Ken's Words of Wisdom**

Be honest: Do the right thing or lose channel credibility and respect.

---

## *Golden Rule 1:* Be Honest and Accurate—Even If It's Painful

*Being completely honest with distributors is one of the most important ingredients in building a lasting, trusting COD partnership.* If you are dishonest or withhold information even one time, your future messages will be closely scrutinized and viewed with suspicion. But tell the truth consistently, and your distributors will begin to respect and trust you. When you have bad news, make sure your channel hears it directly from you, not from a competitor or other third party. Share news—good or bad—promptly. And practice honesty daily throughout your entire organization.

## *Golden Rule 2:* Communicate With Every Level of Personnel to Ensure the Most Complete and Accurate Transmission of Your Channel Information Flow

*Everyone employed by your distributor, from the CEO to the salesperson in the field, is selling for you.* All of them are your customers. Communicate with everyone, and you create strong backers who will enthusiastically support your product marketing efforts within the distributor's organization.

---

**Ken's Words of Wisdom**

❑ Always consider the entire channel equation (manufacturer = channel = end user) prior to taking any managerial action.
❑ Use the infamous "channel telegraph" to your advantage.
❑ Keep in close contact with other friendly channel marketing managers in your industry or marketplace.

---

## *Golden Rule 3:* Consider the Needs of Your Channel Before You Implement New Policies

*Whether you're forecasting next year's sales or contemplating a price increase or a new product, check with your channel first.* By all means avoid the "ivory tower" attitude that the factory/manufacturer knows best. Listen to and consider your distributors' opinions. After all, they know their marketplace and their customers.

Leaving your distributors out of the decision-making process is flirting with disaster. First, it conveys a clear message of disrespect to your distributors. Second, it imperils your future success. Imagine the consequences of raising a price and finding out too late that it is more than the market is willing to pay. Or imagine the consequences of developing and attempting to launch a new product that rots in a warehouse because the channel is not equipped to sell it or doesn't want to. Always, always seek out your channel's opinion *before* you implement any new prices, products, or important policy changes.

### *Golden Rule 4:* Use the Channel Telegraph Judiciously

*The infamous channel telegraph does exist. Distributors, especially eagles, are in constant contact with each other.* They apprise each other of the latest positive or negative manufacturer developments. This channel telegraph quickly broadcasts news about you and your actions. That's why it is judicious to think through any policy or procedure before it is implemented. Act incorrectly, and everyone soon knows.

On the other hand, you can take advantage of the channel telegraph to transmit abbreviated but important messages to your channel. Before you do, review the exact content of your message to be sure that no misinterpretation is possible. Remember, once you release the information, it will be passed on through distributors who may add their own poetic interpretations. Obviously, it is unwise to communicate especially sensitive or detailed subjects this way. And carefully choose the person to whom you initially disseminate the channel telegraph message. Look for someone with credibility and authority who will convey the information in a positive way: a true bell cow.

### *Golden Rule 5:* Communicate With Other Friendly Channel Marketing Managers in Your Industry or Marketplace

*This golden rule governs your relationship with your peers. Don't seal yourself off from other channel managers.* Get out there and trade information! Of course, you should never divulge company secrets, but sharing your insights lets you glean customer and marketplace trend data that can help you compile accurate sales forecasts, take advantage of market opportunities, guard against glitches, keep up on news of distributors, and gather news of direct competitors. Budget some of your time for fostering and developing these very useful intrachannel lines of communication.

## Effective Channel Communications Mechanisms

Four communications tools can definitely help you nurture relationships with your channel members:

1.  Field visits by manufacturer personnel
2.  Joint sales calls
3.  Channel Advisory Councils
4.  A media communications program

Sales training can also be an effective channel communications tool, but since its primary function is to motivate, it is discussed in Chapter 11.

## Field Visits by Manufacturer Personnel

Regular field visits by company management offer several benefits. First, they show that you are sincerely interested in the success of the manufacturer-distributor relationship. When personnel from your company invest time in a personal visit, distributors can't help but be impressed with the depth of your commitment.

Second, they introduce your personnel to the business situation of your channel members—an asset when a problem arises. Third, they make your company's expertise available to your distributor. Your credit manager might make suggestions on handling problem customers. Your materials handling expert might share techniques for cutting costs and increasing on-time deliveries.

Follow these guidelines for a successful field visit program:

1.  *Always make each visit meaningful to the distributor.* Carefully plan each trip's agenda so it is not looked upon as mere "social noise" or a waste of valuable time. If your visits do not have some purpose, you will not be invited back again.

2.  *Prepare your colleagues before the trip by explaining the basics of channel marketing.* Someone who is not involved in channel marketing may be unaware of the hot spots and make grandiose promises that you can't honor. For example, say your distributor mentions features it would like added to your product. "No problem," your engineering director replies. No problem from an engineering standpoint—but what if the new feature adds costs that the channel is unwilling to assume in the form of an increased price? Before any field visit, brief your colleagues on the positive and negative issues that exist in a channel relationship. Then establish guidelines so that no casual or grandiose promises are made to appease or impress a distributor. And accompany your visitors *at all* times.

3.  *Set up visits for key personnel by all parts of your company, but don't bring them along on the same visit.* Showing up with a "posse" scares your distributor, and they will wonder what you have in mind. Termination, perhaps? Establish a schedule of quarterly or bimonthly visits for key

managers. In January, you might want to set the stage by bringing your CEO on a tour of your top tier of distributors. Introducing one "el supremo" to another is a great way to underscore the importance of a distributor's contributions. In March, bring along your credit manager. In May, have your engineering manager discuss present and future products. Ask your product manager to review overall product line and product mix strategies in September. In November, introduce your customer service manager to key distributors. Other personnel you may want to include in visits are your financial manager, physical distribution manager, regional and sales managers, vice president of sales and marketing, technical support manager, manufacturing manager, and MIS director.

Besides impressing channel members with your commitment, field visits can also help improve your distributors' skill levels. Sharing company expertise in such areas as warehouse and shipping can benefit both of you. Key personnel can also help broker a resolution to a conflict. If a distributor is haggling over a difficult credit situation, a visit by your credit manager may be able to clear up the problem.

4. *Key sales and marketing events are natural reasons to schedule a visit.* Consider lining up field visits during:

- ❏ New product introductions
- ❏ Regional sales meetings
- ❏ Sales and product training
- ❏ Sales contests and other promotional announcements
- ❏ Major policy changes

Consider scheduling these on the critical event chart discussed later in this chapter.

5. Consider swapping personnel for a few months, especially with your top tier of distributors. Send one of your sales or marketing people to the distributor for three to six months, and add one of the distributor's key people to your organization. An exchange like this deepens the channel relationship by helping both parties experience each other's business challenges. When both sides better understand the other's trials and tribulations, mutually beneficial and supportive policies can be treated and implemented. Give it a try!

## Joint Sales Calls

*Joint sales calls are a win-win situation.* You benefit because direct access to the distributor's sales force lets you increase its salespeople's knowledge about your product or service and helps them feel more comfortable selling it. The distributor benefits because your expertise makes the sale easier, and your presence tells the end customer that the distributor has factory/manufacturer support. Your presence lets the distributor say, "Buy from me, and you'll get support from me and the factory."

How easily you can schedule joint calls depends on the importance of your line to the distributor. If your company's products are highly profitable, are easy to sell, help open doors, or make up a considerable percentage of total sales, your distributor will be eager to give you access to its foot soldiers. Hot qualified leads also help.

When you go along on the sale, take the supporting role. Remember that the individual you are calling on is the distributor's valued customer. If you intentionally or unintentionally try to take over the sale, your relationship with the distributor will suffer. Your distributor's salesperson wants to be perceived as the person in charge. Don't challenge that role.

Before the sales visit, talk with the salesperson to decide what your exact role will be. Will you be the factory expert, the product expert, or a team member? Don't preempt the salesperson. Above all, don't interfere with pricing. Pricing is the responsibility of the distributor salesperson and you should not meddle.

Immediately after the call, have a cup of coffee and review the sale with the salesperson. Discuss how serious the prospect is, and determine the next step. Ask how you can provide additional support. *Don't* critique the salesperson's performance. Leave that to the distributor's sales manager. Then be sure to schedule more calls for the future.

## Channel Advisory Councils

A Channel Advisory Council is one of the most powerful communications tools at your disposal. Not only does it tell your eagle distributors that you value their input and excellent performance, but it also enables you to quickly spread the word about new products and policies.

Recruit from six to twelve members of your channel, depending on the size of your organization. Choose all types and sizes of distributors so that a variety of experience levels is represented. Seek out active members that can contribute to meaningful discussions—not those wallflowers that just stock your product and don't do much. You want movers and shakers that can participate in a positive manner. Rotate membership by electing new members each year. Consider designating one- and two-year terms so that membership can be refreshed without sacrificing continuity.

Make joining your Advisory Council sound like a privilege by giving it a name like Blue Chip Council, President's Club, Distributors of the Year Club, or The Eagles' Club.

Once a year, convene members for a one- to three-day meeting. Depending on your budget, plan either a "Ritz-Carlton" or a "Motel 6" meeting. Pay all or a portion of the distributors' travel, lodging, and food costs. Mix business with social activities to promote relationships, cooperation, and channel bonding.

Structure your program around a general schedule, and announce that it is your intention to cover certain subjects during the course of the day. However, don't set a precisely timed agenda. Invite distributors to add topics they want discussed, and schedule time when they can ask questions or revisit topics of concern in an open forum. Topics can include:

☐ New products
☐ New markets
☐ Competitive activity
☐ Policies and procedures
☐ Sales promotional plans
☐ Sales and marketing strategies
☐ Product quality
☐ Sales and marketing support
☐ Technical support
☐ Information technology
☐ Media communications
☐ Overall channel management

Invite internal marketing and nonmarketing company managers to participate, making sure to rehearse what they will discuss prior to the meeting. No loose cannons, please!

Set the tone for your meeting by opening with a statement about the ethical, legal, and professional standards that are to be followed while the council is in session. To avoid wasting time on a problem that pertains to only one distributor, you might urge participants to stick to subjects of interest to everyone and to see you privately about individual issues. It's a good idea to clarify that legal matters should be discussed in private, and pricing issues should not be discussed at all. (Chapter 12 explains how you can run afoul of the law by discussing prices in a group setting.) Encourage everyone to keep the meeting on a positive note and to make the most of chances to get to know one another.

It is most important to stress that you will follow up and report back to the group on any statements or promises made during the meeting. If you don't follow through, your distributors will regard Channel Advisory Council meetings as mere social affairs rather than a forum for solving business problems.

---

**Communicating With End Users**

It is hard to communicate with end users because your distributors may not want to reveal their customers' names. If you get the names, you can solicit end users' opinions through a mail survey, focus groups, telephone or face-to-face interviews, or an End User Advisory Council. Be careful, though. Distributors will be alarmed if you try to talk directly to their customers without telling them first. Advise distributors of your plans up front, or better yet, include them. Tell them what you want to find out, and reassure them that you will pass along the results of your communications to them.

An End User Advisory Council can give you feedback on your marketing tactics and strategies, tell you how end users use your products, and spark ideas for new products. Again, tell your channel before your attempt to implement such a council. If your plans generate high levels of anxiety or negative feeling, consider dropping your plans. There are other, less alienating ways to find out or confirm your end users' satisfaction requirements.

---

## A Media Communications Program

Distributors receive hundreds of sales leads each week from the manufacturers they represent. They quickly learn which companies have qualified those leads and which ones are wasting their time with casual, meaningless inquiries. These leads are usually discarded, for it doesn't make sense to pass along unqualified leads that would waste their salespeople's valuable selling time.

If you want your distributors to take your leads seriously, supply them with a steady source of bona fide, closable leads. Begin by deciding which media communications program elements you are going to use:

❐ National space advertising in leading trade and market magazines
❐ Direct mail campaigns
❐ Telemarketing efforts
❐ Public relations news releases
❐ National exhibits
❐ Product literature

Once you determine how often you will use each element, "calcul-estimate" the number of leads generated by magazine ads by contacting the editor for readership information. Explain the number, appearance, size, and schedule of planned ad insertions, and ask for the response likely to be generated by each source. Using the publication's database, the editor can probably project how many leads will be typically generated in the distributor's geographic market. You can "calcul-estimate" the number of other leads from direct mail, public relations releases, and exhibits in the same basic manner.

If your distributors ask how many leads they'll receive, tell them how many leads your program is likely to generate for their respective territories. But I recommend you not give a hard number, but rather state a range (e.g.: "In a twelve-month period, I feel that we'll generate 400 to 800 qualified sales leads"). Also explain how you plan to qualify them. There are three ways to qualify responses to your media communications program:

1. Designate someone on your staff to call and interview each prospect. This is the fastest way to find out whether a prospect is serious.

2. Develop a two-step lead-generation package that you can handle by mail. When you receive a coupon or an inquiry, send back a packet of information that includes a questionnaire or a post-paid postcard for the prospect to complete. Those who return the questionnaire are hot prospects.

3. Turn your leads over to an inquiry handling service (IHS). For three dollars to five dollars a lead, these companies can do a superior job of qualifying your leads. Although their prices are steep, using an IHS may be more cost-efficient than allocating internal staff time and telephone lines to lead qualification.

It is absolutely essential to qualify all leads before turning them over to your distributors. I once watched the owner of a regional distributor throw a thick bundle of unqualified leads into the circular files. Spare yourself this trauma by qualifying everything—and letting your distributors know that you do.

## Five Channel Management Mechanisms

Communication with your channel is not enough. You must also manage your channel. There are five tools or mechanisms that a channelmaster can use to manage a channel. They are:

1. A business policy statement that clearly states how manufacturer and distributor will do business together
2. A mutually agreed-upon contract that legally formalizes the business relationship
3. Compensation

4. Sales force management
5. A minimarketing plan

The first two tools—business policies and contracts—are both discussed in Chapter 8. They are essential management and communications tools. You are asking for trouble if you try to manage a channel without these documents. The Number 1 reason for channel conflict is in the interpretation—or misinterpretation—of policies and conflicts. Trying to operate without them is just like opening Pandora's Box.

The third tool, compensation, is an effective way to direct sales and marketing efforts to reach a mutual goal. Most manufacturers offer *cost-based compensation* to pay distributors for such regular channel tasks as making sales, handling orders, or extending credit. *Value-based compensation* encourages your distributors to generate effort and results over and above those specified by the contract. For example, you might agree to pay a distributor a 2 percent rebate on all sales if it increases sales 15 percent in the coming fiscal year. Or you might offer a 1 percent rebate to distributors that submit a minimarketing plan for the coming year. Value-based compensation is a powerful management tool that is also a motivational tool. It is discussed in detail in Chapter 11.

The fourth and fifth management tools merit detailed discussion.

## Sales Force Management

Without question, the ultimate success or failure of your channel marketing program rests with your field salespeople, and management of them is the fourth tool. Your field salespeople are literally the *last* lines of communication and management between the manufacturer and the distributor, and they are responsible for implementing your business policies and procedures. Your salespeople need to be company representatives, channel defenders, trainers, and field sales managers, all wrapped up in one convenient package.

---

**Ken's Words of Wisdom**

Have both the direct sales force and the indirect channel of distribution report to one functional manager.

---

As *company representatives*, salespeople must understand, support, and execute your company's business philosophy. As *channel defenders*, salespeople work to achieve satisfaction for their distributor. They stand up for the distributor's rights and seek to resolve conflicts in an equitable and acceptable manner. Their credibility with the distributor is earned only after a number of conflicts have been successfully resolved.

As *trainers*, your salespeople must teach, coach, and train your channel members in how to proficiently sell your products. Do not release any sales personnel to manage distributors until you are completely satisfied with their training abilities!

Finally, as *field sales managers*, your salespeople manage their assigned territories. Their managerial responsibilities include but are not limited to:

- ❐ Monitoring distributor performance vis à vis the negotiated quota
- ❐ Supporting distributor sales through joint sales calls, qualified lead disbursement, product expertise, sales contests, and motivation
- ❐ Penetrating present markets
- ❐ Launching new products
- ❐ Developing new markets
- ❐ Ensuring that the needs of key end users are met by both manufacturer and distributor
- ❐ Composing and executing local marketing strategies and tactics
- ❐ Communicating national and regional sales and marketing information, including customer testimonials, sales success stories, marketing trends, and emerging market opportunities

## A Minimarketing Plan

Although most manufacturers have a formal marketing plan, most distributors don't. As entrepreneurs, many shy away from this kind of structure and discipline. Also, they don't have the time to develop a formal plan for each of the dozens or hundreds of companies they represent. To ensure that you and your distributor meet your mutual goals, develop a minimarketing plan that targets key business issues and goals and commits both of you to certain actions.

The sample minimarketing plan shown in Exhibit 9-1 is short but powerful. This document—directed at an industrial electronics company—states a clear objective: to increase sales by 15 percent. It includes strategies that describe *how* this objective is to be accomplished. And it includes tactics or action plans for carrying out those strategies. It also tells who is responsible for implementing each tactic/action plan and when it is to be accomplished.

Depending on your experience in writing marketing plans and the complexity of the channel marketing situation, your plan should not take more than three months to develop. If you are too busy to draft a minimarketing plan with each of your distributors, shoot for the top-tier 20 percent that make up 80 percent of your sales. Ask your local salespeople to help

**Exhibit 9-1.** Sample channel minimarketing plan for an industrial electronics distributor.

___

**Objective**

- Increase sales next year by 15 percent

**Strategies**

- Commit to a guaranteed product and sales training schedule
- Support two new product launches
- Aggressively pursue entering one new market
- Participate in our value-based compensation incentive program
- Allocate one salesperson to be a specialist for our product line

**Tactics/Action Plans**

- Full-day, quarterly sales training sessions in March, June, August, and October (*responsibility of our sales, marketing, and technical personnel*)
- One new product launch in February and one in August (*responsibility of product manager*)
- Enter the medical market in May with a specialist salesperson and local marketing blitz (*responsibility of channelmaster*)
- Quarterly value-based compensation program performance reviews to ensure securing the year-end rebate of 2 percent of total sales (*responsibility of channelmaster*)
- In January, specify the salesperson to be exclusively assigned to our product line (*responsibility of channelmaster*)

___

draft the plan. Their insights will add important local color to the final document.

As a final incentive, tie distributor compensation to these goals. Use value-based compensation to pay them for developing a minimarketing plan and for achieving its goals.

# The Critical Event Chart

It helps to have a way to plan a year's worth of sales and marketing activities without letting anything slip through the crack. One tactic is to construct a critical event chart (see the sample in Exhibit 9-2). When your marketing plan is ready for implementation, list your critical events on the chart, and post it in a visible spot. Use it to monitor the progress of these events and ensure their accomplishment. This is an excellent tool for maximum channel efficiency!

**Exhibit 9-2.** Critical event chart for channel of distribution operations.

| Event | J | F | M | A | M | J | J | A | S | O | N | D | Future Requirements | Comments |
|---|---|---|---|---|---|---|---|---|---|---|---|---|---|---|
| COD Training | | | | | | | | | | | | | | |
| National | x | | | | | | | | | | | | Ongoing | |
| Regional | | | x | | | | | | x | | x | x | Ongoing | |
| Local | x | x | x | x | x | x | x | x | x | x | x | x | Continual | |
| New Market Development | | | x | | | x | | | x | | | x | | |
| New Product Introductions | x | x | | | | | | | x | | x | x | As appropriate | |
| COD Macroinfluence Review | | | x | | | | | | x | | x | x | Ongoing | |
| COD Business Policy Review and Revision | x | | | | | x | | | | | x | | As necessary | |
| Competitive Monitoring/Planning | x | | | | | | x | | | x | | | Continual | |
| Channel Audits | x | x | x | x | x | x | x | x | x | x | x | x | Continual | |
| 80/20 COD Program | x | x | x | x | x | x | x | x | x | x | x | x | Continuous | |
| COD Advisory Council Meeting | x | | | | | | | | | | | | Once a year | |
| COD Advisory Council Meeting Updates | | | x | | x | | | | x | | | x | And as necessary | |
| COD Performance Evaluations | | | x | | x | | | | x | | | x | As necessary | |
| Implementation of Appropriate COD Changes | x | | | x | | | x | | | x | | | As necessary | |
| Cobranding Program | | | x | | | x | | | x | | | x | As appropriate | |
| Review of Annual COD Agreements | | | | | | | | | | | | x | Once a year | |
| Antitrust Update Meeting | | | | | | | | | | | | x | Once a year | |
| Review of Internal COD Support System | x | x | x | x | x | x | x | x | x | x | x | x | Continual | |
| Annual COD Marketing Plan | | | | | | | | | | | | | | |
| 1st Draft Pass | | | | | | x | | | | | | | | |
| 2nd Draft Pass | | | | | | | | x | | | | | | |
| Executive Staff Presentation/Approval | | | | | | | | | x | | | | | |
| Beginning of Execution | | | | | | | | | | | | x | | |

# Reducing Conflict Between Direct and Indirect Channels

Your company's direct and indirect channels of distribution do not automatically work together peacefully. But you can ensure cooperation by involving your direct sales force in the distributor selection process and making sure that both direct and indirect channels report to the same functional sales and marketing executive. To create maximum harmony between the two channels, institute a compensation program that rewards direct salespeople for all distributor sales within their assigned territory. By doing so, you make the distributor less of an adversary to the salespeople and create a partnership of sorts.

Make sure to explain the program carefully to the direct salespeople and your distributors. Explain that in order to earn this extra compensation, your direct salespeople must actively support the sales efforts of distributors by regularly conducting product and sales training meetings as well as participating in joint sales calls. Both of these activities can be verified on call reports and through conversations with distributor management.

Make sure the direct sales force understands that it will receive a lesser amount of commission because the distributor is carrying out the majority of the sales effort. On the other hand, be sure to point out how salespeople benefit from the distributor's presence. For starters, the salespeople will earn a commission on sales to accounts with small to medium revenue potential that the salespeople cannot afford to sell. And because you have chosen distributors carefully, there should be no undue conflict over who sells what account.

While there will always be friction between direct and indirect channels, your professional management can minimize it.

# Evaluating Your Channel

The last important piece of a channelmaster's communications and management strategy is to fairly and accurately evaluate each distributor's sales and marketing performance each year.

## The Channel Audit

To evaluate your channel, conduct face-to-face quarterly audits with your most important distributors. A quarterly audit is a check-and-balance vehicle that lets you and your distributor probe the health of your business relationship and take corrective action to improve it.

A channel audit encourages dialogue between you and your distributors, who are extremely busy balancing the needs of their many manufacturers. The audit provides a structure in which you and your distributor can evaluate and constructively criticize or compliment your policies. It can pinpoint strong areas, flush out problems that the distributor may be reluctant to discuss, or reveal profitable new product and new market ideas. And it can help you review every aspect of the distributor's performance during the previous twelve months. Both sides have a chance to air their points of view. Generally, the audit leads to a plan of action that improves the overall quality of the relationship.

During one channel audit, my distributor took the time to point out how incorporating an additional feature into one of my products would enhance its operational ability and make it very attractive to an entirely new market. I quickly acted on the suggestion and soon found the two of us approaching all-new customers. If we had not sat down for that meeting, I seriously doubt I would have learned about the idea.

Excellent channel relationships can't be sustained and developed by memos and phone conversations. Now and then you have to see the whites of each other's eyes. A channel audit meeting tells your distributors that you are serious about your relationship and sincerely want the best for it. In my opinion, too few manufacturers conduct channel audits. I heartily recommend adding this to your arsenal of management tools.

However, a channel audit meeting may never be more than a pipe dream if you are not a major player. Like everything else in channel marketing, your ability to command face-to-face time with your channel members depends on your importance to your distributors. Therefore, schedule channel audit meetings only with the top 20 percent of your distributors. Evaluate less important relationships with mail surveys.

Cover these topics during the channel audit:

❑ Overall policies and procedures
❑ Sales force performance
❑ New product performance
❑ Existing product performance
❑ Senior management contract/relationship
❑ Competitive activity
❑ New emerging markets
❑ Other miscellaneous complaints and compliments

## Audit, Then Evaluate

The channel audit helps you find out the state of the union between you and your distributor. With that information in hand, you can more accurately evaluate that distributor's performance. To do so, you need to develop a set of evaluation criteria that you apply to each of your distributors to judge performance. A detailed and complete channel member evaluation covers the following points:

❐ *Historical sales performance.* Review performance over one year, two years, and five years.

❐ *Performance compared against other channel members.* Compare similarly sized distributors in areas with equivalent sales potential. For example, your distributors in Minneapolis and Detroit have the same buying potential index, but the distributor in Detroit is doing five times the business of the one in Minneapolis. Why? Is something very wrong, or very right? Find out!

❐ *Performance compared to quota.* Is the distributor above the mutually agreed quota or below it?

❐ *Specific market sales.* Does the distributor have any vertical market expertise?

❐ *Specific product sales.* Does it have any specialized product success?

❐ *Specific product group sales.* Is there any product mix support present?

❐ *Profit contribution.* How profitable is the total sales revenue generated from each distributor?

❐ *International sales.* Measure this if it applies.

❐ *Selling capabilities.* What is the distributor's overall quality level?

❐ *Inventory management.* What is the level of expertise?

❐ *Future growth potential.* Will the distributor fit your future product and marketing strategies and plans?

❐ *Repair/service.* Evaluate this if appropriate.

❐ *Distributor performance compared to industry performance.* Does the distributor's total product category sales performance match the industry or market's growth?

❐ *Extraordinary cooperation.* Has the distributor voluntarily submitted competitive information, new product ideas, or emerging market data?

❐ *Product line growth compared to distributor sales performance.* Does your company's total product category sales performance match the distributor's sales performance? If not, why not?

❐ *Overall evaluation of marketing activities.* What is the quality of the distributor's local marketing efforts (direct mail, use of COOP advertising, telemarketing, advertising, exhibition)?

❏ *Business policies.* Is the distributor easy or difficult to do business with?

❏ *Shipment to end users.* Does it meet the industry delivery standards?

❏ *Revenue per FTE (full-time employee).* How does this compare to other distributors?

❏ *Average account size.* Does the distributor adequately cover small and large accounts, or does the distributor concentrate on one size?

❏ *Average sale.* How does the dollar amount of a typical sale compare to your other distributors?

❏ *Revenue per salesperson.* This is always an interesting comparison. Ask your distributor for its ground-zero revenue target for its salespeople. How does it compare to other distributors? Keep in mind that not all territories are equal. A sales dollar in Omaha may be much harder to earn than a sales dollar in Chicago. But if your distributor in Atlanta sells $300,000 per salesperson, and your distributor in Boston sells $750,000 per salesperson, be sure to ask why.

❏ *Business closeness.* How well do your two managements work together? How solid is the relationship? Overall, how comfortable do you feel about actually conducting business with the distributor?

Include other industry- or market-specific factors that are important to you, and develop a list of those criteria that are *most* important to you. Apply them equally to every member of your distribution channel. Showing favoritism to a particular distributor may land you in ethical, conflictual, and legal trouble.

## Changing Channels

---

### Ken's Words of Wisdom

Never be afraid to make a channel of distribution change, but execute it with a great deal of forethought and sensitivity.

---

Sometimes changes in buying patterns, product lines, or markets make it necessary to leave behind a well-worn and beloved channel of distribution. This is hard for everybody in the channel, which is teeming with business and personal friendships. Yet a channel manager needs the courage, foresight, and experience to know when to change channels. One of the true disasters of channel management is blindly sticking to a traditional channel long after its usefulness is gone. That is why you must perform Step 11 of the Channel Design Sequence: monitoring and evaluating the channel structure.

There is no golden solution to this perplexing and emotional problem. Your only tool is to remain aware of such macroinfluences as the appearance of new and improved CODs or new technologies that cause massive channel change. When you see them, you have to assess whether you can stick with your present channels, reorganize them, or create entirely new channels of distribution.

---

### Reasons for a Channel Change

- New products
- Changes in manufacturer policy
- Changes in distributor policy
- Changes in distributor status
- Poor evaluation
- Changes in buying behavior
- New forms of technology

- New markets
- Mergers and acquisitions
- New geographic market areas
- Major environmental changes
- Conflict or other behavioral problems
- New forms of distribution

---

## *CASE:* BE TRUE TO THYSELF, CHANNELMASTER

As a true channelmaster, you firmly believe in being truthful to your distributors even when the news is not favorable. But recently, your company—an old-line, prestigious manufacturer of office equipment—has experienced a number of internal problems that are beginning to raise some serious questions about your corporation's overall management capability.

For starters, product quality has declined, as a result of improperly administered manufacturing cost-cutting measures. Late product deliveries have caused your distributors to miss customer shipment deadlines and, as a result, to lose profit. Because of the high turnover of sales and marketing managers, inaccurate and not entirely truthful information has flowed to your channel of distribution. It's no wonder distributors are beginning to suspect that your company's management just doesn't care about its distributor sales organization. Worst of all, just last week, two of your top twenty distributors signed with your "death wish category" of competition—a first in your channel. "Death wish category" refers to those of your field opponents who pose the most serious threat to your business future. Under what circumstances could you trust a distributor who also carries a "death wish" competitor? It's just too compromising.

It's your job to change this negative course. Explain how you will do so, using all of your formal and informal channel communications and management abilities.

**Case interpretational points:**

❏ Can this channel relationship be saved? If so, how? Be specific.
❏ What communication strategies should be created and implemented?
❏ What do you think your competitor is doing? How should you combat their channel moves?
❏ What's the real problem?

# Chapter 10

# Channel Conflict and Power

---

**Ken's Words of Wisdom**

❐ Invest in brand power for more channel influence and power.
❐ Some conflict is, in fact, healthy.

---

Power and conflict go hand in hand. When a conflict arises, you need to deal from a position of strength. That strength often determines whether a conflict is resolved in your favor or the distributor's. The more important you are to a distributor, the more it will abide by the policies and judgments you make to resolve conflicts.

That's why it is critically important to know exactly how much power is on your side of the manufacturer-distributor relationship. Inaccurate assessments of power lead to all sorts of problems. Don't waste time wondering why your distributors aren't giving you the star status attention you believe you deserve. Realistically assess your power status in your channel, and then develop marketing strategies that help you achieve a disproportionate share of resources to earn your rank. You can also institute programs that maintain or increase your power without taking you into the territory of channel arrogance—the arrogance that comes from taking advantage of your power to enforce policies that penalize and agitate distributors. This is a prime example of when a manufacturer has extreme brand power with end users, and uses this sales pull through to force the channel to do its bidding.

# Channel Power

Manufacturers have channel power when their products are important in some way to their distributors. Power is earned if your company's products are highly profitable or make up a considerable percentage of a distributor's total sales. The larger your company's share of sales revenue, the more power you have. (Knowing this, many distributors cautiously limit your percentage of sales, so the balance of power doesn't tip too heavily in your direction.)

Power is also yours if your products are easy to sell, because inventory turns are more frequent, product moves through the channel faster, and cash and profits are generated more easily. And products that help open doors to new customers add to your power as well.

Brand power is another significant source of channel influence. Procter & Gamble, Maytag, and Mercedes are market leaders that everyone wants to carry. Every computer dealer wants to be an IBM-authorized distributor—practically the Papal Stamp of the Vatican in the computer market. Brand-power products help distributors sell. Little wonder they are so highly sought after. If you have brand power, your product is more accepted by your distributors. Conversely, if you want to have more power with your channel, build your brand power. You won't do it overnight, however, for the battle for the consumer's mind takes time to wage and win through space advertising, direct mail, exhibitions, and, most important, a highly prized product along with brand recognition and preference.

Channel members also have power—sometimes much, much more than the manufacturer. For example, no one manufacturer has power over Grainger, the world's largest industrial distributor. Whatever Grainger wants, Grainger gets. The same goes for Radio Shack, Wal-Mart, Kmart, and most category-killer retailers. Many manufacturers literally *do* kiss the ground under these power retailers in order to participate in these channels.

## Building and Applying Power

As Louis Stern, Professor of Marketing at Northwestern University's J. L. Kellogg Graduate School of Marketing, states, *"The fact that a channel member has power sources simply indicates that it has potential for influence."* In other words, having a channel power source doesn't mean that you automatically have to employ your channel power. But identifying your sources of power lets you discover the power arsenal at your disposal.

From that arsenal, you can pick your most influential weapons and use them strategically to enhance your position.

The *proper* application of channel power helps you achieve a disproportionate share of resource commitment from your distributors. I stress *proper* because power can be and is often abused. For example, a manufacturer representing 40 percent of a certain distributor's annual sales revenue that "strongly suggests" that the distributor not engage in exploratory discussions with a new competitor is abusing its power. So is a manufacturer with high brand power that coerces a distributor to take in a high inventory level of slow-moving consumer product and also to commit a significant amount of shelf space to the product.

Abusing your power is a definite taboo. While it may bring you some short-term satisfaction, in the long run it erodes your channel relationships. Abuse your power, and no matter how valuable you are to your distributor, you will eventually be terminated when a new revenue-producing product line is found.

There are three ways to build channel power:

1. *Make your products easier to sell.* Invest in marketing programs that boost your brand power. Use channel marketing efforts such as rebates, end user advertising, and direct mail, or use strategies such as training. (See Chapter 11 for details on these techniques.)

2. *Use rewards.* Motivate distributors to perform by creating a unique package of channel enrichments, tailored to a particular distributor. Mix and match from these effective and attention-getting reward vehicles:

❑ Compensation issued
❑ Products assigned
❑ Territory authorized
❑ Support given
❑ Recognition rendered

3. *Use coercion.* This short-term power play is not an option for the ethical channelmaster. No one likes to be forced to do something he or she doesn't want to do. While necessity may make a distributor succumb to a manufacturer's demands, you'd better believe that manufacturer will be placed on the "to-be-dropped-at-a-later-date" list. As soon as a suitable replacement product line is found, the distributor will enthusiastically exercise the termination for convenience clause in its contract. What goes around comes around. Don't coerce. It's self-defeating.

# Channel Conflict

As a channelmaster, conflicts are part of your everyday life. Channel conflict does not go away if ignored. In fact, it surely grows worse. That's why it is your responsibility to resolve conflicts equitably and quickly.

The best way to resolve conflict is to prevent it altogether. Many of the clashes discussed in this chapter can be prevented by formulating clear policies at the beginning of the relationship and enforcing them consistently. If you distribute the business policy statement discussed in Chapter 8 among all your distributors, all channel participants know how to steer clear of hazardous issues.

But sometimes conflict does arise, and as channelmaster you must take corrective action. Your action will have one of three effects on your channel:

1. *No effect.* If your decision is obviously opaque and meaningless, your distributors will perceive you as a weak administrator. Your credibility and their respect will diminish.

2. *Negative effect.* If your resolution is not equitable and is antidistributor, your problem-solving reputation will suffer. Likewise, an image to avoid. Be just and impartial, channelmaster, by supporting your distributors in your conflict settlements.

3. *Positive effect.* If you reach and implement a decision that is logical, correct, and fair to all three parts of the channel equation—manufacturer, distributor, and end user—you and your company will earn a reputation as a knowledgeable and trustworthy channel partner.

When your resolution is sure to have a positive effect, let everyone know. Get the word out through your field sales force, by publishing a memo, or by discussing the decision at sales meetings, training sessions, field visits, Advisory Councils, and other such manufacturer-distributor gatherings. You might also consider using the infamous channel telegraph to transmit the good news by informing respected distributors of the results of your decisive action. They will in turn communicate this information to their counterparts.

If conflict crops up frequently, your distributors will suspect that you are not really committed to managing the channel. They will also find it increasingly difficult to do business with you. When that happens, your product line priority will be reduced, and your distributor may start looking around for replacements from another, less troublesome source. Avoid this tragedy by acting swiftly and fairly.

## The 20 Percent/80 Percent Consideration

While it is important to reduce conflict among all of your channel members, it is especially important to focus on the 20 percent of your distributors that generate 80 percent of your sales revenue and profits. Because they are leaders, they can play an influential role in issues involving power and conflict with the remainder of your channel of distribution.

I recall a situation in which a distributor was dishonestly misusing special bidpriced product intended to be sold to one specific customer. This product, priced low to meet the competition, was mysteriously showing up in various parts of the United States, taking away business that my ethical distributors rightfully deserved. A thorough investigation identified the violator. As soon as that distributor was terminated, I notified the "twelve apostles" on my Distributor Advisory Council, who together represented over 80 percent of my sales revenue. I could almost hear the managerial applause at the other end of the telephone! I asked them to pass the word on to their counterparts. My conflict resolution report card received an A+ that day.

# How to Deal With Channel Conflict

Channel conflict comes in many sizes and shapes. Paradoxically, sometimes it is strategically invigorating to permit a limited amount of channel conflict to exist. Some channel conflict might very well indicate that you are getting incredibly good sales coverage, as two authorized distributors compete for the same account's business. However, it is important to realize that too much conflict can be destructive and time-consuming, draining away important hours from your managerial time.

### *Forms of Channel Conflict*

- ❏ Over-saturation/over-distribution
- ❏ Stocking levels
- ❏ Direct vs. individual channels
- ❏ Regional vs. national distribution
- ❏ Large account coverage
- ❏ Split compensation
- ❏ Sales quotas
- ❏ Territories: geographic, product, or market specific
- ❏ Market life cycle channel transition
- ❏ New market development
- ❏ New product launches

❒ Channel tasks to be performed
❒ Technology required
❒ Training
❒ Channel border skirmishes
❒ The phantom channel/gray marketing
❒ Refusal to be locked into one supplier
❒ Overselling without regard to availability
❒ Bureaucratic vs. entrepreneurial philosophies
❒ Pricing issues
❒ Sizes of profit margins/compensation
❒ Competition over resources
❒ Transshipping
❒ Assigned markets

The key factor is to *manage* conflict, not permit it to rage out of control. The following sections offer advice on how to resolve the most common channel conflicts.

## Oversaturation/Overdistribution

This common conflict is created when the manufacturer authorizes several distributors in a single territory, causing distributors to literally fight for every scrap of business for your overdistributed product. The consequences of this dubious business strategy are price deterioration, end user confusion, and fever-pitch channel member dissatisfaction. Eventually, either the eagle distributor or the manufacturer runs out of patience and ends the relationship. Exhibit 10-1 shows the sequence of destruction caused by oversaturation/overdistribution.

The best way to settle this conflict is to avoid it altogether. Don't spread your business among several distributors in a single territory. Stick to the eagles. By choosing the very best distributor candidate and forming the best possible partnership bond, you achieve the most profitable and productive sales revenue results.

## Stocking Levels

While there is no question that one of the primary responsibilities of a distributor is to maintain a reasonable and proper inventory of a manufacturer's product to adequately meet local market demands, conflicts arise when distributors do not commit to the stocking level the manufacturer desires. To prevent this dilemma, seek mutual agreement on the inventory to be carried. Try to demand certain levels, and you are sure to create hard

**Exhibit 10-1.** The negative effects of oversaturation/
overdistribution in channels of distribution.

Multiple distributors engage each other in the same authorized territory.

⇩

Distributors start to discount manufacturer's products.

⇩

Distributors' profits commensurately decrease.

⇩

Overall distributor confidence in manufacturer declines.

⇩

Distributors further discount products.

⇩

Distributors' support to end users decreases.

⇩

Customer satisfaction erodes.

⇩

Confused and irritated end users buy competitive product.

⇩

Either manufacturer or distributors decide to terminate the relationship.

feelings among all channel members that could cause a channel relationship to sour.

## Direct vs. Indirect Channels

This conflict eternal is inevitable. A direct and an indirect sales force do not cooperate 100 percent of the time, and their internal cultural and business differences clash at some point. Duplicate account coverage, pricing wars, carrying competitive product lines, and lack of direct control with the indirect channel are just a few of the conflicts ready to burst out at any time.

Nonetheless, there are ways to minimize (but never totally neutralize) these potentially explosive business feelings. To start with, clearly and concisely state up front all policies and regulations that affect both organizations, paying particular attention to potentially sensitive issues. By clarifying the ground rules, both the direct and indirect sales forces can predict the outcomes of certain specified field activities and functions. For example, make sure the distributor's contract lists those corporations that, because of their national account status and customer satisfaction requirements, are dealt with by the direct sales force. Or create a partnering atmosphere by compensating the direct sales force for all indirect sales that occur within its respective geographic territories, provided that the direct sales force performs certain regular support activities, such as local product training; giving sales/marketing advice on direct mail, telemarketing, and other marketing activities; and joint customer presentations.

Be sure to establish the frequency of contact between your direct sales force and distributor—say, sales/product training at least once per quarter or four local direct mailings a year. Check call reports to confirm that these activities are occurring, and conduct periodic meetings to discuss the level of support. These actions will reduce, but not alleviate, the traditional hostility between your direct and indirect sales forces—especially if both report to one senior marketing manager, who can deal with channel collisions quickly and fairly.

## Regional vs. National Distributors

Regional distributors are not affectionately inclined toward their national counterparts and often refer to them as "box pushers" whose deeper discounts and price-aggressive tactics threaten their local-market reputation and performance. These big, powerful, national distributors, on the other hand, simply don't care about regional distributors because they are not a serious threat to their business livelihood.

In order to maximize sales and profits from both distributor types, you have to manage intrachannel conflict between regionals and nationals. One way to do so is to sign up regional distributors *before* approaching nationals. In that way, you have your regional market coverage in place before going about establishing national distributor alliances. If you start with national distributors, you will find that regional distributors will be more reluctant to sign with you.

The only real way to manage this form of channel conflict is to adhere tightly to your distributor selection criteria for both regional and national distributors, so that all the distributors you select will be of the highest quality, and watch your business philosophy of maintaining price integrity (a quality product and service should also have a quality price throughout all levels of the channel).

## Large-Account Coverage

Large corporate customers naturally want to deal directly with manufacturers, in order to secure higher purchase volumes, better pricing, and corporate account support. But a distributor may feel that it is fully capable of selling your products to a large corporation and request that you direct the business through it. If you choose to deal directly with the large customer, your distributor might very well attempt to sell that same account a competitive product. This type of activity breeds multiple conflicts and great customer confusion. That's why it's best to establish a large-account policy up front, and then stick with it. Be up front with your plans for dealing with these accounts in your printed business policies. Some channelmasters actually have a distributor contract addendum listing those companies that deal direct, thereby preventing distributors from wasting valuable sales time on a corporate customer.

## Split Compensation

Unfortunately, there will never be a solution for this sensitive subject—at least not one that is totally acceptable to all parties. Let's say that Kmart management wants attention in its Troy, Michigan, headquarters but also wants local distributors to support each of its field store locations. Conflict typically arises when the distributor that covers Kmart headquarters feels that it should get the entire compensation, when actually the local distributors deserve a share, too. It's up to you, channelmaster, to decide what the compensation split should be and to explain and administer it fairly.

The final compensation award decision should be based on which party really exerted the most sales effort, has the most account control, or is most desired by the customer. If necessary, verify these efforts with the actual end user. It is advisable also to plainly state your company's operating procedures on split compensation in your business policies and distributor agreement.

## Sales Quotas

Quotas should never be force-fed to distributors. If a quota seems arbitrary or unattainable, distributors simply ignore it. You get far better results if you develop sales quotas together and mount a team effort to reach them.

There are two ways to develop a team approach to quotas. First, attempt to assign *mutually agreed-upon* quotas in three different measures: total dollars/units/models. If possible, segment the quotas by month, by quarter, or by fiscal year. Most likely, you'll have to work in annual terms, but the more chronologically precise you are, the more accurate sales and profit forecasts, manufacturing plans, and other business documents will be. Second, try to build a minimarketing plan around a quota. Use it as a objective, and tie in related strategies and tactics. This two-pronged approach tells distributors: "Pick up your paddle, we're all in the same canoe."

## Territories: Geographic, Product-Specific, or Market-Specific?

What happens when a rebellious distributor sells outside its authorized primary sales area—whether geographic or specific to a product or market—and the assaulted distributor complains to you about the unauthorized sales transgression? Not only are there two irritated parties—you and the second distributor—but there is a high risk that this classic form of channel conflict will escalate and get out of control when other distributors find out about your lack of managerial attention.

Therefore, territorial disputes must be dealt with firmly and quickly, through a well-planned and executed dialogue with all concerned parties. Better yet, avoid conflict by making sure your distributors have a clear understanding of their assigned geographic, product, and market areas. Remind them that their sales quota performance will be measured for purchase orders generated in this territory and nowhere else.

## Market Life Cycle Channel Transition

Conflict can arise as a market moves through its life cycle, and end user buying behavior and requirements change. As channel tasks change, compensation levels may decrease. It is your responsibility as manufacturer to guide your distributors through these sensitive changes by keeping them aware of (1) the end user buying behavioral changes in each phase, and (2) the specific roles they must play and, in turn, be monetarily rewarded for. Reduced compensation is very difficult for a distributor to adjust to. Channel members are sometimes hard-pressed to accept the fact that times and customers' desires have in fact changed. But the channel of distribution must adapt or perish. (For a graphic view of the market life cycle, see Exhibit 10-2.)

## New Market Development

Your distributors sell your product to the elementary school market—but you want to get your product into secondary, collegiate, and vocational education institutions. You encourage your distributors to move out of

**Exhibit 10-2.** The market life cycle.

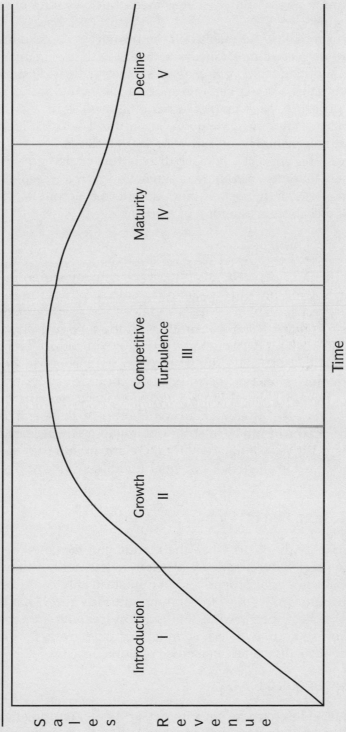

| Sales | | | | |
|---|---|---|---|---|
| Revenue | | | | |
| Introduction | Growth | Competitive Turbulence | Maturity | Decline |
| I | II | III | IV | V |

Time

*Source:* Frank Lynn and Associates, Chicago.

their comfort zone and into these new areas, but they strongly resist. Alas, conflict begins.

The sad moral of this tale is that the primary responsibility for developing new markets almost always remains with the manufacturer. Try seeing the situation from your channel's point of view. Distributors must spread their sales and marketing resources over a multitude of principals and their products. New market development takes time away from this process and does not yield the quick-turnaround sales dividends that are realized in their primary, comfort-zone marketplaces.

To avoid this conflict, don't ask distributors to do your work for you. Develop new markets on your own. When you have succeeded in developing new markets, either retain them as internal accounts, or turn them over to the distributors as a form of a business gift.

## New Product Launches

It's also difficult to persuade distributors to actively support a new product launch. The reasons are the same: The sales time consumed by such an effort may affect sales of other lines and does not yield immediate results, or even results that are commensurate with the time invested.

Instead of asking distributors to *push* a new product, employ marketing strategies that *pull* the product through your channel. Intensive new product training, monetary incentives, and contests can incite distributors to sell your new products. Meanwhile, aggressive space advertising, direct mail, exhibition, rebates, and other promotions can cause end users to "call out" for the product from the distributor. Engaging these marketing efforts produces a positive, winning environment for manufacturer, distributor, and end user when there is a potential for dissension over new product launches.

## Channel Tasks to Be Performed

Channel collision happens when the manufacturer wants the distributor to conduct specific tasks and the distributor has neither the willingness, desire, nor resources to properly and enthusiastically conform. For example, a distributor may refuse to conduct quarterly direct mail campaigns when you request them. Avoid this clash by seeking an explicit written and oral understanding of each channel member's roles and responsibilities prior to formalizing any business relationship.

## Technology Required

Electronic Data Interchange, the internet, and other exciting new technologies are alluring—but does the cost of installing them and educating users equal the business benefits realized by both parties? Talk to your channel before you acquire or install new equipment. If you don't agree on the mutual benefits of these technological requirements, you risk conflict over technologies that don't match or expensive equipment that is not used.

New developments like vendor-managed inventory (VMI) also require detailed dialogue before they can be efficiently employed. With VMI, a local distributor's physical inventories are automatically replenished when a mutually agreed-upon minimum level is reached. VMI works when channel members have high confidence in each other and desire a long-range partnership. It doesn't work when it is imposed by one party on the other.

## Training

As a rule, manufacturers want to conduct more training than distributors are willing to commit to. For as with other resources, the channel must use time available for training to its advantage. While manufacturers may have difficulty accepting this, they should take whatever time is given them. Better yet, instead of haggling over training, discuss and agree to an annual training program. A twelve-month commitment is a much more effective way to manage a sales and product training program, as compared to the "we'll call you when we have some open time" approach from the distributor.

## Channel Border Skirmishes

A limited number of channel border skirmishes (when two authorized distributors compete for the same customer's business) might very well indicate that you are getting aggressive sales coverage. But too many battles, and an out-of-managerial-control condition may erupt. Do not allow these sales confrontations to be the rule, but the exception.

## The Phantom Channel

A phantom channel occurs when an unauthorized distributor unethically acquires your product from one of your authorized channel members, and then resells it to its customers. The first you hear about it is when a valued member of your authorized channel stridently complains about losing sales revenue to a phantom and demands that you end the sales conflict.

You have two options: (1) You can correct the situation by enforcing strict sales and marketing policies that prohibit unauthorized sales, or (2) you can do nothing, hoping that the situation will go away, and knowing that either way you benefit from additional sales revenue. The latter approach is not recommended. It's cynical, and it's eventually the kiss of death to valued long-term relationships. Your authorized distributors will see that you are not their ally, and they will give their valuable resources to a more supportive partner, and start to de-emphasize your product line within their sales organization.

An ethical channelmaster would try to unmask the phantom distributor. If you discover who the violator is, then you might consider invoking the termination for convenience clause and ending the relationship. End of relationship, end of conflict.

## Refusal to Be Locked Into One Supplier

While manufacturers would always prefer to receive the distributor's primary product line ranking, that often is not possible. Many distributors are reluctant to put all of their channel "eggs in one basket" with any one manufacturer, and so they do not permit any one manufacturer to exceed a certain percentage of their total sales revenue and profits. They reason that if there is a sudden parting of the ways, the loss of that line would not cripple their overall business. You want them to sell only *your* products, and they are "gun shy" to commit to only one supplier. Conflict erupts.

## Overselling Without Regard to Availability

This form of channel struggle occurs when a distributor, after being informed that a popular or new product is available only in limited quantities, purposely cultivates significant end user purchase orders and turns over the delivery requirement to the manufacturer. Shifting the full burden of order fulfillment to the supplier is not a fair or positive relationship-building practice, but it happens every day.

It's possible to control this problem by limiting this type of COD exposure. For example, in 1996, Hewlett-Packard announced that it would initially offer its newly introduced and potentially very popular home computer product line only through the national power retailer Circuit City. When production capability caught up with demand, HP would open the products to the rest of its channel. HP hoped this strategy would prevent product availability problems that had previously plagued their prime competitors, IBM and Compaq. The downside of this double-edged sword is that channel members that do not have access to this exciting new product line will feel deprived of significant revenue.

## Bureaucratic vs. Entrepreneurial Business Philosophies

Manufacturers, by their very nature, operate in a bureaucratic managerial environment, while distributors are frequently entrepreneurial. These two distinct cultures have ample opportunity to clash. While manufacturers function in disciplined, sometimes very tightly controlled surroundings, distributors work in a more fluid and flexible atmosphere. Where manufacturers have layers of management and adhere to scores of procedures, distributor operations—which are smaller and likely family-owned—conduct business in a seat-of-the-pants fashion. To prevent channel discord, always be aware of this important cultural difference, and try to adjust to it when dealing with your distributors. Follow the example of Miller Brewing, which instituted a program designed to reduce the trust gap between the corporation and its 600-plus distributors by better understanding how its channel works.

## Pricing Issues

While manufacturers would like to exert some control over pricing levels in the channel, they are sometimes prevented by ethics and laws from regulating the pricing practices of their distributors. The frustration engendered by this lack of control often leads to conflict. A wise channelmaster is aware of all antitrust issues that may arise and adheres to the appropriate legal and ethical regulations. See Chapter 12 for a detailed discussion of this sensitive area.

## Size of Profit Margins/Compensation

Making money is the primary business objective of all distributors. No wonder conflict often erupts over compensation and profit margins. Remember, distribution is a cost-transfer business. Your channel members should be fairly compensated for their efforts.

Conflict over compensation also breaks out when a manufacturer discovers it cannot afford the already established margin requirements of distributors in a primary channel, and is thus shut out of a highly prized channel target. Not a positive situation, but one that can be overcome by concentrating sales and marketing efforts on a secondary channel of distribution to reach the desired marketplace.

## Competition Over Resources

Frequently, this form of channel conflict entails two or more distributors competing for preferential and priority resources from the same manufacturers—perhaps limited quantities of a highly salable new product, or a sales- and profit-producing training program that is provided to one distributor and not the other. While your COD should always be fairly treated, resource competition clashes do occur. The only way to manage this form of conflict is to allocate your resources consistently and fairly.

## Transshipping

Out-of-authorized-territory product shipments by distributors undercut the best of your strategic channel plans. Most of these transgressions are intentional and certainly should not be encouraged by the manufacturer. Conflict between the warring distributors is very difficult to control. Remember your legalities, channelmaster, but deal with this challenge by addressing the problem with the concerned parties and attempting to mediate a mutually agreeable solution.

## Assigned Markets

While distributors primarily want to conduct business within their comfort zone market segments, they may feel shunned when they are not invited to sell into new, exciting, and potentially profitable markets. If you choose other types of distributors to tackle a new market, the rejected or not selected distributors may object to and contest the manufacturer's new market award decision.

To minimize conflict, give everyone a chance to meet the requirements of entering the new market. Tell your existing distributors the criteria you are looking for, and invite them to apply before forming a new distributor organization. Not all of your existing distributors will agree with your final decision, but if you include them in the process, they will have to admit that they were equitably treated.

To obtain a snapshot of strife in your own channel of distribution, complete this rather simple seven-question "Strife-o-Meter." If you answer *yes* to two questions or fewer, conflict is not a strategic issue for you. But if you answer *yes* to three or more questions, conflict could be impacting your business. And if you answer *yes* to five or more questions, conflict may be undermining your channel strategy and must be managed immediately. Based on the results of this quiz, audit your market position and enact strategies to manage destructive conflict.

#### IS CHANNEL CONFLICT A STRATEGIC ISSUE IN YOUR BUSINESS TODAY?

Take a moment to consider the following questions:

|  | Yes | No |
|---|---|---|
| 1. Have you recently seen your market move through a "transition" point (e.g., from introduction to growth, from growth to maturity)? | ☐ | ☐ |

|  | **Yes** | **No** |
|---|---|---|
| 2. Have you made any recent changes to your channel strategy (e.g., adding channel members, adding new types of channels)? | ☐ | ☐ |
| 3. Have requests from the direct sales force or channels for special prices increased significantly? | ☐ | ☐ |
| 4. Have gross margins eroded significantly in any customer or channel segments? | ☐ | ☐ |
| 5. Have you seen a decrease in dollar revenue per direct sales rep and/or dollar revenue per channel location? | ☐ | ☐ |
| 6. Have you experienced significant loss of market share or declines in customer satisfaction in any customer segments? | ☐ | ☐ |
| 7. Have you experienced a decrease in your number of channels as a result of channels dropping your line? | ☐ | ☐ |

SOURCE: Reprinted with permission, Frank Lynn and Associates, Inc., ©1992.

In conclusion, remember that channel conflict and power are quite natural events that must be managed by every channelmaster. Always attempt to deal with these critical business issues in an impartial way. Keep in mind that your distributors are watching your managerial actions (or lack thereof) and making judgments about the way you deal with conflict and use power. Your credentials as a channel marketing manager—as well as your distributors' future growth decisions for your product line—depend on how deftly you meet the power and conflict challenge.

## *CASE:* IF YOU DANCE WITH THE CHANNEL BEAR, THE BEAR LEADS

In terms of channel power, your company is positioned as a secondary, add-on product line by your 105 industrial MRO (maintenance, repair, and operation) distributors that represent you in the United States. Your product line of industrial chemicals:

- ❏ Has consistently high quality
- ❏ Exceeds the channel's economic (profit) requirements
- ❏ Is a full product mix that satisfies almost all customer needs in your chemical category

In addition, your internal sales and technical support, while very conservative, is considered one of most competent in the industry. However, because of your "starch collar" internal environment, all levels of management are not only hesitant but resistant to any business change. This is reflected in your growth rates. While your part of the MRO chemical industry is growing at an impressive 15 percent per year, your company's sales revenue is increasing at a mere 3 percent annually.

As an aggressive channelmaster, you realize that you must deal with a number of positive and negative managerial issues if your company is to see the year 2000. Some serious sales and marketing changes must be made.

**Enter the "channel bear" . . .**

The most powerful and profitable, revenue-rich, national MRO distributor approaches your company to form a business alliance of sorts. It will guarantee an annual sales level equal to a total of 30 percent of your present 105 regional distributors, if you give it a 15 percent discount over your best existing pricing schedule. A 30 percent sales increase! Alignment with a national distributor power! Just what's needed to put some new marketing life into this internal and external channel of distribution situation! Or is it?

Comment on what you would do to correct your future channel's business direction.

**Case interpretational points:**

❑ Always consider the conflictual effect this kind of situation (national versus regional distributors) will have on your entire channel of distribution.

❑ Do a risk analysis that compares benefits to be derived to the conflictual, negative affects that will be generated. Consider short- and long-range consequences.

❑ Consider your internal corporate culture as you contemplate your decision.

# Chapter 11

# Channel of Distribution Motivational Concepts and Processes

As a channelmaster, you are continually competing for resources with all of the other manufacturers your distributors represent. As I have stressed many times, the best way to obtain the greatest share of resources is to create successful channel partnerships—partnerships that focus on coordinated business actions that achieve fair, consistent, and mutual objectives.

When working relationships are in good order, creative motivational strategies and tactics can add a kick that increases those resource commitments. But they are not a substitute! Focus first on your relationship, and then build motivational programs.

## Push and Pull Strategies

There are two kinds of promotional activities: (1) those that *push* products through your channel, and (2) those that *pull* products through your channel. Exhibit 11-1 illustrates the activity flow of each effort.

A *push* strategy is any marketing activity that entices your COD to sell your products rather than those of other manufacturers the channel represents. In other words, these types of promotions *push* your product through the channel. Push strategy examples are:

❏ *Travel incentive programs* that award an all-expense-paid trip to a domestic or foreign destination for meeting a quota during a specified period of time.

❏ *Merchandise programs* that reward salespeople for performance with items such as televisions, sporting goods, clothing, and gourmet foods.

**Exhibit 11-1. Push and pull promotional activities.**

Push Strategy

Manufacturer ← Demand → Channel of Distribution ← Demand → End User

Sales Promotional Marketing Activities

Pull Strategy

Manufacturer → Demand → Channel of Distribution → Demand → End User

Sales Promotional Marketing Activities

❏ *Training programs* that increase the distributor salespeople's comfort level with your products, thereby making it easy to sell the products to their customers and reap compensation (commission, bonus) accordingly.

❏ *Monetary SPIFFS (special promotional incentive factory funds)* that draw specific attention to certain models or groups of units in your product line. For instance, for the next thirty days, you will pay a $30 per unit SPIFF bonus for each particular model a distributor salesperson sells. Two tremendous advantages of this type of program are that it can be launched with very little administrative work and can be communicated quickly to your channel.

❏ *Special discounts or allowances* that draw special attention to your product line through a limited-time offer. For example, a manufacturer might announce that, for the next sixty days, its channel will receive an additional 10 percent discount off the best published price on any order. Or all orders for immediate shipment entered in the next thirty days will receive an additional sixty days of payment dating on top of your normal one-month billing cycle.

❏ *Local COOP advertising efforts* (direct mail, exhibitions, space advertising) that produce local market quality sales leads that materialize into real purchases.

A *pull* strategy motivates the end user to approach your channel of distribution and "call out" for your product. A customer that asks for your product won't be satisfied with anything else—so your distributor must sell your product in order to fulfill its customer's demand. This kind of strategy *pulls* your product through the channel. Pull strategy examples are:

❏ *Space advertising* in leading publications that generates qualified customer inquiries that produce actual purchases of your products.

❏ *Public relations releases* announcing new products or features, which cause potential end users to request further information or a demonstration from your distributor.

❏ *Rebate programs* offering a limited-time, factory-issued cash rebate to end users that purchase your product from your channel of distribution.

❏ *Exhibitions* where end users spend time in your exhibit booth expressing an interest in your displayed product line. These face-to-face discussions can produce excellent, qualified sales leads as your booth personnel directly communicate with customers and can immediately record the level of purchasing seriousness observed.

❏ *Direct-mail campaigns* targeted at qualified individuals who request further contact.

❏ *End user seminars* conducted by your staff and attended by individuals who have, by their presence and time commitment, expressed a sincere interest in your company's products and as a result of the seminar, proceed to your channel to acquire your product.

❏ *Telemarketing efforts* that can supply your distributor with telephone-qualified sales leads that will culminate in actual purchases.

❏ *Internet exposure* via a Web page illustrating the features and benefits of your product line and that directs visitors to local distributors for further information.

❏ *Radio and television advertising* that promotes your products to potential end users that then contact your COD for additional details and sales information.

Should you conduct both push and pull strategies at the same time? Of course! In fact, it is interesting to note that qualified sales leads are a pull and a push strategy at the same time. Leads *pull* because they represent buyers that are interested in purchasing your product instead of another manufacturer's. They *push* because they induce your distributor to sell your product instead of someone else's. Don't forget: You're competing for their resource commitment.

This chapter focuses on two programs that *push* your products through your channel: (1) incentive programs, and (2) sales training.

# Incentive Programs

## Your Channel's Motivational Personality

Before you can design a successful motivational program, you must understand the motivational personality of your channel of distribution. What works well in one industry doesn't necessarily perform favorably in another. For example, in the computer industry, travel incentive programs featuring exotic or hard-to-get-to destinations are particularly effective in motivating distributors and value-added resellers. But an industry with a very starch collar culture might not even think of using such a dynamic program. Make sure your plans match your industry's "excitement factor." If your company and your distributors are on the conservative side, use a conservative motivational program.

Investigate programs that have been used successfully by other manufacturers. Identify the most effective and accepted concepts, and then design a program that improves on them. That way, your motivational efforts will reach a higher level of motivational excellence and capture the sales and marketing attention of your channel.

It is also wise to continually monitor other manufacturers' motivational programs. Doing so helps you identify new imaginative and inventive concepts and avoid duplicating a worn-out motivational idea that would produce lukewarm sales results at best.

Find out how your distributors compensate their salespeople, and tailor your motivational plans accordingly. In this way, you more closely and strategically match your distributor's business direction. For example, if your distributors base compensation on sales revenue growth, your monetary contest could reward them for exceeding a timed quota—e.g., a $250 award for a 10 percent revenue increase over an individual salesperson's monthly quota of your products, or a $500 bonus for a three-month program.

Vary your motivational program calendar each year. Always scheduling motivational efforts for the same period may lead to "sandbagging"— when distributors hold back orders anticipating the start of a regularly scheduled promotion. This peak-and-valley phenomenon can be easily avoided by not conducting the same type of motivational offering at the identical time each year.

Always use the following three-part motivational program formula when composing contest regulations because you certainly do not want to be criticized for giving rewards that are too easy to earn and do not produce favorable and profitable sales results:

$$E = R = R$$

Efforts = Results = Rewards

In other words, make sure that the rewards you give out are in proportion to the results obtained from the efforts exerted. Don't make it too easy for a distributor salesperson to earn a reward from your incentive program!

Direct your distributor's sales efforts not only to meet but exceed the end users' satisfaction requirements for your product. Remember, no channel marketing strategy or motivational program can be intelligently conceived and executed unless you have a rock-solid understanding of what the end user needs and wants from your channel of distribution and then match inducements to convince the customer to purchase your product from your distributors.

Involve all three parts of the channel equation (manufacturer, chan-

## Successful Sales Motivational Program Sequence

Follow these nine steps of creating and administering a sales motivational program and you'll be assured of successful motivational program planning and implementation.

Step 1: *Set your objectives.*
Step 2: *Count the costs.*
Step 3: *Write down the rules.*
Step 4: *Choose the awards.*
Step 5: *Spread the word.*
Step 6: *Attend to administration.*
Step 7: *Sum up and report your success.*
Step 8: *Issue the award(s).*
Step 9: *Review your overall motivational strategy for any future improvements.*

## Motivating With Value-Based Compensation

Value-based compensation can help motivate your channel members to go the distance and perform strategic and tactical tasks over and above those specified in their contract. For example, as an incentive to increase sales, you might offer to pay a 2 percent rebate for all sales to any distributor that increases sales 15 percent over the previous year. You can also use value-based compensation to motivate distributors to:

❒ Submit a mutually acceptable minimarketing plan.
❒ Submit a mutually acceptable minimarketing plan *and* then achieve its objectives with the strategies and tactics the plan specifies.
❒ Supply point-of-sale information, such as customer name, product and model purchased, price paid, and other pertinent details (it's the rare distributor that volunteers this information without an incentive).
❒ Agree to commit a certain number or quality of resources, e.g., a specific dollar volume or unit volume of physical inventory of your products at its location for twelve months, a bimonthly training meeting for its sales force, participation in a product certification course, or a certain number of joint sales calls per month.
❒ Sell highly profitable but difficult-to-sell items in your product line.
❒ Develop new markets.
❒ Launch new products.
❒ Install computer and information technology that complements your system.

These activities can be compensated with a sales rebate or a specific dollar "bounty." A distributor might receive a 2 percent rebate on sales for submitting a minimarketing plan, be paid $300 for each employee it sends to a certification course, or be paid $25 for each joint sales call. Value-based compensation can also be used to reimburse distributors for employing a "specialist" for your product line: 100 percent of salary and expenses for a full-time specialist, 50 percent of expenses for a part-time specialist.

You can't offer value-based compensation for every single one of these items, or you give away the store. But by focusing on objectives that are strategically important, you can create a win-win program that helps you achieve a disproportionate share of the distributor's resources—and makes your distributor happy, too.

nel, and end user) in the motivational program to create a balanced program that produces completely successful results. For example, running both push and pull strategies at the same time helps you boost excitement among manufacturer, channel, and end users alike.

## Four Key Elements of a Sales Motivational Program

Every motivational program has four key elements:

1. Motivational objectives
2. Potential participants
3. Possible rewards
4. Administrative policies

### Motivational Objectives

Always determine a clear goal for your motivational program. Unless you set one, you never know whether you reach it! Possible goals for your program include:

- ❏ Exceeding assigned quotas
- ❏ Offsetting competition
- ❏ Selling existing products
- ❏ Bolstering slow sales season
- ❏ Improving channel morale
- ❏ Moving slow-selling products
- ❏ Reaching new customers
- ❏ Increasing overall sales volume
- ❏ Selling new products

- ❏ Moving full product line
- ❏ Entering new markets
- ❏ Encouraging team selling

You achieve more if you combine two or three objectives into your motivational program and tailor your awards program to match them. For example, one contest could combine these three goals:

1. Exceeding assigned quota: receives a silver-level contest award
2. Moving full product line and exceeding assigned quota: receives a gold-level contest award
3. Reaching new markets combined with the two above objectives: receives a platinum-level contest award

## Potential Participants

To get everyone to buy into your promotion, include all levels and types of personnel: senior, middle, and operational management; technical and sales support personnel; and your foot soldiers—the field salespeople. If you focus your promotion on one or two levels only, you can easily trigger an internal blockade that can thwart your contest. Don't overlook anyone who contributes to or influences your company's product sales success. Include telemarketing personnel who are in frequent telephone contact with your customers and support personnel whose recommendations are trusted by customers. You might want to design a program that blends the efforts of outside salespeople with those of telemarketing staff and technical support specialists. By rewarding all three of these important distributor areas, you can be assured that all three will strive to attain one common goal: to sell more of your product to more of their customers.

## Possible Rewards

There are many different ways to reward participants in your motivational programs. Here are some possible rewards:

- ❏ Cash
- ❏ Dinner for two
- ❏ Weekend for two
- ❏ Clothing
- ❏ Home repair and maintenance items
- ❏ Appliances
- ❏ Gift certificates
- ❏ Home accessories

- ❑ Cultural awards (play, opera, or symphony tickets)
- ❑ Incentive merchandise
- ❑ Incentive travel programs
- ❑ Gourmet food
- ❑ Electronics
- ❑ Popular, state-of-the-art items
- ❑ Automotive accessories
- ❑ Business accessories
- ❑ Professional house repairs and improvements

It's a good idea to offer a single category of reward in each program—i.e., offering only cash or only dinners out as the rewards in a particular contest. The exception would be when the reward is some form of home maintenance item (tools, lawn mowers, lawn tractors), home accessory (refrigerators, stoves, washing machines, microwave ovens), or professional home repair and improvement (a fireplace, a full year of lawn maintenance or snow removal, house painting, a new deck or patio, bathroom tiling, new kitchen cabinets). Here, you can offer a range of items that winners can choose from.

Look for incentive award companies that offer merchandise at special incentive program prices—generally well below retail. To find them, ask the Promotional Marketing Association of America (at 257 Park Avenue South, 11th Floor, New York, NY 10010; 212-420-1100, fax 212-533-7622) for a directory of its membership. You can also attend a trade show where companies and suppliers of incentive programs and merchandise exhibit their products and creative services. The major such shows include:

**The Annual Premium Incentive Show**
(America's Selling and Marketing Megashow)
*Contact:* Miller Freeman, Inc.
1 Penn Plaza, 11th Floor
New York, NY 10019
800-951-1314, 212-869-1300, fax 212-768-0015

**California Premium Show**
*Contact:* Premium Marketing Corporation
1611 North San Fernando Boulevard
Burbank, CA 91504
818-841-7130, fax 818-841-7130

**EIBTM** (European Incentive Business Travel & Meetings Exposition)
Geneva, Switzerland
(011)(44)273-735-253

**The Motivation Show**
(Includes the National Premium/Incentive Show and the Incentive
  Travel & Meeting Executives EXPO)
*Contact:* Hall-Ericson, Inc.
150 Burlington Avenue
Clarendon Hills, IL 60514
800-752-6312, 630-850-7779, fax 708-850-7843

I recommend that any channelmaster responsible for promotional
programs attend The Motivation Show. Held in Chicago, it is the world's
largest exhibit of incentive ideas and well worth a day of your time.

## Administrative Policies

Before you initiate your program, make sure that everyone in your
company and in the distributor's company fully understands how the contest works and how rewards will be obtained. Information up front prevents the promotion tragedy that occurs when a distributor salesperson
exerts a great deal of effort to sell your product and then finds out that he
or she has misinterpreted your program regulations. This kind of unfortunate situation actually demotivates your distributor's salespeople. Don't
let it happen to you! Clearly communicate how your incentives will be
earned and when they will be awarded.

## Checklist for a Successful Promotion

Make sure you do the following things for your motivational and promotional plans to succeed:

❒ *Have fair, equitable, and clearly stated promotional regulations and award
amounts.* That way, no unfortunate misunderstandings can occur and the
value of the awards is established.

❒ *Offer frequent rewards.* Give awards out monthly or bimonthly to
generate excitement by reminding participants of their success as frequently as possible.

❒ *Make all levels of distributor personnel eligible.* Then there will be no
internal distributor roadblocks to your program's success, and all contrib-
uting parties are acknowledged.

❒ *Administer your program in a professional way.* This keeps your image
on a pedestal-like level.

❒ *Ensure that there is an adequate promotional expense budget.* The most
workable budget allocates 75 percent of expenses for rewards, 15 percent
for communication and promotion, and 10 percent for administration.

❏ *Award as many individuals as possible.* Your program should be spread throughout the distributor's entire organization.

❏ *Publicize winners throughout the organization.* Recognition should be properly rendered. Put winners' names on plaques or certificates that are prominently displayed.

❏ *Recognize winners on paper and through publications.* Use newsletters, e-mails, fax memos, or the internet to formally announce the winners.

❏ *Always match your rewards to your target audience's wants, needs, and desires.* For example, distributor salespeople who already travel the world frequently may not be interested in a trip to the Bahamas.

❏ *Dispatch periodic teaser communications to contest participants and their spouses. This helps generate an even higher level of enthusiasm.*

❏ *Establish and adhere to a specific promotional time period.* This ensures that there is a "captured time" of enthusiasm.

❏ *Make your motivational programs set you apart from your direct and indirect competitors.* Remember, your direct and indirect competitors are vying for your distributors' resource commitment. Use creative, attention-getting incentive programs that help you stand out from the crowd.

❏ *Make sure your budget is large enough to pay for your promotion.* Many channel motivational programs fail because shortsighted financial planning forces manufacturers to terminate their programs.

❏ *Assess the results.* When your promotion ends, assess its results and report them to appropriate individuals within your company. Your internal managers have every right to evaluate program performance. If you aren't proactive in communicating the results, you may find yourself in a reactive mode when the president or comptroller asks for a program report. You should also report the results to your distributors, especially if your sales promotion is a tremendous success. Reporting back great results motivates distributors to participate in future programs as well.

## Promotional Trade Organizations

There are several organizations that stand ready to help a channelmaster create a successful motivational or sales promotional program. Contact them for unique sales and profit-producing channel incentive programs.

**Association of Incentive Marketing**
1620 Route 22
Union, NJ 07083
908-687-3090, fax 908-687-0977

**Association of Retail Marketing Services**
3 Caro Court
Red Bank, NJ 07701
908-842-5070, fax 908-219-1938

**Council of Sales Promotion Agencies**
750 Summer Street
Stamford, CT 06901
203-325-3911, fax 203-969-1499

**Incentive Manufacturers Representatives Association**
1805 North Mill Street, Suite A
Naperville, IL 60563
630-369-3773

**Promotional Marketing Association of America**
257 Park Avenue South, 11th Floor
New York, NY 10010
212-420-1100, fax 212-533-7622

**Promotional Products Association International**
3125 Skyway Circle North
Irving, TX 75038
972-252-0404, fax 972-594-7224

**Society of Incentive Travel Executives**
21 West 38th Street, 10th Floor
New York, NY 10018
212-575-0910, fax 212-575-1838

These organizations are there to serve the incentive buying public and, for the most part, offer their informational services free of charge.

## Cobranding

---

### Ken's Words of Wisdom

Whenever possible, seek out and employ comarketing or cobranding alliances with similar companies using the same channel of distribution.

---

Cobranding and comarketing alliances are hot new marketing strategies worth trying in the channel environment. Under these alliances, two companies with great reputations get together and either comarket their products (comarketing) or jointly produce a third product (cobranding). There are some prominent examples. By serving Starbucks Coffee, United Airlines meets its customer demand for quality caffeine, and Starbucks gets extra publicity and reaches a whole new market. By setting up Bank of America kiosks in their stores, Jewel Food Stores meets its customers' needs for convenient banking, and Bank of America reaches new retail customers.

This approach can be just as powerful in the industrial market, and it can also be applied to promotions. Try pooling your efforts with another manufacturer and rewarding your distributors with an additional 5 percent discount on all purchase orders that list certain products from both manufacturers. Or share space advertising costs and run a pull through campaign that generates leads for your channel member. The possibilities—and the benefits—are endless. Use your imagination, and both partners will earn extra channel power.

# Sales and Product Training

Sales and product training programs can be tremendous motivational vehicles, especially when combined with other push strategies. They instill your distributor salespeople with confidence, thereby making your products easier and more comfortable for them to sell, and enable salespeople to earn more "bags of gold" in the form of increased compensation.

As Exhibit 11-2 shows, there are nine important factors to consider in designing a training program. Let's examine them.

## 1. What Are the Training Program Objectives?

Not every training program has the same objective. Is your goal to introduce a new product? Provide general sales know-how? Determine your objective first, and then decide what blend of training will best help you reach that objective. Eight possible objectives follow.

❒ *Initial distributor start-up product and sales indoctrination.* Make a good first impression! It is imperative that you deliver the highest level of instructional excellence and value to your channel during start-up training. If you waste their time, your distributors will not invite you back. Your goal should be to deliver a meaningful program that can be put to work immediately so that they can more easily sell your products to their customers and earn a monetary award.

Be sure to include positive testimonials from end users and other distributors. Whatever you do, don't let a factory person stand up and recite

**Exhibit 11-2.** Factors to consider in designing a training program.

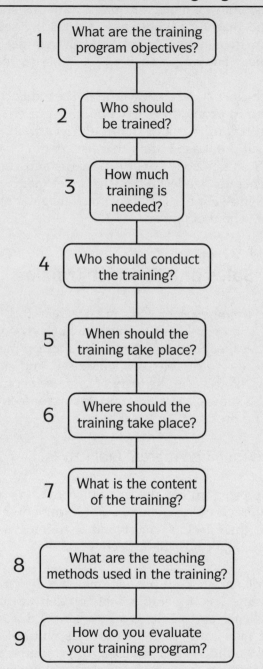

1 — What are the training program objectives?

2 — Who should be trained?

3 — How much training is needed?

4 — Who should conduct the training?

5 — When should the training take place?

6 — Where should the training take place?

7 — What is the content of the training?

8 — What are the teaching methods used in the training?

9 — How do you evaluate your training program?

the features and benefits of your product line from a piece of your company literature. Instead, tell your distributors how they can efficiently sell your products. Give them examples of how their brother and sister distributors have achieved sales success with your product line.

❐ *Ongoing product and sales training programs.* Ongoing training should strive to provide regularly scheduled training sessions designed to weave your products' features and benefits into the sales fabric of your distributor's sales force. To firm up this very important resource commitment, seek to establish a fixed training schedule with your distributors. For example, in the fourth quarter of the year, reach an agreement to conduct training sessions in a specific month of every quarter in the coming year. Confirm the training commitment in writing, and share a recommended agenda for each of the meetings.

❐ *New product launches.* Sales training can help make a new product that is important to you a priority for your distributor as well. The goal of new product training should be to make salespeople as familiar and as comfortable with the new product as possible, so that your distributor salespeople will not have to devote extra sales presentation time to the new product. Reduce that missionary new product sales effort by increasing their comfort level with your new product.

Combining such training with some type of limited-time promotional incentive can gain the enthusiastic attention of the sales force. Why not offer a per-unit SPIFF bonus for each new model sold during the first ninety days after the product's introduction?

❐ *New market penetration.* Like launching a new product, penetrating a new market requires additional sales work—and your distributor needs encouragement to do it. Devote this training to educating the sales force about the new market. Save the salespeople time by telling them what they need to know in order to successfully sell this market as soon—and as confidently—as possible. Again, linking training with an incentive program is a good way to induce your channel to pursue customers in your targeted new market. If you have a travel incentive program, try giving double-dollar credit for all new market sales, thus making it easier for reps to attain the trip award.

❐ *Overall positioning of your company and product line/mix.* Positioning your company as a market leader is a goal you should continually work toward achieving. High-quality, professional sales and product training produces professional sales results from your distributor and salespeople—thus establishing your company as a competent and authoritative corporation in the markets that both you and your channel serve.

❐ *Competitive analysis.* No products are sold in a vacuum. That's why all training *must* include a segment on competitive analysis. Use Chapter 4 to formulate this part of your training program as it relates to a competitive study of the corporations that are your field opponents. Also include a model-by-model comparison of your competitors' products.

❐ *Sales skills training.* You'll be head and shoulders above your opponents if you offer your distributor's sales personnel generic but professional sales skills education in areas that will enhance their overall occupational competency. Be sure to discuss how your product will be specifically presented in all of the phases of a typical sales process. Exhibit 11-3 illustrates the different phases.

Go ahead and use internal personnel, but if you can afford it, bring in outside experts to cover such specific areas as time and territory planning and customer relationship management. Some companies actually charge their distributors a nominal sum to attend these sessions.

❐ *Business management skills training (financial management, credit, billing, inventory management).* Show your concern for the business welfare of the distributor by including a series of business management skills topics in the total channel training program. Sessions in financial management, credit policies, billing procedures, and inventory management would be excellent subjects to incorporate in the agenda. Again, why not charge for attendance?

All of these objectives can be met through one of the four basic sales training formats: (1) national, (2) regional, (3) local, and (4) on-the-job (OJT) training. National sales training should be held once a year, at a national trade show or sales meeting. Smaller, regional sales training meetings allow more interactive response through open forums or break-out sessions. They make an excellent follow-up to national sales training. Local sales training offers very customized distributor training. On-the-job training is most intensive, because it pairs a factory salesperson with a distributor's salesperson on calls to customers.

## 2. Who Should Be Trained?

Before you offer training, decide whom you want to attend the sessions. Of course, you want to train anyone who is in frontline sales contact with the end user. This includes internal and external salespeople, customer service and technical support personnel, and sales and marketing managers. Consider also those individuals who have indirect or operational relationships with the end users, such as personnel in credit, billing, warehouse, and procurement.

**Exhibit 11-3.**  **The phases of the selling process.**

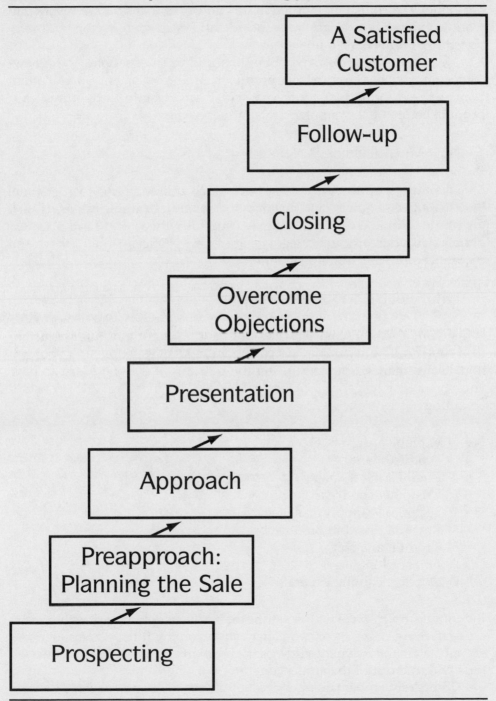

Initially, the distributor may allow you to train only frontline sales personnel. Graciously accept any time and personnel you are given, and work to expand your program to include others as you develop your relationship with the distributor.

Keep an eye out for newly hired distributor salespeople. These newcomers most likely require basic product training. By paying special attention to these individuals, you can win them over to supporting your product before other manufacturers influence them.

## 3. How Much Training Is Needed?

This is entirely up to you. Assess how much training your total channel of distribution requires, and evaluate the separate training needs of each distributor. Some channel members—especially those that have prior experience in your product category—are more proficient than others and require less of your training attention.

## 4. Who Should Conduct the Training?

While you, as channelmaster, certainly play a role in any training activities, you should always include your own field salespeople and your national sales manager in conducting the training. It's a good idea to have your president or general manager kick off the meeting. Also consider including:

❐ National sales manager
❐ Product manager
❐ Engineering manager
❐ Customer service manager
❐ Technical support manager
❐ Physical distribution director
❐ Credit manager
❐ Financial manager
❐ Outside training experts

*Always* try to involve the distributor's salespeople by arranging interactive training activities or spontaneously involving them in the program's events. Their involvement adds peer credibility to your instructional efforts with the rest of the audience.

To prevent embarrassing moments, *always* drill and rehearse the presentations of each of your factory or corporate participants well in advance of any training session. Don't let anyone promise new product features or improvements or innocently discuss sensitive issues. Remember, your distributors hold you to any commitments made during training sessions, even if they are off the cuff.

## 5. When Should the Training Take Place?

Training, in some form (national, regional, individual customer calls), should take place as often as possible! Any productive form of sales training is always advantageous to both the distributor and manufacturer.

Strive to offer some type of product or sales training communication *monthly* with your most important distributors. Cover other distributors quarterly if possible. Use a critical event chart to plan a year of training events at a time, so you can see at a glance what kind of training is to be offered, and where.

Try to offer training in full- or half-day sessions. If your distributor won't commit business hours to training, settle for conducting training before or after the business day, during lunch, or on a weekend.

Special conditions may cause you to add unscheduled training sessions or move previously scheduled sessions forward. For example, an unexpected competitive threat may require immediate field training action. A new product may become available sooner than expected, or a product quality issue may arise—either would demand immediate training attention.

## 6. Where Should the Training Take Place?

The best place to conduct training is someplace where there are absolutely no interruptions. Try to convince distributor management to let you present training off its premises. That way, you can better control the meeting's agenda. As a second choice, strive for the most professional and quiet environment possible at the distributor's place of business—perhaps an isolated meeting room or a conference area removed from business distraction. By all means, stay away from telephones, computers, and fax machines. They only disrupt the flow of your program.

## 7. What Is the Content of the Training?

The subject matter of your sales training program depends on your goals and on the knowledge level of your audience. Some distributors require more intensive instruction than others. Assess the skill level of the overall group and then of the individual sales to prepare a package that makes the most sense for manufacturer and distributor alike. Secure the distributor's approval and commitment by discussing the training plan format before-hand with the distributor's management.

Training topics can include:

❑ Case studies of other distributors that have successfully sold your products
❑ Testimonials about your products
❑ Product knowledge and sales application
❑ The manufacturer's company
❑ Competitive products and companies
❑ Typical customers and markets
❑ Selling and business skills
❑ Vertical market applications

Mix and match these to prepare a meaningful agenda that will hold the interest of distributor personnel while providing them with the knowledge they need to sell your products effectively to their customers. Vary the subjects from training session to training session.

## 8. What Are the Teaching Methods Used in the Training?

Training does not necessarily mean a group lecture or demonstration. Teaching methods also include:

❑ Interactive lectures
❑ Group discussions
❑ Videocassettes
❑ Compact disks
❑ Demonstrations
❑ Role playing
❑ Audiocassettes
❑ Video-enhanced training
❑ Computer-assisted training
❑ Teleconferencing
❑ Actual OJT customer calls
❑ Internet
❑ e-mail

Try to blend as many of these teaching methods as possible into your total training program, making sure each technique relates to the others so that your session has a logical and continuous flow. You might begin with an interactive lecture and follow it up with group discussions, demonstrations, role playing, and OJT training to enhance and expand your initial training message. Audiovisuals and prepared handouts increase the amount of information retained.

## 9. How Do You Evaluate Your Training Program?

Continually monitor the progress of your training program to enforce a check-and-balance evaluation plan. Some suggestions are:

1. Observe the overall mood of the audience at each session to identify what level of enthusiasm and interest is being generated as a result of your training.
2. Ask for verbal and written feedback from each distributor salesperson and manager.
3. Ask your internal company managers who participate in the meeting to express their opinion of the effectiveness of the training.
4. Watch for any improvements in sales performance that could be attributed to a specific product or subject covered at one of your gatherings.

If you find out that your training sessions are not perceived as effective, take steps to improve them as soon as possible—or you may be turned down the next time you request training time from your distributors.

## Other Training Guidelines

❏ Take the time to prepare a meeting binder into which you place all training materials in the sequence in which you will discuss the various subjects.
❏ Provide food and refreshments if appropriate.
❏ Be professional and seek credibility at all times.
❏ Use a VIP guest speaker (e.g., the president of your company or a noted expert in the distributor's area of business management).
❏ Use hands-on demonstrations, which are superior teaching methods.
❏ Make sure that videos do not exceed fifteen minutes in length.
❏ See that overall, information transmitted is readily usable in the field.
❏ Stress how other distributors are successfully selling your product or service.
❏ Follow up on issues discussed and questions raised via postmeeting communications.

- ❐ Leave samples or demonstration equipment behind after the meeting.
- ❐ Motivate attendees by issuing certificates of completion (such as ''Master Salesperson'' diplomas).
- ❐ Give a remembrance gift after each session.
- ❐ Attempt to go on joint customer calls immediately after the training session to implement information and strategies discussed.

---

### What to Look For in Selecting an ''Off-Campus'' Meeting Location

Use this list to avoid disasters that can sabotage your meeting. Check all eight of these points with the off-campus location manager before you agree to conduct your training at a particular facility. Always inspect the meeting location to ascertain that the facility adequately meets your requirements.

- ❐ Avoid a hotel in an undesirable or inconvenient area. It may cast a pall over your meeting's atmosphere.
- ❐ Stay away from hotels under renovation or near construction sites. Construction or renovation noise disturbs your attendees and draws their attention away from your presentation.
- ❐ Find out who else is using the facility. Are opposing distributors or regional and national competitors planning to use the room next door at the same time? If so, switch your location to prevent confrontations or disruptions.
- ❐ See that meeting room capacity charts are accurate. A room that is smaller than you expected may not lend itself to active participation in group training activities and certainly gives your attendees a ''sardine can'' mentality.
- ❐ Make sure no local protests or labor strikes are going on to disrupt your meeting.
- ❐ Ask about hotel security. A safety or security problem could turn out to have disastrous results.
- ❐ Double-check your bill to make sure it is accurate. Hidden charges and billing errors can inflate your meeting costs.
- ❐ Make sure there are enough telephones nearby! A shortage of phones forces your attendees to leave the area to communicate with their customers or check their voicemail. Who knows when they will be back?

---

In the last analysis, how you mix and match motivational tactics and strategies is entirely up to you. The proficiency of your selection greatly enhances your ability to obtain and maintain a disproportionate share of your distributor's resource commitment—the most important part of a channelmaster's managerial charter.

### *CASE:* THE TWO-CADILLAC/ONE-BOAT DISTRIBUTOR SYNDROME

In channel marketing, one often comes across a distributor who, by his own standards, considers himself to be at the apex of success in the marketplace he serves. This is commonly referred to as the Two-Cadillac/One-Boat Success Syndrome.

Gulfview is such a distributor. The company is located in the Southern State of Destin, and is one of the most loyal and committed members of the channel organization. In the past two years, the company has generated $4.5 million in annual sales revenue. The company is quite pleased with its performance, and has no desire to grow any larger revenue-wise. The company is a tight, family-owned business, headed by a fifty-seven-year-old founder and his two daughters (who are being managerially phased into the business and are the clear heirs apparent). You have solid statistical (and other) verified information that the Destin area should be producing at least $7 million per year in distribution revenue. To date, you have had an excellent "business closeness" relationship with Gulfview, and have had four meetings to discuss this matter—but to no avail. You are at your wit's end, and it's clear to both you and your supervisor that something must be done.

**Case interpretational points:**

❑ What should you do now? What's your plan?
❑ Do you have any concerns over your competitor's reaction to your corrective plan? If so, what are they?

# Chapter 12

# Legalities

Of all areas of sales and marketing, channel of distribution management offers the greatest danger of potential legal entanglement. To help you steer on the right side of the law, this chapter acquaints you with the major antitrust laws and outlines danger zones in which legal issues can easily arise. In addition, there is an appendix, "Antitrust Laws: Summary for Managers," written by antitrust attorney Richard O. Becker, to provide further information.

## Principal U.S. Antitrust Laws

The U.S. antitrust laws exist to create, foster, and protect unreasonable restraint on competition. They are primarily designed to protect the channel of distribution and the final end user, not the manufacturer. Because of this regulatory alignment, it behooves you to acquaint yourself with the basics to avoid running afoul of antitrust law.

Four primary antitrust laws govern channels of distribution. (These laws are covered in greater detail in the appendix to this chapter.)

1. *The Sherman Antitrust Act* prohibits any unreasonable restraint of interstate and foreign commerce. It states that it is a criminal act to have a monopoly on interstate or foreign commerce.
2. *The Clayton Act* prohibits actions intended to significantly lessen competition, such as exclusive dealing, tying contracts, and collusion between competitors.

3. *The Robinson-Patman Act* prohibits price discrimination and governs the allocation of promotion allowances and efforts.
4. *The Federal Trade Commission Act* deals with unfair competition within all levels of the channel of distribution.

If you violate antitrust laws, you can suffer substantial penalties. Each offense is punishable by up to three years in prison, personal fines of up to $350,000, and corporate fines of $10 million or more. In 1996 the Department of Justice levied an antitrust penalty of $100 million on the Archer/Daniels/Midland Company for price-fixing violations—an all-time high!

Antitrust litigation is also an expensive business. Attorney fees can be substantial. Depositions and court appearances take time away from your primary managerial responsibilities and add stress to an already pressure-filled job.

Your chances of drawing the attention of the Department of Justice are increasing as more government agencies investigate violations and enforce antitrust laws. Besides the Department of Justice, these enforcers include the Federal Trade Commission, the National Association of Attorney Generals, state attorney generals, and private parties.

Violations often occur when companies are unaware of changes in antitrust laws. Note that you may also conduct business in a certain way to conform to an antitrust law, when you are unaware that there has been a change in the antitrust law that would allow you to act differently. Antitrust laws, both at the federal and state levels, are constantly being modified to meet today's rapidly changing business world. Their interpretation also changes. It is important for you, your managers, and your corporate counsel to stay abreast of legal amendments and interpretations that may affect the way you conceive and implement your channel marketing strategies.

To protect yourself, you should *always* be an active participant in any discussion or decision regarding actions that may involve corporate antitrust matters. For example, any internal pricing action must involve the company channelmaster because both the ethical and legal implementation of this policy is predominantly up to that individual.

Companies switching from direct to indirect CODs are often unaware of the antitrust law pitfalls that they now face. It is hard for these companies to accept the stark reality that distributors are not like their direct employed force—the actions of distributor salespeople cannot be controlled by the manufacturer.

Sometimes antitrust litigation occurs as a result of channel conflict. Price fixing, the most frequently prosecuted of all violations, is a good example of a conflict between two distributors that may eventually land you—the manufacturer—in a legal battle. Say that two competing distributors agree to bid the same price for the same product to the same cus-tomer—but the manufacturer knows nothing about it. If the Department of Justice gets wind of this, it's quite likely that the authorities will come searching around *your* office to find out what you knew and when. This happened to me once. Eventually, I was proved innocent—but not until I had spent six months giving depositions and going to court. A real time drain on a busy channelmaster!

Every angle of channel management has legal implications, from se-lecting and terminating distributors to managing conflict or just adminis-tering your business. Couple these legal implications with the complexity of the COD business environment, and it's no wonder the channelmaster faces potentially dangerous situations that could very easily evolve into legal entanglements.

What's even more frustrating is that many of us often see flagrant and open antitrust violations that no one does anything about. That may be true, but it's no excuse to step on the wrong side of the law. Everything eventually comes full circle, and most antitrust violators are eventually brought to task. The ones you see today just haven't been caught yet!

---

### Per se vs. Rule of Reason

There are two methods of interpreting law: *per se* versus *rule of reason*. *Per se* means that by the mere act, an action clearly breaks the law. For exam-ple, price fixing is illegal at all times. The *rule of reason* means taking all competitive factors into consideration and then determining whether an ac-tion is legal or illegal. For example, territorial restraint that causes an unrea-sonable repression of competition between distributors is determined by rule of reason.

---

## The Legal Meter

The Legal Meter shown in Exhibit 12-1 is a whimsical but useful tool that helps you measure your comfort level about decisions with legal implica-tions. You should of course never go into the "Clearly Illegal" area. And while you should primarily strive to stay in the "Clearly Legal" area, many of your actions will land you squarely in the "Gray Area." The Gray Area is not illegal, but when you venture there, you should conduct a risk-benefit analysis to decide whether to proceed. If you think you hear the thin legal ice beneath you breaking, stop and go seek legal counsel. By legal counsel, I don't mean an everyday lawyer. I mean an experienced antitrust attorney who knows what's going on *today* in antitrust and chan-nel law.

**Exhibit 12-1.**  The Legal Meter.

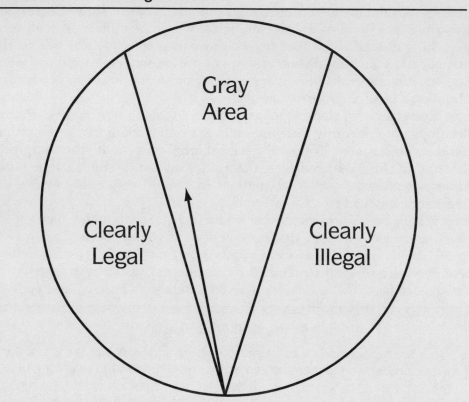

For example, let's say that the Chicago public school system, one of your top five end users in the country, issues a bid for 3,000 overhead projectors. Dealer A, one of your authorized Chicago-area dealers that is a preferred supplier by the Chicago Board of Education, contacts you and requests special pricing assistance. You must then reach a business decision where you substantiate that a true "meeting competition" situation exists. In other words, the competitive situation does indeed justify your special pricing. You decide that such a situation does exist. Feeling good about your decision, you issue a special bid to Dealer A.

The next day, your other authorized Chicago-area dealer, Dealer B, calls and requests the same special pricing assistance. However, this much smaller company is authorized to sell your products only to religious schools and cannot prove to you that it knows anything about doing business with the Chicago Board of Education. Dealer B contends that because religious schools are quite similar to their public school counterparts, it is capable of satisfying the Board of Education's desires. Knowing that

Dealer B pays you and other manufacturers slowly, you wonder whether Dealer B has the financial stability to handle the high-revenue volume that would occur with this transaction.

Are you obliged to offer the same special pricing to Dealer B? If you do it, and Dealer B aggravates the situation by giving away your product, you will have a very intense channel conflict on your hands as you seek to placate the justifiably disturbed Dealer A. On the other hand, if you don't give a special price to Dealer B, are you opening yourself up to a price discrimination charge? Once you have made the decision that is best for business, will you be able to justify it legally?

Caution, channelmaster, you are entering the Gray Area of the Legal Meter! Stop and seek the advice of your antitrust attorney before you react to Dealer B's request for special pricing. It's much better to be legally safe than illegally sorry.

## Key Legal Issues and Potential Transgressions

There are a number of situations that most frequently land a channelmaster in a tenuous legal position. When you encounter any of these, stop, look, listen—and check with your lawyer if you feel you are venturing too far into the Legal Meter's Gray Area!

### Collusive Actions

Any two or more members of a channel of distribution that collude to take a mutually agreed upon action that could possibly cause some irreparable harm (loss of business, customers, or reputation; bankruptcy) to another company may be taken to court to pay damages. Think long and hard before you engage in any potentially collusive actions.

### Dual Distribution

It is not illegal to sell your products through more than one authorized distributor in a sales territory, but the law dictates that you treat each of those distributors equally when it comes to enforcing business policies and procedures. To prevent problems, it is usually advisable to limit the number of authorized distributors you have in a geographic territory or market. Assign enough distributors to achieve the desired sales revenue, profit targets, and end user customer satisfaction requirements, and no more. Why open a Pandora's Box by having too many distributors, thus making yourself a target for charges of unfair treatment? It doesn't make COD marketing sense.

## Exclusive Dealing

Asking distributors to stock your products instead of your competitors' is enforceable as long as it is specified and agreed to in the channel contract and openly stated in published policies. Often a noncompete clause is used to clearly spell out the terms and conditions under which your distributor agrees to exclusivity.

As with dual distribution, exclusive dealing is not illegal *per se*, as long as it is stated and agreed to up front by both parties. The test falls under the rule of reason, where it is determined how much of a market is foreclosed to any one distributor, causing a noncompetitive situation to occur. Without an agreement, it is easy to move from the Gray Area into the Clearly Illegal area of the Legal Meter. Problems arise when, in the heat of channel competition, you take some action to prohibit your distributor or your competitor from doing business with each other by issuing a threat to terminate the distributor if it deals with the competitor. Don't do it. It's much too dangerous.

Prevent problems with exclusive dealing by clearly addressing it in your contract—and backing up this very astute business decision with the right administrative documentation.

## Full-Line Forcing

Full-line forcing occurs when a manufacturer insists that a distributor carry and sell its entire product line or product mix, causing an unfair business burden on the distributor. There are channel business methods that can accomplish your goal of full-line support without full-line forcing. They are:

❐ Making it a condition of doing business, and clearly stating so in your distributor contract
❐ Offering encouragement through economic incentives

Stay on the safe side by using the word *encouragement* instead of forcing the issue. A manufacturer can tactically and strategically "encourage" distributors to purchase and support its full line by giving them an incentive to do so. For example, you can:

❐ Offer higher compensation for the products that are more difficult to sell.
❐ Combine intensive "comfort level" product and sales training with increased sales and marketing support targeted toward the more difficult-to-market units.

❑ Give extra promotional credit for full-line purchases (here, *encouragement* can be a legally safe and sales-motivating word).
❑ Pay a higher discount for purchase orders that represent your full product line.
❑ Create strong end user demand for your entire line through space ads, direct mail, and other pull-through promotion activities.

## Preferential Treatment/Secretive Behavior

Here's a situation that develops when a manufacturer has more than one authorized distributor in a territory. Because you're human, chances are you sometimes prefer one distributor over the other. No problem—unless the other dealer feels that it is being deprived of some sales or marketing advantages that the one you like better is receiving, and that because these positive leverages are not available, its sales and profits are being impaired and injured.

So go ahead and develop friendly relationships—but don't meet collusively and plan anything that lets one distributor come out ahead or puts the other out of business so the one you like can be an exclusive dealer. Those kinds of actions are damaging, disruptive, and illegal.

## Price Discrimination

While it is perfectly legal and ethical to issue different pricing schedules to different distributors, be sure you can justify them. The key is to make sure that your pricing schedules do not substantially hinder, reduce, or prohibit free-enterprise competition. The test is when having two different prices for two different distributors causes an injury to competition. Always keep this important prerequisite in mind before you grant any special form of pricing. Here are some legally acceptable reasons for issuing different pricing to different distributors:

❑ You do so to meet the competition's price.
❑ There is a cost justification (cost economics).
❑ You do so in exchange for getting the distributor to perform required services (functional discounts).
❑ The prices are actually available to all parties.

It's always a good idea to justify a pricing decision on paper. For example, keep a form on hand that you can give any distributor that requests special pricing. (See Exhibit 12-2 for a sample of such a form.) You want distributors to demonstrate that they're not just trying to line their pockets with extra profits but are indeed facing a "meeting competition"

**Exhibit 12-2.**  **A sample special pricing form.**

Date _____

        Actual end user                           Distributor(s) involved

_____            _____

_____            _____

_____            _____

_____            _____

Product specified _____

Company specified _____

Quantity specified:

Quantity in initial shipment: _____ units

Quantity in total contract: _____ units

Manufacturer information:

Model: _____

List price $ _____

Net price $ _____

Competitor information:

Model: _____

List price $ _____

Net price $ _____

Special pricing information:

Projected competitive pricing:

Distributor's estimate $ _____

Manufacturer's estimate $ _____

Special pricing issue $ _____

Regional Sales Manager/Director/VP/ _____

Final report: _____

Competitor's pricing/$                   /Awarded to: _____

situation. On the special pricing form, have the distributor provide such competitive information as the name of the competitor, the competitive model in question, the quantity involved, and the price it thinks will close the sale. If your distributor can't answer these questions, chances are good it is just trying to get a better deal and really knows very little about whether this is a "meeting competition" situation.

To prevent legal problems about special pricing decisions, give two copies of the special pricing form to the distributor, and ask it to file one and return the other to you after the business is awarded. Keep a third copy in your files, preferably in one labeled with the end user's name. It's imperative that all parts and sections of the competitive pricing form be fully completed. It's a given, of course, that all information gathered on this form is highly confidential.

## Price Fixing

Price fixing involves an agreement by two or more competitors to raise, lower, or stabilize prices. The most frequently prosecuted type of antitrust violation, it comes in two variations: horizontal and vertical. Horizontal price fixing, as Exhibit 12-3 shows, happens between two companies at the same level in the channel. For example, two competing dealers may get together and agree to raise, lower, or stabilize prices for a specific model, without the manufacturer's involvement. Or two manufacturers can make a similar decision about their products.

Vertical price fixing, shown in Exhibit 12-4, occurs when a manufacturer coerces the channel distributor to bid a certain price. A type of vertical price fixing is resale price maintenance (see Exhibit 12-5), which occurs when a manufacturer tells a distributor what price to resell its product at. Accompanied by an agreement, such coerced price maintenance may not necessarily be an illegal act, as when a manufacturer orders its distributor to sell only at list price with absolutely no discounting, under threat of immediate termination of its contract. In Gray Area situations such as this, it is always advisable to get good legal advice.

Price fixing of either type gets you in trouble every time. Remember, when a distributor stocks your product, it *owns* it. That means it has the power to make pricing decisions about that product. Your attempts to control or influence that process may be illegal. Stay in the Clearly Legal section of the Legal Meter on this one, channelmaster.

"Loose lips sink ships"—and careless channelmasters. Price signaling, a form of price fixing, can happen inadvertently if you make statements about prices in a group environment. Imagine that you, an industry market leader, are participating in a major trade show. Exhausted after a

*(text continues on page 201)*

**Exhibit 12-3.** Horizontal price fixing.

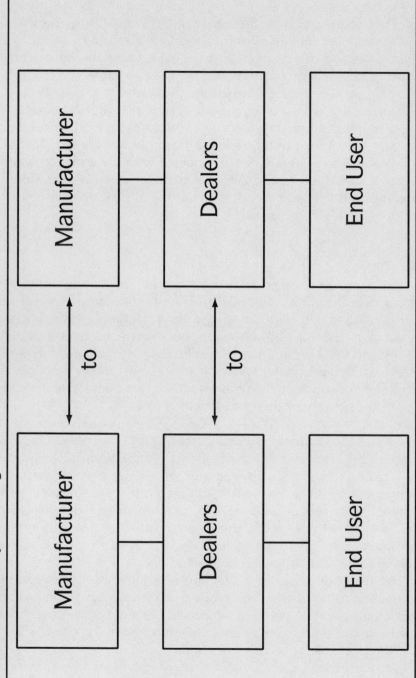

**Exhibit 12-4.** Vertical price fixing.

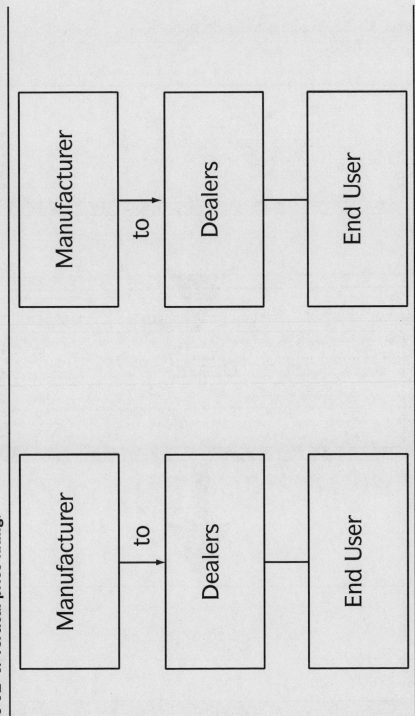

**Exhibit 12-5.**  Resale price maintenance.

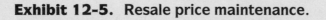

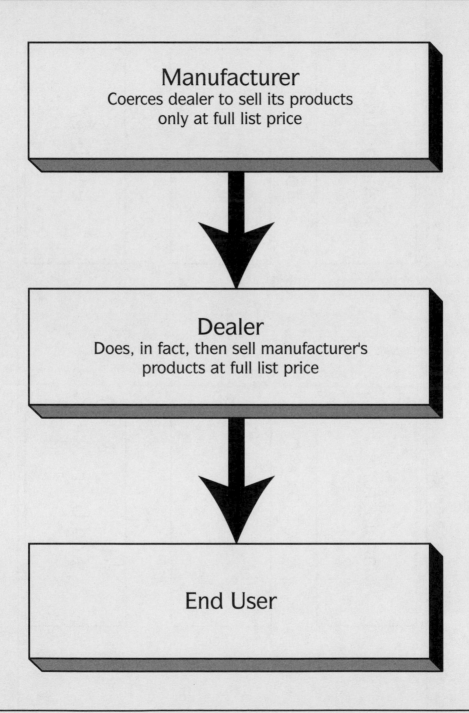

# Manufacturer
Coerces dealer to sell its products
only at full list price

# Dealer
Does, in fact, then sell manufacturer's
products at full list price

# End User

full day of booth duty, you're waiting for the hotel elevator when your two biggest competitors approach. The three of you board the elevator in silence, but as the elevator rises, you mutter, "Boy, these falling prices are killing us. I'm going to pull prices up and hold them." A week later, you raise prices. A week after that, so do your competitors. The attorney general's office is very suspicious about this apparent coincidence. The authorities subpoena your expense report, and then they discover that all three of you were at the trade show and the New York Hilton at the same time. Get ready to answer some rather penetrating questions!

Stay out of potential trouble by refusing to talk about prices in front of a group, channelmaster. The less said, the better, when it comes to price signaling.

## Refusal to Deal

A refusal to deal charge may be made when a manufacturer hastily turns down an illegitimate, renegade distributor's request to become a fully authorized representative, after the distributor claims that it has the necessary qualifications to properly service a manufacturer's product line and end users. To avoid this charge, never turn anyone down quickly. Have a clear set of channel selection criteria readily available. Ask the applicant to complete an application. Be sure your application requests information about the applicant's sales and marketing plans for your products, so you can see what it plans to do with your line.

In the vast majority of instances, the applicant won't bother to submit a completed application with a marketing plan or contact you again. If a written application is rendered, then evaluate the distributor against your list of criteria, and make a fair and equitable decision. After all, every channel has turnover, and a wise channelmaster always has a backup plan. Your applicant may not be illegitimate or renegade and may prove to have qualities or create talents you need now or in the future.

## Resale Restrictions

Resale restrictions come in two basic forms:

1. Price restrictions, such as price fixing and resale price maintenance
2. Nonprice restrictions, such as territorial constraints or account limitation

Say that a distributor authorized to sell only in Denver begins to ship into your Salt Lake City distributor's territory. It's certainly within your rights to have a serious discussion in which you share your aggrieved feelings about the situation, and you can, under the rule of reason and economic incentive, prohibit a channel member from selling outside its territory or accounts. But partner your disapproval with a threat, and your distributor may say, "I'll see you in court."

The best way to avoid this situation is to select distributors that don't violate territories. During your selection process, you can find out which ones have no respect for authorized territories or clients. Think twice before you sign them.

## Tying Agreements

A tying agreement becomes a legal issue when a manufacturer requires that a distributor buy slow-moving Product B in order to also obtain market power via high-profit, fast-turnover Product A. Forcing the tie-in purchase restricts the channel's choice of purchase. Tying agreements, shown in Exhibit 12-6, happen every day, but they may not be legal if the distributor is forced to carry Product B. They *are* legal if you can accomplish the dual purchase through creative promotional activities. Encourage, don't force, and you'll stay on the right side of the law.

## Vertical Integration

In this uncommon situation, the manufacturer actually owns a distributor. The term *captive channel* best describes the concept of vertical integration. A manufacturer may legally own a distributor, providing it treats that distributor the same way it treats the rest of its channel. Independent distributors may feel that the captive distributor gets preferential treatment. Suspicion of preferential treatment may lead to charges that the vertical relationship is causing an independent distributor irreparable harm in its own sales revenue performance potential.

When there is vertical integration, the manufacturer must be doubly cautious about apportioning channel support to avoid charges of unfair treatment, channel conflict, and legal entanglement.

# How to Communicate Legally

Follow these communications guidelines to reduce the chances of ending up in legal trouble.

1. *Watch what you say, and write it down!* An accurate, written record is your best defense in case legal proceedings arise—presuming, of course, that you are following the law. Without documentation, an "agreement"

**Exhibit 12-6.** Tying agreements.

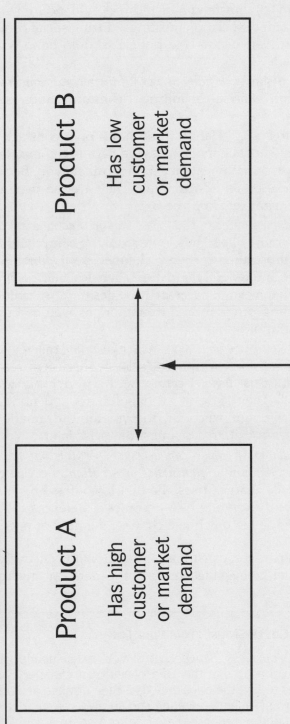

Product B

Has low customer or market demand

Product A

Has high customer or market demand

Distributor cannot buy Product A without also buying Product B

may be entirely proved by circumstantial or indirect evidence, including casual remarks made at trade association meetings, during social contacts, or during telephone calls. Agreements and policies should be in writing and clearly stated!

2. *Remember that there is no such thing as an "off the record" conversation or a "gentlemen's agreement."* Formal or informal communication can be used as evidence in court.

3. *Consider your "marginalia."* Handwritten notes on a contract, special pricing form, letter, memo, telephone message pad, fax, computer record, or any other business communication can incriminate you. Be aware of any notes that you make on any documents. They are the paper trail that could be admissible in any legal proceeding.

4. *If your company is a market leader, be advised that your actions are highly visible.* Market leaders are more likely than lower-ranking companies to be closely scrutinized and prosecuted by your channel, your competitors, and, most important, state and federal regulatory agencies. Success breeds many forms of attention that may not necessarily be desired. Use prudence in your sales and marketing program and execution, as well as in your internal and external communications.

5. *If a questionable discussion begins, halt it with a clear and concise "legalistic plea."* For example, if someone begins to carelessly discuss prices, say, "According to the U.S. antitrust laws, I cannot and will not talk to you about price-fixing issues." Then leave in an expeditious and noticeable manner. Slam a door, raise your voice, or do something dramatic that makes people remember your exit, in case questions arise later.

6. *Note that "close business friends" can become "very distant acquaintances" when one is granted immunity to antitrust prosecution in exchange for testimony.* When an antitrust charge arises, the first to confess gets immunity from prosecution—and everyone else becomes a defendant. Think about that before you confide too much in a channel member or peer.

When a legal question arises, consult an attorney who is actively engaged in antitrust channel counseling and is up-to-date on any recent changes in the law.

---

**How to Get the Most From Your Lawyer**

❏ *Choose a good "business" lawyer.* It should be someone who knows business and who practices in the area of antitrust channels. Ask around among colleagues to find the ones they use, then arrange an initial interview. A fifteen- or twenty-minute meeting should give you an idea of the person's background and experience. Feel free to prepare a couple of questions in advance or to mention a few specific issues you need help with.

This gives you a feeling for the lawyer's experience and helps you determine whether you have a good personal fit with the attorney. There is generally no charge for the interview.

❏ *Choose a lawyer who knows channels and channel law.* Confirm the attorney's familiarity with this area in your initial interview.

❏ *Remember, you are the client.* Your lawyer's advice is a valuable asset, but you make the decision. You can ask his or her opinion or advice, but the ultimate decision and legal consequences are yours. It's really no different from any other business decision you have to make, except the consequences may be more severe. Pick the wrong product or the wrong price, and sales plummet. Make the wrong channel decision, and—well, you pay the fine or go to jail.

❏ *Involve counsel early in your plans.* It's more difficult and expensive for a lawyer to come on board once a decision has been implemented and a problem has developed. Involve your attorney at the beginning. Tap his or her experience and expertise as you develop your programs, so you can develop sophisticated alternatives if business or legal obstacles arise.

❏ *Remember that communication and education go both ways.* You and your lawyer should communicate as clearly and frequently as you can. Be clear about your expectations, short- and long-term goals, and how you would like to accomplish them. Be candid about known or suspected business and legal risks. Don't make your lawyer guess or waste time while he or she discovers them! Say, ''My goal is exclusive distributors but I know there are risks, such as. . . .'' Educate your lawyer by talking about your business and passing along articles about channel issues that may be of interest. Likewise, ask your lawyer to help educate you by passing along legal news that affects your business.

❏ *Ask questions—especially ''why?''* Don't just accept your lawyer's opinion. Too many people simply shrug their shoulders and accept it as ''legal.'' If your lawyer says you can't do something or that there is a risk, ask why. What about the situation can't you do? How else can you meet your objectives? What if . . . ? Being a client means you have the right to ask questions. Being a businessperson means you should keep asking them, and you and your attorney together may generate alternatives and find a legally acceptable solution that also makes business sense.

❏ *Avoid legalese.* Insist on plain English in all discussions with your counsel. All agreements and questions should be in language both parties can understand. Don't be embarrassed if you don't understand something. Ask your lawyer to say it again using business language. You're paying for the advice, so you deserve to understand it! Likewise, don't pepper your speech with business jargon that confuses your lawyer. And avoid using legal terms yourself. If you are using them inaccurately, you may mislead both of you.

SOURCE: Richard O. Becker, Attorney-at-Law, Glenview, Illinois    Phone: 847-729-8366

# Terminating a Distributor

Termination is a fact of channel life. It is also an area rife with misunder-standing, conflict, and potential legal complications. That's why it is easier not to select a distributor than it is to terminate, as attorney Richard O. Becker, source for much of this chapter, always counsels me. A careful selection process clearly identifies troublemakers that you should stay away from. Why be forced to terminate a business relationship when, by investing a little more managerial time up front, you can find positive, long-lasting channel partners?

However, when you are forced to terminate, don't burn your channel bridges. You may find yourself wanting to do business with the terminated distributor again some day. That's why it is important to conduct the ter-mination with high ethics, proper legal procedures, and channel sensitiv-ity. In the ever-changing world of COD marketing, negative situations can easily evolve into positive ones. A distributor's management philosophies and attitudes may change for the better, enabling the wise channelmaster to reconsider the "fallen eagle."

### *Termination Guidelines*

1. Have clear and objective criteria/expectations in writing. See Chapter 9 for guidelines on establishing criteria to evaluate your channel members.

2. Always try to repair or improve the negative situation before you terminate a distributor. Develop a plan of corrective action, and agree on steps you and the distributor should take to correct problems. Follow up your meetings with letters and memos summarizing the problem and specifying how it is to be solved. Allow plenty of time for the distributor to make these corrections before you proceed to termination. "By sundown tomorrow" is not an appropriate deadline. "By the end of this quarter" is much more realistic. Always involve your field sales manager in your remediation efforts.

3. Evaluate the emotional volatility of the distributor representative's personality before you begin termination proceedings. Will both parties treat termination in a businesslike way, or will the person scream, "You can't do this to me, and I'm going to fight you for all it's worth"? If the termination is likely to be troublesome, be extra cautious about building your evaluation and termination file. You have to be able to back up your assertion that the distributor is not meeting your standards.

4. Before you proceed with termination, consult an experienced and up-to-date antitrust attorney. Follow his or her advice to the letter, particu-

larly when dealing with a potential troublemaker. Try to negotiate a hostile termination without legal advice and without an adequate evaluation file, and you might even find yourself on the wrong end of a difficult and expensive lawsuit.

5. Make realistic and fair disengagement arrangements to take back the terminated distributor's physical inventory of your products, literature, and sales support items such as banners, certificates, and so on.

6. Consider the effect of the termination on the other distributors in your channel, especially the 20 percent of your channel that gives you 80 percent of your sales revenue. Will the effect be negative or positive? Inform the other distributors of the decision as soon as you can, using the channel to your communicative advantage.

7. Deliver the termination notice in a face-to-face meeting. If that is not possible, use registered or certified mail.

8. After the termination, take time to reflect on what really went wrong in the relationship. Use what you discover to prevent future channel mismatches and mistakes.

Termination is never a pleasant decision and is never easy to carry out. But it's a tragic mistake to stay with a distributor that cannot or will not perform to your business standards. Doing so could tarnish your entire channel image. Never let a "bad apple" compromise your commitment to excellence. Careful attention to channel design and selection can reduce the number of terminations you find yourself handling.

# International Antitrust Legislation

## Export Trading Company Act of 1982

One piece of legislation that applies to export trading actually *reverses* the usual interpretation of antitrust law. The following excerpt from a U.S. Department of Commerce brochure explains the law, called the Export Trading Company Act of 1982.

> In today's global marketplace more and more U.S. firms are exporting—frequently in the face of intense competition from foreign suppliers. Authorized by the Export Trading Company Act of 1982, the Export Trade Certificate of Review Program provides a way for exporters to gain a competitive edge in selling U.S. goods and services around the world. The Certificate of Review

provides exporters with an antitrust "insurance policy" intended to foster joint export activities where economies of scale and risk diversification can be achieved. Any exporter, or group of exporters, not just an Export Trading Company (ETC), may apply for a certificate.

*The export trade certificate of review program permits U.S. firms to join together to export, cutting costs and gaining a competitive edge in world markets.*

Joint exporting allows exporters to:

❏ Present a full line of complementary products.
❏ Respond to and win large orders.
❏ Share the costs of market research, transportation, insurance, overseas warehousing, and after-sales services.
❏ Share the costs of overseas representation.

A Certificate of Review provides antitrust protection to companies that join together in exporting. Firms with certificates can engage in joint export activities such as:

❏ Setting prices
❏ Allocating customers or markets
❏ Sharing market information
❏ Sharing product information
❏ Bidding on large contracts
❏ Operating join facilities in export markets

The Certificate of Review provides immunity from federal and state government antitrust actions, both civil and criminal. For more information and a more detailed brochure contact:

The Office of Export Trading Company Affairs (OETCA)
U.S. Department of Commerce
Washington, DC 20230
202-482-5131

Additional export data can be found in the *Export Trading Company Guidebook,* available through the U.S. Government Printing Office at 202-783-3238 or through G.P.O. bookstores in several metropolitan areas (local numbers are listed under Federal Government in your local telephone directory). The guidebook is intended to assist those who are considering starting or expanding exporting through the various forms of an ETC as encouraged by the ETC Act. It will also facilitate your review of the ETC Act and export trading options and serve as a planning tool for your business by showing you what it takes to export profitability and how to start doing it.*

## Other Pertinent Laws

Channelmasters should be aware of four other legal areas that pertain to global channel management:

1. The Export Control Law, which restricts some types of technology being shipped overseas
2. The Foreign Corrupt Practices Act, which basically says you can't bribe anybody in your business dealings
3. The Antiboycott Law, which prohibits companies from refusing to do business with a particular company
4. See "Appendix B: International Laws Affecting Channel of Distribution Relations" for specific country-by-country laws.

### *CASE:* WATCH YOUR LEGALITIES

Your company, one of the top three in your consumer products marketplace, is in the process of reducing the number of wholesalers and distributors it does business with in order to reduce channel support costs. You have confirmed that your end user customers are clearly going through a buying behavioral change, now appearing to purchase your product in larger bulk quantity at more deeply discounted prices. Some of your past pricing practices have been called both predatory (to your competitors) and collusive (within your channel of distribution). These accusations have not been proven, and no legal action of any kind has been instituted.

Now an interesting channel contact occurs. Three of your largest wholesalers, representing 25 percent of your total sales revenue, call and ask you to attend a closed-door meeting at a plush local resort. They indicate that they want to discuss the following topics:

❑ A special product assortment available to only these three wholesalers

---

*U.S. Department of Commerce, *A Competitive Edge for U.S. Exports: The Export Trade Certificate of Review Program.*

- ❐ Special promotional allowances and considerations (cooperative advertising, training, qualified sales leads, and so on)
- ❐ Special high-volume discounts for these wholesalers alone

In return, they promise to carry no competitive product lines and immediately terminate relationships with those competitors whose products they now carry. They also agree to maintain a mutually agreed-upon inventory of your products, as well as to share information about customer product and purchase references, customer pricing habits, and new market data, which they have not previously made available to you. Now, your channel cauldron is boiling over with sales, marketing, and legalistic activities.

Answer these questions:

1. Should you attend this meeting?
2. If so, how should you prepare?
3. Who should attend with you?
4. What agreement or proposals should be discussed?
5. What about your future strategic channel plans?

React, channelmaster—but watch your legalities!

**Case interpretational points:**

- ❐ What are the legal issues you should be aware of?
- ❐ Does any collusive and secretive behavior on different channel members' parts worry you?
- ❐ Are there any end user buying behavioral changes happening that concern you?
- ❐ What, overall, in your channelmaster opinion, is the present and future quality of the business relationship between the manufacturer and the distributors?
- ❐ What are the primary competitive influences? Predict their reactions.

# Antitrust Laws: Summary for Managers

*Richard O. Becker*
*Attorney-at-Law*
*916 Wedgewood Drive*
*Glenview, IL 60025*

*847-729-8366*

I.  ## THE ANTITRUST LAWS

**General Statement.** The federal antitrust laws consist of a series
of statutes enacted to foster free and open competition unfettered
by artificial, restrictive arrangements. These laws provide the foundation upon which the free-enterprise system rests: The four federal laws are the **Sherman Act** (1890), the **Clayton Act** (1914),
the **Robinson-Patman Act** (1936) (actually a part of the Clayton
Act), and the **Federal Trade Commission Act** (1914). All states
also have antitrust statutes. For the most part, the statutes themselves are brief and couched in broad or general terms. Often the
cases decided under them must be reviewed to determine whether
a proposed course of action will violate the law. Generally speaking, conduct which may be lawful under one set of circumstances
can be unlawful under another, and quick and easy answers to
many antitrust questions are not often possible.

A.  **The SHERMAN ACT** is a federal statute which prohibits conspiracies, combinations, or contracts that result in unreasonable restraints of trade. It also prohibits conspiracies and
attempts to monopolize a market or the actual monopolization
of a market by one firm.

B.  **The CLAYTON ACT** is a federal statute which prohibits certain
distribution practices, as well as mergers, acquisitions, and
joint ventures which may substantially lessen competition or
tend to create a monopoly. It also establishes notification requirements and a waiting period for certain mergers and acquisitions.

C.  **The ROBINSON-PATMAN ACT** is a federal statute which prohibits discrimination, in connection with the sale of goods, with
regard to price and promotional allowances and services.

D.  **The FEDERAL TRADE COMMISSION ACT** is a federal statute
which prohibits unfair and deceptive practices by business-
men. In essence, it imposes a standard of ethical practice
which forbids such things as false advertising, misrepresenta-

— 2 —

tion, and disparagement of competitor's products, acquisition of competitor's secrets by unfair means, and any other practice which could be viewed as contrary to acceptable business moral standards.

E. **STATE ANTITRUST LAWS** have been passed by all states forbidding many of the same kinds of conduct as that prohibited by the federal antitrust laws. These state laws, however, also reach purely local business activities that the federal antitrust laws, which require some relationship to interstate commerce as a prerequisite, may not reach.

## II. THE ANTITRUST ENFORCERS

The UNITED STATES JUSTICE DEPARTMENT (DOJ) and the FEDERAL TRADE COMMISSION (FTC) are the government agencies which enforce the federal antitrust laws.

STATE ATTORNEY GENERALS enforce state antitrust laws.

PRIVATE PARTIES, such as competitors, customers, or suppliers who claim injury from violations of the antitrust laws, can sue the alleged violator for treble their damages, and such private cases are an essential part of the enforcement scheme.

## III. PENALTIES

A. <u>Felony</u>—Violation of certain antitrust acts is a crime and can now result in a **felony conviction**

B. <u>Incarceration</u>—An individual can be imprisoned for a period not exceeding three years. In recent years the Justice Department has sought and obtained a significant number of jail sentences in antitrust cases.

C. <u>Fines</u>—A corporation may have to pay as much as ten million dollars in fines, and an individual may have to pay $350,000 per violation.

D. **Civil Damages**—Other than injunctive relief, violators of the antitrust laws can also be sued for **damages**, and the antitrust laws require that as a form of punishment the damages be **trebled**. Multi-million dollar damage awards or settlements are not considered unusual in antitrust cases.

E. **Attorney Fees**—Private parties suing for damages are entitled to recover their **attorney fees** if they successfully show a violation, and these attorney's fees can be **enormous**.

F. **Restrictions on Business Activity**—Besides criminal penalties and monetary damages, injunctive relief may be obtained which frequently prohibits business conduct beyond the specific conduct charged as illegal. Once any illegality is found, the enforcement agencies and the courts feel free to impose additional restrictions to protect against the possibility of some future violation. Even in settlement, such as through a CONSENT DECREE (which is a settlement agreement approved by the court or ordered by the FTC), business conduct not directly challenged by the complaint may be prohibited.

G. **Additional Burdens**—Parties defending antitrust charges expend enormous sums in **legal fees and costs**. Massive amounts of the time of company officials must also be devoted to the **non-productive work** of aiding in the defense of an antitrust case. It is not unusual for company officials to undergo questioning in pretrial discovery for weeks at a time. Furthermore, in many antitrust cases, an exceedingly large volume of company documents must be produced to the other side in the case for inspection and copying. Frequently, hundreds of thousands, if not millions, of pages of documents are involved.

H. **Bad Publicity**—Obviously, neither companies nor individuals gain any benefit from stories published in newspapers and magazines that they have been accused of or have been found guilty of committing a crime.

— 4 —

IV.   **PROOF**

It is important not only to avoid potential antitrust violations, but any behavior which could be construed to be improper.

Most criminal acts are not proven by eyewitnesses, but are proven by circumstantial evidence (i.e., an act is inferred from the facts and circumstances). An antitrust violation is no different and can be proven by the piecing together of a circumstantial pattern. No express admission or first hand evidence of a violation is essential. The antitrust laws pierce behind the formalities of any business transaction or arrangement to see what actual practices are involved. An informal understanding to do something illegal is every bit as bad as a formal agreement to do the same thing.

V.   **COMMUNICATION, CORRESPONDENCE AND MEMORANDA**

Every communication, oral or written, relating to the corporation's business can be obtained in a discovery proceeding in connection with a government investigation or private litigation. Company personnel may be required under oath to testify as to oral communication. Documents, even though personal or confidential, are also subject to discovery. Calendars and diaries have also been included in documents that must be produced. Only written or oral communications in confidence with attorneys for the purpose of legal advice are fairly certain to be spared production. It is important to realize that carelessly written documents, taken out of context and viewed as isolated documents, may give someone not familiar with the facts a wrong impression that could lead to costly investigations and litigation.

VI.   **PURPOSE AND APPLICATION OF THE ANTITRUST LAWS**

A.   **The Importance of Competition**

The antitrust laws are meant to protect and encourage competition based on price, quality and service. They are not concerned with what may seem to be beneficial or advisable for any one firm.

## B. Per Se Violations

Some practices have been found by the courts to be sufficiently anti-competitive by their very nature to be declared automatically illegal no matter what the justification of the firms involved. These practices are said to be **Per Se** violations of the antitrust laws.

## C. Rule of Reason

Some business practices, unlike those which are per se illegal, may or may not be illegal depending upon the business purpose for the practice and their effect on competition in light of the complete factual context in which they take place. This analysis on the basis of all the facts to determine legality is an application of the **Rule of Reason**. It should be remembered, however, that the perspective of the Rule of Reason is not what is reasonable in a single firm's view, but rather what is reasonable in terms of protection and encouragement of competition in the industry. Furthermore, the analysis is made after the conduct alleged has taken place, and this hindsight may encompass factors that may not have been known at the time of the conduct.

## D. Horizontal as Distinguished From Vertical Conduct

In antitrust law, HORIZONTAL CONDUCT refers to the activity of firms in competition with one another or, in other words, on the same level of distribution in any given market. On the other hand, VERTICAL CONDUCT refers to the conduct of firms on different levels of the same distribution system. Horizontal conduct is ordinarily believed to be more anti-competitive than vertical conduct and this is more likely to result in application of **per se** illegality rules and criminal indictments.

—6—

VII.  **POTENTIALLY UNLAWFUL CONDUCT**

The following types of conduct are frequently the basis for antitrust law violations. They are described here so that management may recognize areas of concern and seek advice from legal counsel. The list is by no means all inclusive. The antitrust laws are complex and very often more than one law is applicable. It is the obligation of every Company executive to immediately confer with legal counsel about all business matters with antitrust implications no matter how minimal the executive believes the impact. The purpose of the following description of antitrust violations is meant to increase the sensitivity of Company executives to such antitrust implications.

A.  **Contacts with Competitors that Limit Competition**

It is **per se** illegal under the SHERMAN ACT to engage in any joint or collusive contacts or activities with competitors with the purpose or effect of limiting competition. Even a simple conversation on competitive subjects followed by actions using the information discussed can be sufficient evidence of an understanding or agreement to impose liability. Any discussions with competitors or contacts with competitors at trade association functions should be carefully limited under the advice of counsel.

B.  **Price Fixing**

It is **per se** illegal under the SHERMAN ACT to agree formally or informally with competitors about prices or any other term of sale (horizontal price fixing). Although price fixing seems straightforward, what has actually been held to comprise price fixing is very broad. It is not limited to fixing, but any stabilizing effect, and it is not limited to affecting just higher prices, but any artificial change in market price.

C.  ## Customer and Territory Allocation

It is **per se** illegal under the SHERMAN ACT to agree formally or informally with competitors on the allocation of customers, whether by name or class. Similarly, it is illegal for competitors to allocate among themselves territories in which each will compete or not compete.

D.  ## Boycotts

It is **per se** illegal under the SHERMAN ACT to agree formally or informally with others to boycott or refrain from dealing with any individual, partnership, or corporation.

E.  ## Refusal to Deal

Ordinarily, it is a seller's right to determine initially for itself with whom it will deal, and if all a disappointed prospective buyer can show is a unilateral refusal to deal, there is no anti-trust violation. There may be exceptions in monopoly situations or if the refusal to deal is a vehicle for violating a particular antitrust prohibition. An initial refusal to deal with a prospective buyer is less likely to run a risk of an antitrust violation than the termination of an existing relationship. The same rules are applied to refusals to deal with a supplier.

F.  ## Resale Price Maintenance

It is **per se** illegal under the SHERMAN ACT for a seller to agree formally or informally with a purchaser on the price at which a product purchased shall be resold. This conduct is illegal whether the agreement is voluntary or coerced (directly or indirectly) by the seller, and is considered vertical price fix-ing. A seller may suggest resale prices, but it cannot insist (directly or indirectly) upon adherence to them. This rule does not apply if the distribution of the goods is not consummated through a sale and re-sale, but rather through the use of agents or a consignment system.

## G. Resale Restrictions other Than Price

It is also illegal under the SHERMAN ACT for a seller to impose (directly or indirectly) or agree (formally or informally) with a purchaser (**vertical**) on any non-price resale restriction **if** the result **unreasonably restrains competition**, i.e., the restriction does not meet the **Rule of Reason**. Among the restrictions subject to this test are limitations on the category or type of customers, specific customer by name, or geographic area into which the products can be resold. These rules are applicable whether they are coerced by the seller or voluntary, or even if they are sought by the purchaser.

The reasonableness of these restrictions often involves complicated issues relating to industry history and structure and the purpose of the restraint. It is **very factually dependent**. Therefore, a determination of the level of risk requires careful factual and legal analysis. Absent economic power in the marketplace, on the basis of this analysis, a manufacturer may generally impose non-price vertical restrictions over its own channels of distribution (**Intra-brand competition**) for the purpose of strengthening competition among competing brand channels of distribution (**Inter-brand competition**).

Also generally lawful are practices limiting the number of distribution outlets (selective distribution), limiting the location of distributor outlets (location clauses), assignment of areas where the distributor must focus its attention (primary areas of responsibility), and requiring dealers to compensate other dealers who provide promotional or post-sale assistance when sales are made in their territories (profit passovers). As with price restrictions, controls over true agency distribution are generally lawful.

—9—

It is worth emphasizing that the Rule of Reason analysis only applies to non-price vertical restrictions. Price-related or horizontal restrictions are **per se** illegal.

## H. Reciprocity

It is **per se** illegal under the SHERMAN ACT for a purchaser to use its economic power in the marketplace to force a supplier to buy its products. Such a buyer cannot condition its purchase on the seller reciprocating, i.e., purchasing from the buyer. Illegal reciprocal dealing could also involve a seller with economic power conditioning product availability on the buyer supplying it with certain goods.

## I. Tie-in Sales

It is **per se** illegal under the CLAYTON ACT for a seller to condition the purchase of one product which has substantial demand or economic power in the marketplace (the **tying product**) on the purchase of another product (the **tied product**). The CLAYTON ACT applies to goods and the SHERMAN ACT prohibits essentially the same conduct when the tie-in sale involves goods or services. Coercion and economic power of the tying product distinguish this transaction from a lawful package sale. However, the distinction depends on the individual facts and "package deals" should be reviewed by legal counsel. Frequently, the very fact that customers feel compelled to accept the tied product in order to get the tying product evidences the requisite economic power and makes the transaction illegal. (Again, there are very limited exceptions to this rule, the application of which requires comprehensive legal analysis.)

A seller may, however, properly insist that its distributor be willing to fulfill the distributor function for more than one of its products. Full line endorsement, however, may be illegal. (These, too, should be reviewed with legal counsel.)

— 10 —

J.  <u>Exclusive Dealing</u>

It may be illegal under the SHERMAN and CLAYTON ACTS for a seller to require a purchaser not to deal in the products of the seller's competitors if the result has an anti-competitive effect. The **Rule of Reason** applies. The SHERMAN ACT also applies to exclusive dealing involving services. Any intention to enter into an exclusive dealing arrangement requires a comprehensive analysis by legal counsel centered on the market position of the seller and the competitive importance of the customers foreclosed from the seller's competitors.

K.  <u>Requirements Contract</u>

It may be illegal under the SHERMAN and CLAYTON ACTS for a seller to require that a purchaser agree to buy all or a large percentage of its requirements for a particular type of product from one supplier. Requirements contracts are very similar to exclusive dealing (if the buyer purchases all its requirements from the seller, the buyer would not deal in products of the seller's competitors). Unless there is substantial foreclosure of competition over a significant period of time, these restrictions have generally been held lawful under the **Rule of Reason**. Any requirements contracts should, however, be discussed with legal counsel prior to implementation.

L.  <u>Price Discrimination</u>

It is illegal under the ROBINSON-PATMAN ACT (an amendment to the CLAYTON ACT) for a seller to discriminate in price (including terms, conditions, services or allowances) between competing purchasers of goods of like grade and quality where it substantially lessens or injures competition. This is a fairly complex and frequently misunderstood statute and legal counsel should be consulted as to its application to particular situations.

— 11 —

1. <u>**Primary Line Discrimination**</u> occurs if the seller discriminates in price between different customers or in different territories in order to hurt the vigor of competition between itself and another seller to the same Customer or in a territory where the discrimination occurs. Here, the injured party is the other seller, not the customer.

2. <u>**Secondary Line Discrimination**</u> occurs if the seller discriminates between two customers who compete and are purchasing the product for resale. Here the injured party is the non-favored customer. (Note that the law makes no distinction between "authorized" Company distributors and any other purchaser for resale.)

3. <u>**Defenses**</u>—Price discriminations may be defended as lawful if:

   a. <u>**Meeting Competition**</u>—the particular low price was necessary to meet, but not beat, a specific price of a competitor;

   b. <u>**Cost Justification**</u>—the lower price can be justified because of a savings in cost to the seller derived from the nature of the specific transaction;

   c. <u>**Functional Discount**</u>—a different price is offered purchasers at different levels of the distribution chain because the purchasers are not competing with each other, or is offered because the favored purchasers are performing functions which the disfavored purchasers do not perform;

   d. <u>**Availability Doctrine**</u>—the alleged discriminatory price was reasonably known to be and actually was available to all competitive purchasers, or

   e. <u>**Statutory Exceptions**</u>—they meet the statutory exceptions applicable to certain sales to government

—12—

agencies or non-profit institutions and sales arising from changing conditions forcing the lowering of prices.

Before granting or offering a lower price in reliance upon one of the defenses or exceptions to the ROBINSON-PATMAN ACT, legal counsel should be consulted.

4. **Unlawful inducement**—A purchaser may violate the ROBINSON-PATMAN ACT by inducing an unlawful price discrimination if it knows the discrimination is in fact unlawful and cannot be justified under the defenses discussed above. In particular, a purchaser should not tell a supplier the supplier must lower its price in order to meet a specific competitive offer unless that representation is, in fact, accurate.

5. **Unreasonably Low Price**—A seller may violate the ROBINSON-PATMAN ACT by selling a product at an "unreasonably low price" for the purpose of destroying or eliminating competition. A price below "cost" is unreasonably low and any sales price that does not include an adequate profit must be carefully reviewed.

## M. Promotional Service and Allowance Discrimination

It is illegal under the ROBINSON-PATMAN ACT for a seller to discriminate between competitive purchasers in the granting of promotional allowances or services. This requires the granting of such allowances and services on a **proportional** basis so that large and small customers can take advantage of them.

## N. Acquisitions and Mergers

The CLAYTON ACT makes corporate acquisitions and mergers illegal if the effect may be to substantially lessen competition or tend to create a monopoly. The **Rule of Reason** applies. The term **market** is a **word of art** in the law referring to the particular product or geographic area of business activity a court would determine to be relevant under the antitrust laws. Business executives should take particular care in using the word and it should be understood that a businessman's use of the word "market" does not necessarily coincide with the definition of the word market under the antitrust laws.

Under the **Hart Scott Rodino** pre merger notification requirements, the CLAYTON ACT requires pre-notification to the Justice Department and the Federal Trade Commission of significant acquisitions and mergers. The procedures include the imposition of a prescribed waiting period prior to consummation of the transaction. The purpose of this procedure is to give enforcement authorities an opportunity to sue to enjoin the transfer. Interest in any potential acquisition or merger should be immediately reviewed with legal counsel to avoid wasted effort.

O.  Monopolies

It is illegal under the SHERMAN ACT to conspire or attempt to monopolize or, in fact, to monopolize. This means a firm with a substantial position in any **market** cannot engage in "predatory" practices or act with the intention to drive competitors out of business. With such a substantial position, many practices that otherwise might be legal may become illegal and classified as predatory. Again, the term "market" is a word of art as noted in paragraph N.

P.  Unfair, False and Deceptive Conduct

The FEDERAL TRADE COMMISSION ACT makes unfair methods of competition and false and deceptive acts and practices illegal. At the beginning of this summary of the antitrust laws, the conduct covered by the Act is briefly mentioned. In essence, it requires ethical business practices with regard to treatment of customers, competitors and suppliers. Executives believe in and must act in accordance with the highest ethical standards.

Q. <u>Patents, Trademarks, Copyrights and Know-How</u>

The patent, trademark, and copyright laws grant certain exclusive rights to their recipients. State common law creates certain rights in trade designations and proprietary know-how. (It is therefore sometimes permissible to include limitations in respect to the manufacture, sale or use of products, machines or processes in agreements licensing the use of patents, trademarks, copyrights, or know-how.) Despite the lawful nature of these exclusive rights, however, agreements (such as licenses) relating to them may fall under the ban of the SHERMAN ACT. (The decisions interpreting the law in this area have been characterized by change and uncertainty. Accordingly, it is most important that, prior to their negotiation and execution, all such agreements should be entered into only with the advice of counsel.)

R. <u>Foreign Transactions</u>

The conduct of business in foreign countries and trade with foreign companies may involve violations of the SHERMAN ACT as well as other antitrust statutes where the questioned activity substantially **affects** or **may affect** either the domestic market or the foreign commerce of the United States. The conduct of a foreign business through a subsidiary will not necessarily insulate either the parent company or the subsidiary from liability for violations. Further, many foreign countries now have laws similar (but not the same) to U.S. antitrust laws which must be taken into consideration. For example, the Treaty of Rome, which created the European Union (formally the European Economic Community), contains provisions, among others, modeled after (but in some instances different from) U.S. antitrust laws. Accordingly, it is not prudent to rely on U.S. antitrust laws when deciding on legality in foreign countries.

—15—

S.  **Antitrust Inquiries**

If anyone representing the Antitrust Division of the Department of Justice, the Federal Trade Commission, any state antitrust enforcement agency, or any attorney not representing
the Company should contact any employee, the person should
be treated with courtesy and referred to Company Counsel.
No information should be given without approval from the
Company's Lawyer.

VIII.  CONCLUSION

Now that you have read this summary of the antitrust laws, please
re-read it. The Company must always use reasonable efforts to be
in full compliance with the antitrust laws without exception.

# Chapter 13

# New and Different Channel Forms and Trends

Channels evolve. On any given day they are roiling with change. Because being an early mover in a new channel can help you seize a strategic advantage, it's important to stay abreast of the new and emerging channels covered in this chapter. They include:

❐ The internet
❐ Synthetic channels of distribution
❐ Situationally adaptive channels
❐ Integrated supply distributors
❐ International channels

This chapter also discusses the value of linking business strategy with information technology. By making the most of information and keeping up-to-date on these dynamic channels, you will be in the best position to decide on their value and act quickly, thus gaining over slower competition.

## The Internet

As the internet and the World Wide Web have grown, companies that initially published Web pages with basic information for prospective customers and investors have added on all manner of bells and whistles. As it has become easier to process monetary transactions on-line, more commerce sites have been established. It is now possible to buy books, investment reports, market research, computer hardware and software, movie tickets, wine, and even cars on-line.

Still, the Web remains an uncharted channel of distribution. Few agree on who is really using the Web and how often. A Commerce/Neilsen survey projected 11.8 million users in 1996, more than double the total for 1995. At the same time, a Georgia Tech survey calculated that 18 million people used the Web in 1996. There is more consensus on the demographics of Web users. Most surveys agree that they are predominantly male, upscale, and well educated. The Commerce/Neilsen survey found that 66 percent of internet users were male, 25 percent had annual incomes exceeding $80,000, and 64 percent had college degrees. The same survey calculates that 2.5 million Web users have purchased products or services over the Net.

For now, the internet is mostly an information medium, offering companies convenient and money-saving ways to disseminate such information as technical manuals and product specifications. As a channelmaster, you should be looking for ways to use the internet to spread the word about your products and services. You should also be reflecting on how your existing channels of distribution will be challenged when the internet becomes a widely accepted transaction medium.

How will buying habits change as the internet matures? Professor Anthony J. Paoni of the J. L. Kellogg Graduate School of Management at Northwestern University believes that it has a great potential to "disintermediate"—new terminology for the old phrase "eliminate the middleman."

For example, newspapers, whose classified sections have traditionally served as matchmakers for buyers and sellers, are now losing business to Web pages that list jobs, real estate, classic cars, and thousands of other kinds of merchandise. The companies posting those pages have successfully disintermediated because they need no longer cough up budgets for classified ads. (They may still want to, but that's another question.)

Disintermediation will have many consequences for both buyer and seller. For example, let's say a consumer can download a movie directly from Paramount Pictures. When a movie can be delivered digitally into your living room, what role will Blockbuster Video play in the channel? The internet may trigger changes in buying behavior that revolutionize the way things are purchased. What about *your* channel? What would happen if your end users could see and almost touch your product on-line? How would it be purchased? How would that affect your existing channel?

Before you establish a presence on the internet, carefully evaluate your position. Can you disintermediate, or are you in danger of being disintermediated yourself? Could the internet somehow cut you out of the supply chain? Can your product or service be acquired directly by consumers? If so, what is the implication to your position in the supply chain?

The internet is exciting, ever changing—and definitely worth monitoring to discover how this COD can fit into your strategic marketing plans.

## Information Technology and Channels of Distribution

The internet is just one of many dazzling new information technologies that have the potential to transform your business. J. L. Kellogg Graduate School of Management at Northwestern University's Professor Anthony J. Paoni, an expert on the linkage between information technology strategies and an organization's business strategy and culture, stresses that the ability to easily access information is a critical success factor in the execution of a strategic marketing plan. He recommends linking your business strategy to information technology in order to strengthen your channel management efforts and let you efficiently and effectively respond to changing market needs—provided that your information technology infrastructure provides information you can use. (See Exhibit 13-1.)

As Bill Gates, founder and chairman of Microsoft, once pointed out, "We are drowning in data and at the same time we are starved for information." Most organizations with channel management strategies have plenty of data stored in mainframe databases, departmental servers, and

**Exhibit 13-1.** The linkage of business strategy, marketing strategy, and information technology strategy.

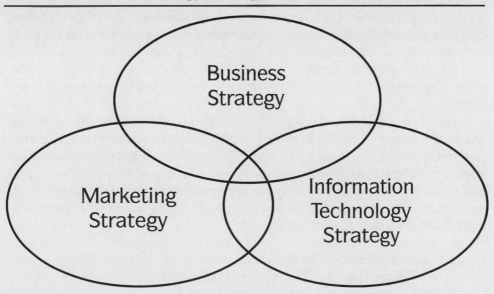

desktop computers. Somewhere in your organization, you have records of historical purchasing quantities, discount schedules, shipment locations, returns, supplier data, manufacturing data describing customer orders, and much more—all in different systems. The challenge is *coordinating, organizing,* and *managing* these data assets so that they can be accessed and manipulated into useful information for decision makers like you.

Combining your organization's vast informational assets with an information technology infrastructure can enable your company to respond to market requirements in an efficient, effective manner. And a change in business strategy *must* be linked to information technology strategy. Consider the case of a $5 billion consumer products company that attempted to implement a new micromarketing strategy. It learned the hard way that there are problems in changing a business strategy that alters the marketing strategy *without* linking the information technology strategy. Was it right to implement a business strategy that would enable the company to respond to market changes more rapidly? Yes. Was it right to implement marketing strategy that would enable it to define, produce, and distribute its products to meet the needs of its micromarkets? Yes. The challenge was that without a linked information technology strategy, the expected business outcome could not be achieved.

When your business, marketing, and information strategies are properly linked, two important results occur (Exhibit 13-2). First, you can greatly enhance your "customer-facing processes"—those external processes that touch your customers. You get the most leverage out of applications that let you serve your customers better.

Second, you begin to acknowledge the value and role of information in the organization. You begin to understand the information required to execute a marketing strategy. You discover what you need to know about your target market to implement a new channel strategy. And you determine where you can get the information to measure the results of the strategy.

Achieving these goals requires a solid infrastructure of information technology. How to build that? Well, it all depends on what you are trying to accomplish. The matrix in Exhibit 13-3 can help you find your answer without wading through hopelessly technical discussions. The horizontal rows answer the question: "Why are we implementing this business strategy/marketing strategy?" The answer can be categorized into four basic business outcomes:

1. To strengthen customer relationships
2. To differentiate or create products or services
3. To enhance supplier relationships
4. To improve cost position

**Exhibit 13-2.** The results of properly linking the business, marketing, and information technology strategies.

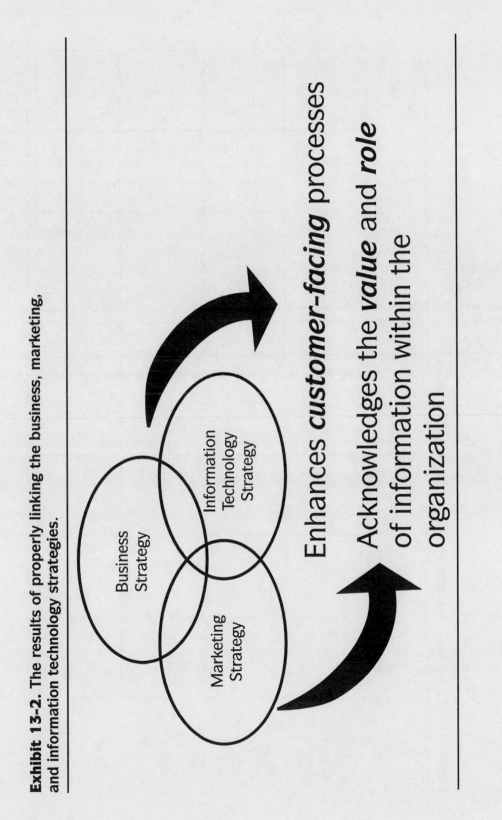

Business Strategy

Information Technology Strategy

Marketing Strategy

Enhances *customer-facing* processes

Acknowledges the *value* and *role* of information within the organization

**Exhibit 13-3.** A matrix for information technology decisions.

| | Displace labor | Enhance analyses | Reduce cycle times | Improve tracking | Improve communications | Integrate work | Transfer Knowledge | Remove middle parties |
|---|---|---|---|---|---|---|---|---|
| Strengthen customer relationships | | | | | | | | |
| Differentiate or create products or services | | | | | | | | |
| Enhance supplier relationships | | | | | | | | |
| Improve cost position | | | | | | | | |

The vertical columns answer the question: "For what purposes are we using technology?" These can be categorized into eight generic uses:

1. To displace labor (i.e., cut labor costs)
2. To enhance analyses (e.g., allow complex tasks to be done more easily. You might set up a software program that speeds up credit authorization decisions by letting the computer make limited decisions based on certain criteria, so that fewer requests need to be handled personally)
3. To reduce cycle times (e.g., improve total time to implement the system's deliverables)
4. To improve tracking (e.g., pinpointing the precise status of an order or delivery)
5. To improve communications (e-mail, etc.)
6. To integrate work (e.g., groupware that lets participants in a nationwide or worldwide project team communicate)
7. To transfer knowledge (so-called "expert systems" that allow transfer of the knowledge of experts into a database)
8. To remove middle parties (i.e., disintermediate or cut out the middleman)

Use this matrix as a decision tool whenever you consider new information technology. Simply check the categories that best explain *what* you are trying to accomplish and *why*. By focusing on the *what* and the *why* and leaving the *how* to the experts, you won't be overwhelmed by technical jargon, and your information technology experts will have a clear idea of their goal.

## Synthetic Channels of Distribution

Also termed the hybrid or fulfillment channel, the synthetic channel of distribution calls for the manufacturer to literally farm out different channel tasks to different companies and organizations that specialize in performing various channel business functions. The synthetic channel is used when a company attempting to enter a new market finds that it is unable to do so, as more powerful suppliers have already locked up eagle distributors. Faced with such a blockade, the manufacturer can delegate the presale, transaction, and postsale customer support activities to different companies.

The greatest advantage of the synthetic channel is that it lets you enter a marketplace from which you are otherwise barred. Once you have established a beachhead, the primary channel may find your products and company appealing and worthy of their resources. But the disadvantages are legion. First, it is harder to control performance and reputation when channel tasks are divided among different companies. It can be more expensive to use a synthetic channel. And managing a synthetic channel takes up a great deal of your time. Instead of dealing with a distributor that handles all functions, you have to divide your time among the companies that are handling each function.

Finally, if product or market specialization is important to you, chances are you won't find them in a synthetic channel. A synthetic channel is a hodgepodge of services performed by different companies that do just what they are asked to do, and no more. Sadly, they lack the passion for your product that a distributor can offer. A synthetic channel can help you get the job done, but not as efficiently or successfully as a bona fide channel.

In order to use this type of channel successfully, you need to assign a synthetic channelmaster to oversee and manage this hybrid operation. Then closely examine the alternatives open to you. Which support activities can your company handle? Which need to be contracted to outside companies? Delegate those activities that your company cannot easily or profitably perform. Here are some suggestions:

❑ Locate and employ sales "guns for hire"—a direct or indirect sales force that closes sales for you. Supply them with qualified sales leads you have generated through direct mail and telemarketing programs.
❑ Use an order fulfillment house to handle the inventory supply, order processing, and product shipment functions.
❑ Contract with an external field service organization to manage product installation, warranties, field repair, and postsales service.

While the synthetic channel of distribution is a fragmented approach to reaching a customer base, it is worth considering if it is the only way you can establish your company and product in a marketplace dominated by your competition.

## Situationally Adaptive Channels

A situationally adaptive channel is an unconventional arrangement in which channel partners share their resources and capabilities in novel ways. Situationally adaptive channels are the specialty of Professor James

Anderson of the J. L. Kellogg Graduate School of Management at North-western University, on whose material this section is based.*

More and more companies are turning to situationally adaptive channels to cope with infrequent but critical situations, such as a rush order on an item that is out of stock or a request for a service that the distributor has never supplied. In these situations, the channel shares its resources to meet the demand. In this collective approach, channel members help one another out instead of losing business to a competitor. By sharing resources and capabilities in novel ways and situations, channel members can take advantage of profit-making opportunities that they could not avail themselves of acting alone.

There are three broad categories of situationally adaptive channels:

1. *Auxiliary support systems* are created to cope with unexpected demands for products or services. In this arrangement, a manufacturer and its resellers agree to share their inventories and support services in crucial situations. For example, if Distributor X has 700 units of a product in stock but receives an order for 1,000 units, it can turn to Distributor Y for the remaining 300 units. Both distributors are compensated based on some previously agreed-to schedule.

This arrangement requires a shared computer system that can monitor product and service availability, process orders, and rapidly deliver products or services from distant locations to customer sites. Very sophisticated systems also monitor and plan inventory and service capabilities for the *entire* channel in order to minimize redundancy and maximize the availability of certain products.

2. *Reseller supply alliances* help companies meet customer demands for broader market offerings. Basically, such an alliance lets a channel provide one-stop shopping. This type of alliance lets a channel member market complementary products and services of a partner company when a customer requests items it does not normally provide. In this situation, companies that carry complementary product lines and support services agree to pool their cooperative resources and capabilities to broaden each others' market offerings.

By doing so, they can meet demand for products and services that fall outside their traditional areas of specialization. In return for their respective contributions, each alliance member gains a share of resulting sales and profits.

*James Anderson and James Narus, ISBM Report 5-1996, Northwestern University, (J. L. Kellogg Graduate School of Management), Wake Forest University, Institute for the Study of Business Markets (Pennsylvania State University), March 1996.

3. *Capabilities-sharing agreements* improve the quality of important services provided by channel members. Under these agreements, the superior service capabilities of one company are substituted for the inferior capabilities of another. The provider of the services is compensated for so doing. Through this kind of agreement, each channel member offers far more high-quality services at far lower costs than it could have acting alone.

All three of these arrangements challenge us to see our channels in new ways. Situationally adaptive channels require cooperation instead of competition, which is challenging for most traditional companies. These arrangements require the channel to see itself as one extended enterprise instead of separate members vying for business. In essence, they turn the channel into a web of capabilities and its members into one extended enterprise.

Situationally adaptive channels are a hard sell, because they offer less clearcut rewards than traditional compensation methods. It is easy to measure success by gross margin on sales. It's harder to measure the softer gains of increased leverage or better cash flow released by lower inventory levels. Also, some channel members may see situationally adaptive channels as a threat to their historic functions, responsibilities, and relationships.

Despite resistance, these strategic alliances and partnerships are likely to become more common in the future, providing a new way of working together for mutual gain. They also lower the cost of business by eliminating redundant inventory and redundant service costs. Obviously, one service pool shared by twenty distributors is less costly and more efficient than twenty separate service organizations. Situationally adaptive channels also mean less business lost when products or services cannot be provided. And they mean an increase in sales, because they enable the distributor to offer a broader selection of products and services than it can on its own. Keep an eye out for these important new arrangements.

## Integrated Supply Distributors

Integrated supply distributors (ISDs) are an emerging powerhouse channel that manufacturers will have to increasingly deal with in the future. An integrated supply distributor acts as the primary or sole source for the maintenance, repair, and operation (MRO) and supply of industrial products to large end users. Because these end users usually operate nationally, the ISDs must have national coverage ability to support their customers. Frequently, ISDs place their own personnel at key end user locations to manage the MRO inventory flow. Prominent ISDs include Fairmont Supply, Cameron and Barkley, Ferguson, Kennametal, W. W. Grainger, Graybar Electric, Strategic Distributors, and GE Supply.

By buying all materials and obtaining all support services from one source, end users reduce the cost of procurement and operation—key objectives of this channel. Both end user and distributor benefit because of a consolidated and more efficient purchasing program, which usually shaves about 15 percent off the cost of a traditional, multisupplier procurement program.

Information technology plays a critical role in the efficiency level of communications between the ISD and its end user customers. Both parties must have equally sophisticated information technology systems to manage the procurement program.

The emergence of integrated supply distributors also affects the traditional balance of power in the channel. Manufacturers often find themselves doing business with ISDs whose sales revenue and channel clout dwarf their own—a frustrating situation to accept. Another double-edged conflict occurs when the manufacturer's traditional COD loses revenue from a previously secure industrial customer to the powerful ISDs, and then the traditional channel finds a manufacturer they represent aligned with the ISD. In addition, some manufacturers see their MRO market share significantly eroded by ISDs that have captured their customers with cost-saving procurement programs.

The number of ISDs is expected to increase as medium-size distributors form collective groups to blend their marketing power. Keep an eye on this trend. Integrated supply will touch and influence almost everyone's MRO lives.


## International Channels

Over the next five years, foreign economic growth and improved access to foreign markets will help U.S. exports grow 8.5 to 10 percent annually. Companies that have already established international channels of distribution will be joined by many more that want to take advantage of this growth.

But the decision to export is a major one. A successful international channel requires a firm commitment and plenty of time and patience. Surveys show that many small and medium-size companies are put off by these perceived barriers to export trading:

❑ Lack of knowledge and expertise about selling overseas
❑ The belief that it is too difficult, risky, and unproductive

❐ The belief that their product is not suitable for export
❐ The difficulties of financing overseas purchases
❐ Complicated logistics involved in moving products to buyers

If your company makes the decision to export, you need to prepare an export plan. Your first step is to develop consensus on your company's goals, objectives, capabilities, and constraints. Basically, you need to go through the Channel Design Sequence (see Chapter 2) and identify your company's goals, your overseas end users' requirements, the competitive environment, and the potential channels available. When these issues are clear, you know which tasks you want your channel to perform. The next step is to decide on one of the following channel structures and determine whether you can meet its economic requirements:

1. A network of export intermediaries that handle marketing functions, while you handle manufacturing, finance, and logistics
2. A network of foreign distributors that take title to your product and manage all channel tasks
3. A foreign factory that manufactures your products for sale in that market

Exhibits 13-4 and 13-5 describe the characteristics and functions of different types of export intermediaries and foreign distributors. Export intermediaries handle international sales and marketing services, leaving manufacturers to handle overseas shipping, letters of credit, bills of lading, and customs preparation and shipping. In contrast, a foreign distributor, like a domestic one, generally takes title to your product and provides sales and marketing services within its country.

## Export Intermediaries

Export intermediaries are specialized companies that market U.S. products and services on behalf of manufacturers, farm groups, and distributors. They generally fall into one of two entities: (1) the export management company (EMC), or (2) the export trading company (ETC).

An export management company acts as the export arm of one or more U.S. manufacturers, helping to establish an international market for the company's products, usually on an exclusive basis. The export trading company, in contrast, acts as an independent distributor, linking buyers and sellers to arrange a specific transaction. ETCs identify what international customers want to buy and work with a variety of U.S. manufacturers to fulfill those requirements. Both EMCs and ETCs are paid a commission by the manufacturers they represent.

# Exhibit 13-4. Characteristics of domestic channels of distributors serving overseas markets.

| Type of Duties | Agent | | | | | | Merchant | | | |
| --- | --- | --- | --- | --- | --- | --- | --- | --- | --- | --- |
| | Export management company | MEA | Brokers | Buying offices | Selling groups | Norazi | Export merchants | Export jobbers | Importers and trading companies | Complementary marketeers |
| Take title | No | No | No | No | No | Yes | Yes | Yes | Yes | Yes |
| Take possession | Yes | Yes | No | Yes | Yes | Yes | Yes | No | Yes | Yes |
| Continuing relationship | Yes | Yes | No | Yes | Yes | No | No | Yes | Yes | Yes |
| Share of foreign output | All | All | Any | Small | All | Small | Any | Small | Any | Most |
| Degree of control by participant | Fair | Fair | None | None | Good | None | None | None | None | Fair |
| Price authority | Advisory | Advisory | Yes (at market level) | Yes (to buy) | Advisory | Yes | Yes | Yes | No | Some |
| Represent buyer, seller, or self | Seller | Seller | Either | Buyer | Seller | Both | Self | Self | Self | Self |
| Number of principals | Few to many | Few to many | Many | Few | Few | Several per transaction | Many | Many | Many | One per product |
| Arrange shipping | Yes | Yes | Not usually | Yes | Yes | Yes | Yes | Yes | Yes | Yes |
| Type of goods | Manufactured goods and commodities | Staples and commodities | Staples and commodities | Staples and commodities | Complementary to their own lines | Contraband | Manufactured goods | Bulky and raw materials | Manufactured goods | Complementary to their own line |
| Breadth of line | Specialtywide | All types of staples | All types of staples | Retail goods | Narrow | NA | Broad | Broad | Broad | Narrow |
| Handle competitive lines | No | No | Yes | Yes—uses many sources | No | Yes | Yes | Yes | Yes | No |
| Extent of promotion and selling effort | Good | Good | One shot | NA | Good | None | None | None | Good | Good |
| Extend credit to principal | Occasionally | Occasionally | Seldom | Seldom | Seldom | No | Occasionally | Seldom | Seldom | Seldom |
| Market information | Fair | Fair | Price and market conditions | For principal, not for manufacturer | Good | None | None | None | Fair | Good |

NA = Not available

Source: Philip Cateora, *International Marketing*, 7th ed. (Homewood, IL: Richard D. Irwin, 1990), p. 607. Copyright © 1990 by Richard D. Irwin. Reprinted by permission.

# Exhibit 13-5. Characteristics of channels of distributors in foreign countries.

| Type of Duties | Agent | | | | Merchant | | | |
| --- | --- | --- | --- | --- | --- | --- | --- | --- |
| | Broker | Manufacturers representative | Managing agent | Comprador | Distributor | Dealer | Import jobber | Wholesaler and retailer |
| Take title | No | No | No | No | Yes | Yes | Yes | Yes |
| Take possession | No | Seldom | Seldom | Yes | Yes | Yes | Yes | Yes |
| Continuing relationship | No | Often | With buyer, not seller | Yes | Yes | Yes | No | Usually not |
| Share of foreign output | Small | All or part for one area | NA | All, for one area | All, for certain countries | For assignment area | Small | Very small |
| Degree of control by principal | Low | Fair | None | Fair | High | High | Low | None |
| Price authority | None | None | None | Partial | Partial | Partial | Full | Full |
| Represent buyer, seller, or self | Either | Seller | Buyer | Seller | Seller | Seller | Self | Self |
| Number of principals | Many | Few | Many | Few | Few | Few major | Many | Many |
| Arrange shipping | No | No | No | No | No | No | No | No |
| Type of goods | Commodities and food | Manufactured goods | All types of manufactured goods | Manufactured goods | Manufactured goods | Manufactured goods | Manufactured goods | Manufactured consumer goods |
| Breadth of line | Broad | Allied lines | Broad | Varies | Narrow to broad | Narrow | Narrow to broad | Narrow to broad |
| Handle competitive lines | Yes | No | Yes | No | No | No | Yes | Yes |
| Extent of promotion and selling effort | None | Fair | None | Fair | Fair | Good | None | Usually none |
| Extend credit to principal | No | No | No | Sometimes | Sometimes | No | No | No |
| Market information | None | Good | None | Good | Fair | Good | None | None |

NA = Not available

Source: Philip Cateora, *International Marketing*, 7th ed. (Homewood, IL: Richard D. Irwin, 1990), p. 607. Copyright © 1990 by Richard D. Irwin. Reprinted by permission.

In effect, the ETC and EMC serve as an international marketing department for small to medium-size manufacturers. However, the manufacturer still must handle the financial aspects of the sales and the logistics of shipping products around the world. A new organization called Global Trade Net (847-253-1565) saves small and medium-size corporations the expense and responsibility for finance and logistics. It works with selected ETCs and EMCs to provide comprehensive overseas coverage, taking title to finished goods at the dock. In effect, it converts the international sale into a domestic transaction for the manufacturer.

## Foreign Distributors

Foreign distributors perform the same channel functions as their domestic counterparts, but in other countries. Setting up a global network of distributors is hard work, but it pays off in results, because you have more control over how your products are sold than you would if you worked through export intermediaries.

To begin with, you need to recognize that each country has its own culture and its own mores. Find out what they are, or risk making "ugly American" blunders. Before you enter any foreign market, research the country in detail to identify the important differences between your channel and marketing strategies and those of the targeted country. Find out everything you can about the following factors:

- ❐ *Culture.* Languages, holidays, religious practices, racial attitudes, traditions, consumer tastes and lifestyles, food habits, mores, and customs
- ❐ *The economy.* Currency, balance of payments, economic conditions, trade alignments
- ❐ *Import/export regulations.* Import restrictions, methods of payment, duty structures, documentation requirements, packaging regulations, weights and measures
- ❐ *Tourist/immigration regulations.* Visa requirements, inoculation requirements, immigration procedures
- ❐ *Politics.* Government, military and political stability
- ❐ *Market conditions.* Local competition, communications facilities
- ❐ *Physical geography.* Climate, temperature, time zone, regions

As a channelmaster, you need to develop a particular strategy for each country and a generalized marketing strategy for each "theater" or region. For example, France, Germany, and Italy are all individual markets, but as members of the European Union, they share some geographic, economic, political, and religious bonds. It would be appropriate to develop a general strategy for all European sales, as well as individual strategies for each country.

The best international manufacturer/distributor relationships have the following characteristics:

❏ *The roles of the foreign distributor are not rigidly set by the manufacturer.* While you should have a basic set of criteria that you want your distributors to meet, you need to be flexible and considerate about the details. Business is simply not the same everywhere in the world. Familiarize yourself with the culture and business practices of each distributor's country, and accommodate your practices accordingly.

❏ *Marketing strategy decisions are made jointly by the manufacturer and the channel of distribution.*

❏ *A high degree of personal contact between the channelmaster and the distributor is mandatory.* An international relationship requires a great deal of business closeness. You need to work even harder to build trust with overseas distributors because, after all, *you* are the foreigner. Personal visits and frequent phone calls are a must.

❏ *Each foreign country is unique and is approached with its uniqueness in mind.*

❏ *Patience, flexibility, and understanding are key factors in establishing and maintaining a strong and lasting channel relationship.*

## Finding Foreign Distributors

There are many sources of information about foreign distributors. Draw information from more than one source in order to verify which distributors are a company's eagles.

❏ *Government sources.* While the U.S. Department of Commerce can provide some overseas names, I have had better luck working with the individual state Departments of Commerce. Other government sources of local-market knowledge are U.S. embassies and consulates, foreign embassies and consulates in the United States, and information readily available at your local library.

❏ *Transportation industry.* Freight forwarders, airlines, and shipping agents are good sources of information. If you, an electronics manufacturer, ship most of your goods to Germany via Lufthansa, ask your Lufthansa representative for the names of companies that receive electronics shipments. This is very interesting information and should not be confidential.

❐ *Institutional contacts.* Talk to commercial banks and foreign banks located in the United States. Attorneys, advertising agents, and international accounting firms may also be good sources.

❐ *Private trade lists.* Dun & Bradstreet and other private consultants publish lists of overseas contacts. Try *American Firms, Subsidiaries and Affiliates Operating in Foreign Countries,* published by the World Trade Academy Press, 50 East 42nd Street, New York, NY 10017.

❐ *Chambers of commerce and trade associations. Check the World Yearbook of Chambers of Commerce,* available in your library's reference section, for the names of foreign chambers of commerce in the United States. Also consult with U.S. chambers of commerce located overseas, as well as world trade centers. Another source is *Trade Directors of the World,* published by Crown Publications, Inc., Queen's Village, NY 11428.

❐ *On-line directories.* Check out the World Wide Web for information on your industry. Information technology distributors, importers, dealers, and resellers are listed on The Channel, an on-line directory subscription service located at http://www.thechannel.com

This book contains an appendix titled "International Laws Affecting Channel of Distribution Relations." You need to be fully aware of laws in the countries you intend to do business with, and this appendix is a good reference.

# Appendix A

# Channel of Distribution Words of Wisdom Glossary

❐ *Never burn your channel bridges.* You never know if in one or two years you'll be reapproaching that same distributor to once again take on your product line. Could be new ownership with a new attitude has turned it around.

❐ *Go regional first, then national when establishing your COD.* It's a channel design fact that it's best to sign your regional complement first, then your national distributors, as the regionals do not like their national counterparts. Why cause unnecessary obstacles to be placed in your path to channel success?

❐ *Watch for "hidden authority" in all channel environments.* The individuals with the apparent titles may not be decision makers.

❐ *Make it as easy to do business with your company as possible.* Review your business policies on a biannual basis to ensure that you are not falling into the trap of being hard to deal with. TLC$^2$ (Tender Loving Channel Care).

❐ *Develop as much of a "business closeness" relationship as possible with the 20 percent of your COD that generates 80 percent of your sales revenue. Get to know them both in a business and social way.* This will pay handsome dividends when you need them.

❐ *Always remember that your distributors are not your direct employees,* and therefore, you must earn your continued share of their sales and marketing commitment.

❐ *Watch your legalities or you might become entangled.* There is nowhere in sales or marketing when a manager could be brought into an antitrust violation proceeding when he or she had absolutely nothing to do with the transgression. For instance, the COD actually violated the antitrust law and every level in the channel was then brought into the litigation.

❏ *Invest in brand power for channel power.* If you are fortunate enough to have a high customers-brand preference, then use it to gain a stronger, more powerful new channel position.

❏ *Go for all the business from your COD. Do not allow "cherry picking."* In other words, ask for, motivate, and expect full product line and product mix support from your distributors.

❏ *Only pick the best "Eagle" COD candidates or risk sales leakage.* Do not succumb to what I call "the warm body syndrome" when being pressured to find a distributor in a primary market. You'll end up rushing into signing a mediocre candidate who generates mediocre sales results. Use the time-proven channel design sequence!

❏ *Always be honest. Do the right thing or you'll lose credibility with your COD.* Tell your distributors the truth about product quality or delivery problems. It is better they hear it from you rather than someone else.

❏ *Direct and indirect COD will always have some level of conflict between them.* I call it "the conflict eternal." Deal with it!

❏ *When a company has both indirect and direct COD, then they should report to one functional manager to resolve issues involving "the conflict eternal."*

❏ *Use the infamous channel telegraph to your communicative advantage.* Within twenty-four hours of your taking a channel action with one distributor, the rest of your COD will know of it.

❏ *Whenever possible, seek out cobranding or comarketing possibilities* where you can combine resources to achieve a mutually beneficial objective.

❏ *The primary business objective of a channelmaster is to achieve a disproportional share of your channel distribution resource commitment.* Always remember that you are competing with every other product line the distributor carries, and it only has so many resources to allocate (inventory, training, local marketing).

❏ *Always anticipate your competitor's actions.* It is always better to be proactive rather than reactive.

❏ *Your major market areas aren't necessarily the ones you first attempt to penetrate.* Because competition may be strongly entrenched, your company might not have the funding to properly support major market demands. You may want to first try out your channel marketing plan in a secondary market to find out if there are any deficiencies.

❏ *Keep in close contact with other friendly channel marketing managers in the same industry.* They might possess or have access to important information that is not available to you (e.g., specific data on a mutual distributor or overall marketplace forecast conditions).

❐ *Manufacturers do not control their channels of distribution, they manage them.* Compared to your direct employed sales force, who, when ordered to perform a sales task (sell at full-list pricing, give competitive feedback) must obey, indirect channels do not have to conform to these directives.

❐ *Some channel conflict is, in fact, "healthy."* Having a limited number of "border wars" over a mutually authorized customer may actually indicate that you're getting great sales coverage.

❐ *Fully understand your own company culture before creating and implementing any COD action.* Avoid internal political warfare by first knowing your company's true commitment toward indirect channels. Quite often, it is very painful for a corporation to change from a direct sales force mentality.

# Appendix B

# International Laws Affecting Channel of Distribution Relations

## Algeria

Sales agreements must be registered. Applicable law: Law #78, 02, 1978, as modified, 1988, 1990.

## Argentina

Antitrust. Applicable law: Law #22, 262, 1980. Criminal Code, Law #22, 802.

Advertising. Disallows the negative use of a competitor's trade name or logo; re: Pepsi Challenge, October 1994.

## Austria

Termination of agents or distributors. Applicable law: Trade Agents Act, 1993, paragraph 25.

SOURCE: William C. Fath, *How to Develop and Manage Successful Distributor Channels in World Markets* (New York: AMACOM, 1995), pp. 156–157. Reprinted by permission.

# Bahrain

Termination of agents or distributors. Applicable law: Amiri Decree #23, 1975, as amended by Legislative Decree #10, 1991 and articles 164–174 and 194–203 of the Law of Commerce, Amiri Decree #7, 1987. Registration of sales agreements is required under the above laws.

# Belgium

Termination of agents or distributors. Applicable law: Unilateral Termination of Indefinite Exclusive Agreements, Law of July 27, 1961, and Law of April 13, 1971, and April 21, 1971.

# Brazil

Antitrust. Applicable law: Law #8, 884, June 11, 1994.
Termination of automotive vehicle distributors. Applicable law: Law #6, 729, November 28, 1979, as amended by Law #8, 132, December 26, 1990.
Termination of independent agents. Applicable law: Law #4, 886, December 10, 1965, as amended by Law #8, 420, May 8, 1992.

# Colombia

Termination of agents or distributors. Applicable law: Commercial Code, articles 1317–1331.

# Costa Rica

Termination of agents or distributors. Applicable law: Law #6209, March 9, 1978, as amended by Executive Decree #8599, May 5, 1978, and Decree #13519-S, April 19, 1982.

# Cyprus

Termination of agents. Applicable law: Laws of Cyprus, section 161–170, chapter 149.

# Dominican Republic

Termination of agents or distributors. Applicable law: Law #173, April 6, 1966, as amended by Law #263, December 31, 1971, Law #622, December 28, 1973, and Law #664, 1977.

# Ecuador

Termination of agents or distributors. Applicable law: Supreme Decree 1038-A, Official Register #245, December 31, 1976.

# El Salvador

Termination of agents or distributors. Applicable law: Commercial Code, articles 392–410 and 1066–1097, as amended by Decree #237, December 23, 1985.

# Finland

Termination of agents. Applicable law: Law #417, May 8, 1992.

# France

Termination of agents or distributors. Applicable law: Decree #58-1345, December 23, 1958, as amended by Law #91-153, June 21, 1991.

# Germany

Termination of agents or distributors. Applicable law: Commercial Code, section 89.

# Greece

Termination of agents. Applicable law: Commercial Code, articles 90–94; Civil Code, articles 211–215; Law 307/76, as amended by Presidential Decrees 407/87 and 219/91.

# Guatemala

Termination of agents or distributors. Applicable law: Decree #78-71, August 25, 1971, Official Gazette, October 1, 1971.

# Honduras

Termination of agents or distributors. Applicable law: Decree #459, November 24, 1977, as amended by Decree #804, September 10, 1979.

# Indonesia

Termination of agents or distributors. Applicable law: Civil Code, article 1266.

Registration of sales agreements. Applicable law: Ministry of Industry Decree #135/Kp/VI/91, June 3, 1991.

# Iraq

Termination of agents or distributors. Applicable law: Supreme Decree 1038-A, Official Register #245, December 31, 1976.

# Israel

Termination of agents. Applicable law: Agency Law of 1965.

# Italy

Termination of agents or distributors. Applicable law: Civil Code, articles 1742–1752, as amended by Law #204, May 3, 1985, and Legislative Decree #303, September, 10, 1991.

# Japan

Registration of sales agreements. Applicable law: Japan Fair Trade Commission, all agreements of more than one year's duration and any agreement that contains resale price restrictions.

# Jordan

Termination of agents or distributors. Applicable law: Article 864, Civil Code, Law #43, 1976; Article 18, Law #44, 1985, Article 97, Commercial Code, Law #12, 1966.
Registration of sales agreements is required under the above laws.

# Kuwait

Termination of agents or distributors. Applicable law: Law #36, 1964; Law #37, 1964; Decree #68, 1980.
Registration of sales agreements is required under the above laws.

# Lebanon

Termination of agents or distributors. Applicable law: Decree #34, 1967, as amended by Decree #9639, 1975.
Registration of sales agreements is required under the above laws.

# Libya

Termination of agents or distributors. Applicable law: Registration of Agreements; Law #33, 1971, and implementing regulations in Decree #40, 1971; Law #87, 1975, and implementing regulations in Decree #73, 1975.

# Myanmar

Nationalization of Enterprises Law, 1962—only the government may be a distributor.

# Netherlands

Termination of agents. Applicable law: Commercial Code, Book I, Title 4, articles 74–74S, as amended, July 5, 1989.

# Nicaragua

Termination of agents or distributors. Applicable law: Decree #13, December 22, 1979, modifying Decree #287, February 2, 1972.

# Norway

Termination of agents. Applicable law: Commercial Agents Act, June 19, 1992.
Termination of distributors. Applicable law: Law of June 1916, as amended by Law of June 1, 1985.

# Oman

Termination of agents or distributors. Applicable law: Royal Decree #26, 1977, Ministerial Order #11, 1985.
Registration of sales agreements is required under the above laws.

# Pakistan

Termination of agents or distributors. Applicable law: Contract Act, 1972, section 205.

# Philippines

Termination of agents or distributors. Applicable law: Presidential Law #1789.

# Portugal

Termination of agents or distributors. Applicable law: Decree Law #176/
86, July 3, 1986.

# Puerto Rico

Termination of agents or distributors. Applicable law: Law #75, June 24,
1964, as amended by 10 L.P.R.A., section 278, 1984; Law #21, December
5, 1990.

# Qatar

Termination of agents or distributors. Applicable law: Law #3, 1985, as
amended by Law #10, 1989, and Law #4, 1986.
Registration of sales agreements is required under the above laws.

# Russia

Termination of agents or distributors. Applicable law: Civil Code, 1964,
and Principles of Civil Legislation, 1991.

# Saudi Arabia

Termination of agents or distributors. Applicable law: Royal Decree M/11,
1962, as amended by Royal Decree M/5, 1969, M/8, 1973, and M/32,
1980, and implementing regulations in Ministerial Decision #1897, 1981.

# South Korea

Registration of sales agreements. Applicable law: Article #24 of the Anti-
Monopoly and Fair Trade Law, 1991, and Article #28 of the implementing Enforcement Decree and Economic Planning Board Notice #50, October 1, 1987.

# Spain

Termination of agents. Applicable law: Law of Agency, February 4, 1949, and article 418a, Swiss Code of Obligations.

# Tanzania

Termination of agents or distributors. Applicable law: Law of Contract Ordinance, 1961.

# Thailand

Termination of agents or distributors. Applicable law: Civil and Commercial Code, section 827.

# Turkey

Termination of agents. Applicable law: Turkish Commercial Code, Book I, chapter VIII, articles 116–134.

# United Arab Emirates

Registration of sales agreements. Applicable law: Federal Law #18, 1981, as amended by Federal Law #14, 1988, and Ministerial Resolution #47, 1989.

# Venezuela

Antitrust, price fixing. Applicable law: Venezuela Antitrust Law, articles 10.1 and 10.2.

Intellectual property. Trademarks and patents are *not* protected after two years of nonuse. Applicable law: Resolution #914, March 29, 1961, Official Gazette, May 10, 1961.

Foreign debt. Applicable law: Resolution #46, November 10, 1994; Official Gazette, November 11, 1994. Foreign debt may not be incurred in commerce without the prior approval of the Minister of Finance.

# Index